WATERFORD

For Dolores, without whose support this book would never have been written.
For Alan and Aoife, and in memory of Larry McCarthy, the ferryman

The Irish Revolution, 1912–23

Waterford

Pat McCarthy

FOUR COURTS PRESS

Set in 10.5 on 12.5 point Ehrhardt for
FOUR COURTS PRESS LTD
7 Malpas Street, Dublin 8, Ireland
fourcourtspress.ie
and in North America for
FOUR COURTS PRESS
c/o ISBS, 920 N.E. 58th Street, Suite 300, Portland, OR 97213.

A catalogue record for this title
is available from the British Library.

ISBN 978–1–84682–410–4

Printed in England
by TJ International, Padstow, Cornwall.

Contents

Illustrations

Credits

Illustrations 1, 2, 3, 5, 6, 13, 15, 16, 17, 18, 19: Poole Collection, National Library of Ireland; 4: Julian Walton, Waterford; cover, 7, 9, 21, 22, 24, 27, 28, 29: Waterford County Museum, Dungarvan; 8, 10, 25, 26: Waterford Museum of Treasures, Waterford; 11, 12: *Freeman's Journal*, National Library of Ireland; 14: Irish ships.com images; 20: De Fuiteoil, *Waterford remembers*; 23: Dermot Power, Waterford.

MAPS

Abbreviations

AOH	Ancient Order of Hibernians
ASRS	Amalgamated Society of Railway Servants
ASU	Active Service Unit
BMH	Bureau of Military History
CAB	Cabinet Records, TNA
Cd, Cmd	Command Paper (British parliamentary papers)
CE	*Cork Examiner*
CI	County Inspector, RIC
CO	Colonial Office, TNA
CSORP	Chief Secretary's Office Registered Papers
DÉ	Dáil Éireann
DI	District Inspector, RIC
DIB	*Dictionary of Irish biography*
DO	*Dungarvan Observer*
FJ	*Freeman's Journal*
GAA	Gaelic Athletic Association
GHQ	General Headquarters
GOC	General Officer Commanding
GPO	General Post Office
Hansard	House of Commons debates
IFS	Irish Free State
IG	Inspector General, RIC
IHS	*Irish Historical Studies*
II	*Irish Independent*
IMA	Irish Military Archives
INL	Irish Nation League
IPP	Irish Parliamentary Party
IRA	Irish Republican Army
IRB	Irish Republican Brotherhood
IRRSA	Irish Railway Record Society Archives
IT	*Irish Times*
ITGWU	Irish Transport and General Workers' Union
IV	*Irish Volunteer*
IWFL	Irish Women's Franchise League
JP	Justice of the Peace
LGB	Local Government Board
ME	*Munster Express*
MP	Member of Parliament

NAI   National Archives of Ireland
NLI   National Library of Ireland
NMI   National Museum of Ireland
NUDL   National Union of Dock Labourers
O/C   Officer Commanding
OPW   Office of Public Works
PR   Proportional Representation
PRONI   Public Record Office of Northern Ireland
RAF   Royal Air Force
RDC   Rural District Council
RFA   Royal Field Artillery
RIC   Royal Irish Constabulary
SF   Sinn Féin
TD   Teachta Dála, member of Dáil Éireann
TNA   The National Archives, London
UCDAD   University College Dublin, Archives Department
UDC   Urban District Council
UIL   United Ireland League
UVF   Ulster Volunteer Force
WCA   Waterford City Archives
WCoA   Waterford County Archives Service
WCL   Waterford City Library
WFA   Waterford Farmers' Association
WN   *Waterford News*
WO   War Office, TNA
WS   Witness Statement to Bureau of Military History
WS   *Waterford Standard*

Acknowledgments

This book is the outcome of a lifelong passion for all things Waterford. Writing it has been a ten-year journey during which I made many friends and accumulated many debts of gratitude. It is not possible to name everyone but without their individual contributions this book would be a poorer volume.

Like all Irish historians I am indebted to the friendly and efficient staffs of libraries and archival repositories. Successive commanding officers and their staffs at the Irish Military Archives responded unfailingly to innumerable requests for documents. Likewise, the staffs of UCD Archives Department, Trinity College Library, the National Library of Ireland, the Representative Church Body Library, Waterford County Archives, Waterford City Archives, Waterford City Library, Waterford Diocesan Archives, Waterford County Museum, the National Museum of Ireland, the National Archives of Ireland, the National Archives, London, the National Army Museum, London, the Irish Railway Record Society Archives and the Keep Military Museum. To all I express my sincere thanks.

For their unfailing support and encouragement I thank my friends and colleagues in the Military History Society of Ireland – particularly Colonel Donal O'Carroll, Dr Harman Murtagh, Dr Ken Ferguson and Anthony Kinsella – and in the Waterford Historical and Archaeological Society, Julian Walton, William Fraher, Donnchadh Ó Ceallacháin and Nioclás Graves.

The maps in this book are the work of Dr Mike Brennan of UCD. His unrivalled expertise in this area has added greatly to the text.

I am particularly grateful to my editors, Professor Mary Ann Lyons and Dr Daithí Ó Corráin, for their professional expertise in guiding me through the process. Special thanks are due to Daithí who devoted many, many hours to editing and condensing various cumbersome drafts into a readable monograph.

My late parents, who gave me a love of learning, and my brothers and sister, who gave me constant support and encouragement, all deserve my thanks.

My wife, Dolores, has encouraged, supported and tolerated my passion for the Déise since we first met. To her and our children, Alan and Aoife, a thousand, thousand thanks for many years of support and tolerance. You made this book possible.

The Irish Revolution, 1912–23 series

Since the turn of the century, a growing number of scholars have been actively researching this seminal period in modern Irish history. More recently, propelled by the increasing availability of new archival material, this endeavour has intensified. This series brings together for the first time the various strands of this exciting and fresh scholarship within a nuanced interpretative framework, making available concise, accessible, scholarly studies of the Irish Revolution experience at a local level to a wide audience.

The approach adopted is both thematic and chronological, addressing the key developments and major issues that occurred at a county level during the tumultuous 1912–23 period. Beginning with an overview of the social, economic and political milieu in the county in 1912, each volume assesses the strength of the home rule movement and unionism, as well as levels of labour and feminist activism. The genesis and organization of paramilitarism from 1913 are traced; responses to the outbreak of the First World War and its impact on politics at a county level are explored; and the significance of the 1916 Rising is assessed. The varying fortunes of constitutional and separatist nationalism are examined. The local experience of the War of Independence, reaction to the Truce and the Anglo-Irish Treaty and the course and consequences of the Civil War are subject to detailed examination and analysis. The result is a compelling account of life in Ireland in this formative era.

Mary Ann Lyons
Department of History
Maynooth University

Daithí Ó Corráin
Department of History
St Patrick's College,
Dublin City University

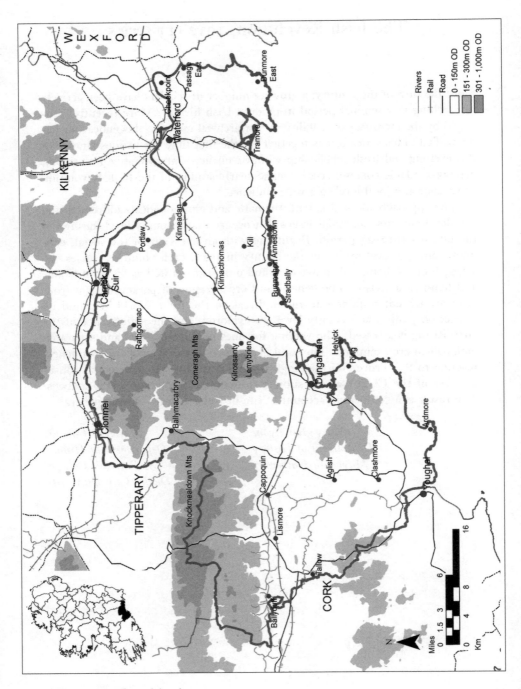

1 Places mentioned in the text

1 'The coming prosperity':[1] Waterford in 1912

At 12.30 p.m. on 10 February 1913 John Redmond, MP, leader of the Irish Parliamentary Party (IPP), arrived by train to his Waterford constituency to a tumultuous welcome. He had come to open the new 'free' bridge, a modern concrete structure, which replaced 'old timbertoes', a toll bridge that had been the only river crossing in the city for more than 120 years. The city was *en fête* and most businesses had responded to the mayor's call to make the occasion a holiday. More than 30,000 people thronged the quays, the approaches to the bridge and the railway station, where Redmond thanked 'those faithful and indulgent supporters of mine who for such a long number of years have honoured me with confidence and trust'. The crowd responded with applause and cries of 'always will'.[2] At the opening of the bridge, to be named 'Redmond Bridge' in his honour, the IPP leader spoke at length about the home rule bill then being debated in the House of Commons:

> That goal for which we have struggled during the past 21 years since I first came to Waterford is within our grasp. We all believe and know that in a few short months an Irish parliament will be sitting in College Green. This beautiful new bridge is a sign of the new commercial life that is before Ireland ... I look forward with confidence to the day that this noble river of yours will run through a really thriving and prosperous city, whose population, drawn from many races and cherishing many different creeds, will on that happy day be working in peace and in unity under the shelter of a free national institution for the welfare of their common country.[3]

He then pressed the button to lower the opening span and formally declared the bridge open to traffic. Redmond did not live to see a home rule parliament. He could not have foreseen the decade of threats of violence, violence and government reaction to violence that engulfed Waterford, Ireland and Europe, a decade during which the IPP disintegrated and new political forces emerged in Ireland. In 1922 Redmond's son, William, represented Waterford in the parliament of a self-governing Irish dominion from which the six counties of Northern Ireland had been excluded. This book charts how Waterford was affected by that tumultuous decade.

As illustrated in map 1, physically Waterford is well defined to the south, east and north by the sea, the River Suir and the Comeragh and Knockmealdown Mountains. In the west of the county the rich farmlands of the Blackwater and Bride river valleys merge seamlessly with neighbouring east Cork. Between the sea and the mountains, up to thirty miles inland, the land is fertile and intensively farmed. By contrast, in the early twentieth century, the mountainous north of the county, about 110,000 acres or 25 per cent of the county, was bare, wind-swept bogland and poor upland grazing. The broad tidal rivers of the Blackwater and Suir facilitated communication and trade and their fertile valleys were home to several members of Ireland's landed ascendancy. Their stately homes and large demesnes bore testimony to their power and influence. The Monavullagh Mountains reach south from the Comeraghs and almost dissect County Waterford. Although both parts of the county had mainly rich farmlands with many landlord mansions and estates, culturally, economically, and politically they differed significantly. Apart from Waterford city, the main population centres were Dungarvan (the administrative centre for the county), Cappoquin, Lismore, Tallow and Tramore.

In 1911 the population of Waterford, city and county, was 83,926, a decrease of 57 per cent since 1841.[4] Emigration accounted for much of the post-Famine decrease. Between 1851 and 1911, a total of 107,336 people (53,554 males and 49,782 females) had emigrated from Waterford, the majority from rural districts.[5] In the same period the proportion of the Waterford population living in urban areas increased from 18 to 46 per cent. This reflected a national trend but can in part be attributed to the expansion in the area of most urban centres under the Local Government (Ireland) Act of 1898.[6] In 1911 Waterford city had a population of 27,464. The next most populous centre was Dungarvan with 4,977 residents, while other towns ranged from a population of 1,644 in Tramore to 849 in Tallow.[7] By 1912 the city and towns provided a range of services for the growing agricultural economy and in turn benefitted from the farming community's prosperity.

Denominationally, Waterford was largely Roman Catholic. The 1911 census recorded that 96 per cent of the county and 92 per cent of the city population were Catholic, with the majority of the balance being Church of Ireland.[8] The Methodist and Presbyterian communities each accounted for about 0.5 per cent of the population of the city and county. There was also a small but influential Quaker community, numbering about 300 people, mainly in the city. The denominational profile of Waterford was similar to that of the adjoining counties of Wexford, Kilkenny, Tipperary and Cork, where Roman Catholics accounted for between 91 and 95 per cent of the population.[9] All of Waterford city and county, as well as part of Tipperary, was situated in the Roman Catholic diocese of Waterford and Lismore. Between 1892 and 1915, the presiding bishop was Richard Sheehan, who was described by the diocesan historian as 'a man of tireless zeal and energy, of broad sympathies and exact information'.[10] Socially conservative, his public pronouncements, like those of his fellow bishops, promoted Catholic claims in the field of educa-

tion and warned against social evils. He constantly exhorted the British government to increase education grants at all levels and took an active part on
local educational bodies such as the technical instruction committee of the
Waterford Central Technical Institute.[11] Sheehan was a close friend of
Redmond and often advised him on educational matters. In 1912 Waterford
and Lismore had 109 diocesan priests and almost 500 regular priests, brothers and nuns.[12] If Bishop Sheehan avoided overt political involvement, the
same could not be said for his priests. Throughout the city and county, parish
priests and curates involved themselves in branches of the United Irish
League (UIL), the local network of the IPP. At one selection convention in
1913, for instance, there were at least fourteen priests among the 145 delegates.[13] Sheehan died in November 1915 and was succeeded four months later
by Bernard Hackett, a Redemptorist priest, who possessed 'a remarkably
quick mind – ready perhaps, rather than profound, with a judgement rather
intuitive than reasoned'.[14] Although his views and public utterances did not
differ significantly from those of his predecessor, he was not a close friend of
Redmond.[15]

Henry Stewart O'Hara was Church of Ireland bishop of the united dioceses of Cashel, Emly, Waterford and Lismore from his consecration in 1900 to
his retirement in 1919. He resided in Waterford. A native of Derry, before
his election to the episcopacy O'Hara had been vicar of Belfast and was
instrumental in the building of St Anne's cathedral, of which he was the first
dean. O'Hara was staunchly unionist and at times outspokenly anti-Catholic.
One fiery sermon preached in Coleraine in 1902 drew the condemnation of
Waterford Corporation and the board of guardians. There was considerable
disquiet even among his own flock in Waterford. Robert Dobbyn, a Church
of Ireland solicitor, noted in his diary how 'the old respectable Protestants are
very indignant as they and the RCs were always good friends'.[16] By 1912,
however, the bishop was acutely conscious that his church was 'but a feeble
minority', and consequently tended to be guarded in his public utterances.[17]
O'Hara had only seventy incumbents to assist him in caring for his widely
dispersed flock and he often preached about the need for vocations and better
stipends for the clergy.[18] R.B. McDowell credits him with 'fusing to an
extraordinary degree fiery enthusiasm for his church with a shrewd grasp of
practical detail'.[19]

In 1912 the economy of Waterford was predominantly agricultural and
serviced the domestic market and, in particular, the expanding British one.
This growing prosperity in the fertile land of south-east Ireland, in Counties
Waterford, Tipperary, Wexford, Kilkenny and Cork, benefitted the emerging
new class of farm owners, their labourers and market towns such as
Dungarvan that served them.[20] As a major port and rail centre with direct lines
to Dublin, Limerick, Kilkenny, Rosslare and Cork, and serving a thriving hin-

terland, Waterford city benefitted significantly from rising Irish agricultural prosperity. The bacon trade was central to the city's economy. Four bacon-curing firms with 850 employees and a further 150 pig-buyers managed an annual kill of about 450,000 pigs, about one-third of the national stock.[21] Most of this produce, together with growing numbers of live cattle, was exported via regular shipping services to Glasgow, Liverpool, Bristol and London. Both city and county had other industries based on the processing of agricultural produce such as corn mills, breweries and creameries.[22] In 1894 a group of Waterford dairy farmers founded the first cooperative creamery in the county in Gaultier and by 1904 there were twenty creameries in Waterford. This lagged far behind neighbouring Tipperary, which had 121 creameries, and it reflected the lesser importance of dairying in County Waterford.[23]

As a maritime county one might have expected Waterford to have a thriving commercial sea fishery. In reality it had an undercapitalized inshore fishing fleet powered by sail. Steam trawlers from as far away as Lowestoft and Aberdeen made sizeable and lucrative catches in the waters off Waterford. This had but a limited impact on the local economy as the trawlers only occasionally put into port to land their catches for transport by rail to London.[24] Local fishermen fished the inshore waters to supply the local markets only. The Blackwater, the Suir and the Bride were noted salmon rivers and sport fishing contributed to an increase in tourism. After agriculture, transport services were a key source of employment for males as railwaymen, dockers, carters and casual labourers, while domestic service was the main outlet for female workers. Across the county there were several reminders of Waterford's strong manufacturing past such as the abandoned cotton mills in Portlaw, the derelict mine workings near Bunmahon and the remains of the shipyards in Waterford city; all bore mute testimony to an earlier industrial heritage. The city's over-reliance on processing agricultural goods was vividly illustrated in March 1913 when a pig brought into Waterford from a Tipperary farm was suspected of having foot and mouth disease. The ensuing two-month ban on all livestock movements in the city and its hinterland led to the closure of the processing factories, widespread lay-offs in the railways and docks, and significant distress in both city and county.[25]

This limited economic activity did not benefit all of Waterford city's citizens equally. At one end of the spectrum, a small cohort of wealthy businessmen lived in substantial residences, mainly on the Dunmore Road. Families such as the Jacobs, who were architects and solicitors; the Goffs, who had shipping, railway and construction interests; and the Strangmans, who were brewers and bacon-curers, dominated the commercial life of the city. Their comfortable and leisurely lifestyle has been captured evocatively in the unpublished diaries of Rosamond Jacob and Emily Ussher, and Annabel Goff-Davis's memoir *Walled gardens*.[26] Sir William G.D. Goff, a Protestant, unionist and a major employer of labour through his various enterprises, was the acknowledged leader and spokesman of this elite. He also served as south-east provincial grand master of the Freemasons and was master of the local Royal Shamrock Lodge No. 32.[27] A thriving middle class comprising traders, shopkeepers and professionals, such as doctors and lawyers, also enjoyed a comfortable lifestyle. Owing to the city's restricted manufacturing base the number of skilled tradesmen was relatively small.

At the opposite end of the socio-economic spectrum were those dependent on casual labour or charity for subsistence. The 1911 census enumerated 8,145 labourers: 1,244 were employed in transport and a further 1,998 classed as general labourers.[28] The female labour force numbered 3,179: 1,258 were domestic servants and 421 worked in dressmaking. In 1911 just over 4 per cent of the Waterford Poor Law Union population, about 1,400 persons, were either workhouse inmates or in receipt of outdoor relief, proportionally greater than the cities of Cork, Limerick and Dublin. Some of the unskilled labourers, who could not find regular employment, lived in appalling slums. A detailed report prepared by the Local Government Board of Ireland (LGB) in 1911 revealed an impoverished underclass living in unsanitary conditions with higher than average infant mortality and deaths from tuberculosis. The inspectors found it 'sad to see some of the children in the poorest houses, with their puny bodies insufficiently clad, with sore eyes and swollen glands, and many other symptoms which are sure tokens of want and misery.'[29] Preoccupied with the daily grind of survival, this deprived cohort unsurprisingly showed little interest in political activism. The 1911 report estimated that no less than 1,470 persons, over 5 per cent of Waterford city's population, lived in these conditions. By comparison, about 20 per cent of Dublin's population lived in similar circumstances.[30] Seán O'Faoláin's bitter description of his native Cork city could be applied with equal force to Waterford city: 'Merely a country town filled with half-rich and pauper-poor, and small merchants and petty tradesmen who ... fatted the priests and kept the monks and nuns and starveling beggars alive, and made those half-rich happy in their half-wealth.'[31]

In rural Waterford prosperity was more evenly spread and poverty less pronounced. The ongoing transfer of land ownership under the land acts, especially the Wyndham Act of 1903, had created a class of prosperous farmers that was well positioned to avail of the market demand for their produce. The average farm size in Waterford was larger than that in neighbouring counties with a higher average valuation and with just over two farm labourers per farm.[32] Under the various land acts up to 1909, the total acreage purchased by tenants was 56 per cent. By contrast, 74 per cent had been purchased in County Cork and 76 per cent in County Kilkenny. The relatively small amount purchased in Waterford did not, however, give rise to agrarian unrest.[33] Most of the workforce in the county were classified as unskilled labourers: in 1911 out of 12,272 male workers, who were not farmers or assisting relatives, 7,351 were agricultural or general labourers. Domestic service remained the principal outlet for female employment with 2,469 or 49 per cent of the rural female workforce engaged in that occupation.[34] These workers had experienced some significant improvements in their living standards. For instance, agricultural labourers benefitted from the provisions of the 1906 Rural Housing Act to the extent that by 1913 over 2,500 cottages, each with a half-acre, had been provided in Waterford county.[35] Nevertheless, earning a living remained a challenge for the majority. This was particularly the case for farm labourers as wage rates in Waterford were the lowest in Munster with outdoor labourers earning between 12 and 15*s.* per week.[36]

Commercial farmers benefitted most from the agricultural prosperity of the early twentieth century, along with middlemen such as pig buyers. At the top of the region's socio-economic pyramid were the landlords and aristocracy in their castles and country houses clustered along the valleys of the Suir, the Bride and the Blackwater. Although a widening of the franchise, disestablishment of the Church of Ireland and land transfers had greatly reduced their power, their status and wealth were undiminished. Sir John Keane of Cappoquin House was the most visible and active of this class and he often spoke publicly on farming issues.[37] His membership of Waterford County Council gave him a platform from which to air his views and to represent the interests of his land-owning class. Committed to maintaining the status quo, the larger landowners viewed themselves as having most to lose in the event of revolutionary change.

The Royal Irish Constabulary (RIC), British army and coastguard had a widespread and visible presence in Waterford. From his headquarters in Lady Lane Barracks in Waterford city, RIC County Inspector (CI) William Hetreed controlled a network of thirty-four barracks, staffed by 238 officers and constables, organized in four districts: Waterford city, Portlaw, Dungarvan and Cappoquin.[38] This enabled him to monitor and report on all activities, political, labour or criminal, although these were evidently few in number as his monthly reports between 1908 and 1912 typically concluded: 'the county is generally peaceable; no indictable offences; no rent troubles; political societies quiet; no boycotting or intimidation; no secret societies in county'.[39] Hetreed was replaced by Robert J. Maunsell in 1918 and in turn he was succeeded by Captain Cornelius O'Beirne in December 1920. There was no tradition of agrarian violence in the county. In 1912 both city and county waited peacefully for home rule and the expected resultant prosperity. The British army did not have a significant presence in the city or county. There were two army barracks in the city, both appropriately on Barrack Street. The Infantry Barracks housed the 72nd Battery, Royal Field Artillery (RFA), part of the XXXVIII Brigade, RFA, which had its headquarters in Fermoy.[40] At the time of the 1911 census the 72nd Battery consisted of 125 officers and men, none of whom were born locally, the majority being English. Further along Barrack Street was the Artillery Barracks, previously the home of the Waterford Militia Artillery. Weekly drills had taken place there for the part-time soldiers of the militia until 1909 when the unit was disbanded. In 1912 the barracks operated on a care and maintenance basis with just four soldiers billeted there. Beyond the county boundary was a string of large military establishments in Fermoy, Tipperary, Cahir and Clonmel. Although Fermoy was the largest, Clonmel was the most important for Waterford. It housed the depot of the local regiment, the Royal Irish, and local recruits enlisted and received their training there. There was a strong tradition of army service in Waterford, especially in the city, reflecting the traditional urban bias in recruiting. Among those who enlisted in 1912 was 12-year-old John Condon from St Thomas's Avenue, who became the youngest British army fatality in the First World War.[41] As a maritime city and county, there was also a tradition of service in the Royal Navy among the seafaring communities along the coast. Seven coastguard stations watched the coast from Ardmore to Dunmore East. The economic benefit of a military presence in the city was recognized and led to occasional calls at corporation meetings for more troops to be stationed in the under-utilized barracks.

Between 1885 and 1918 Waterford was divided into three parliamentary constituencies: Waterford Borough (the city), Waterford County East and Waterford County West (see map 2). In 1912 all three were held by members of the IPP: John Redmond, Patrick Joseph Power and James John O'Shee[42] respectively. Redmond had followed his father into politics and was first elected in 1881. In the bitter aftermath of the 'Parnell split' he sided with his leader. Following Parnell's death on 6 October 1891, Redmond, in an act of electoral bravery, resigned his own seat to contest the by-election in Cork but was defeated. Two months later, in December, he defeated Michael Davitt in Waterford city in a contest marred by street violence and bitter polemics. Davitt ascribed Redmond's triumph to a combination of 'toryism and terrorism', while others characterized Redmond's support as a unique combination of 'fenians and unionists'.[43] Redmond and his supporters celebrated in their stronghold – the hill of Ballybricken. He and the people of Waterford city had forged a bond and Redmondism – a political creed that owed more to loyalty to Redmond, and after his death to his family, than to any ideology – was the dominant political force in the city. This bond was strengthened when Redmond successfully defended members of the Ballybricken Pig Buyers' Association who had been charged with violent conduct during a strike in 1893. As a Parnellite, Redmond was, in the view of the RIC, associated with Fenianism, especially during the 1798 centenary celebrations. However, his speeches showed a total commitment to parliamentary methods and a willingness to

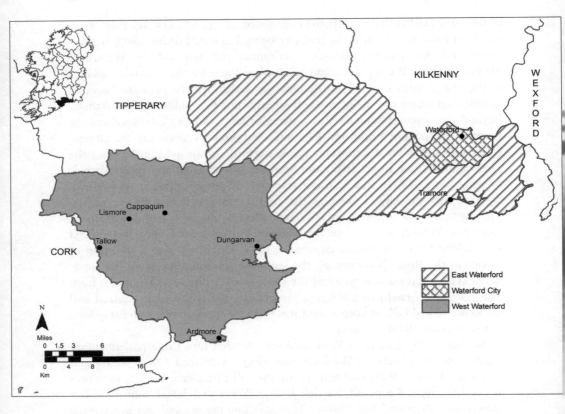

2 Parliamentary constituencies in 1910

extend the olive branch to landlords and unionists. When the IPP reunited in
1900 Redmond was chosen as chairman. He proved a capable incumbent and
kept such personalities as John Dillon, Joe Devlin, Tim Healy and William
O'Brien within the fold, at least most of the time. After the inconclusive general elections in 1910 Redmond found himself holding the balance of power at
Westminster and set about realizing the goal of all-Ireland home rule.

   Until his sudden death in January 1913 Waterford East was represented
by Patrick Joseph Power of Carrickbeg, an anti-Parnellite and a wealthy
landowner with extensive holdings in Waterford and Tipperary. First elected
in 1885, he was returned unopposed in five general elections between 1892
and 1913.[44] Following the resignation of Alfred Webb, a well-known Quaker
nationalist in 1895, Waterford West was represented by J.J. O'Shee, a solicitor by profession who had helped to found the Land and Labour Association
in 1894. In parliament he continued to champion the causes of tenant rights

and labour. In the two general elections of 1910, O'Shee was opposed by candidates who supported William O'Brien, the independent nationalist leader, but on each occasion O'Shee won decisively.[45] The revision of constituencies in advance of the 1918 general election reduced the number of parliamentary constituencies to two: Waterford County (which now encompassed all of Waterford West and most of Waterford East) and Waterford City. The latter was enlarged to include adjoining rural districts to ensure that it met the minimum population requirement of 30,000 for a borough seat.

Power does not seem to have been active locally but he was prominent at public meetings in England in support of home rule. On his death in January 1913 he was described as 'a country gentleman of the good old type' and 'intensely religious'.[46] By contrast, O'Shee pursued local issues with zeal both inside and outside parliament and his efforts were reported extensively in the local press.

After becoming leader of the IPP, Redmond was not a frequent visitor to his constituency due to the pressure of parliamentary business. Instead he relied on a local network to keep him abreast of constituents' concerns and to inform them of his efforts on their behalf. P.A. Murphy, a solicitor, was his principal local agent but others including successive mayors, city and district councillors, newspaper proprietors and priests also laboured on his behalf. The erection of the new bridge over the River Suir was regarded as the result of his efforts to develop the city. At that time Redmond admitted he would have liked to have done more for the 'material benefit' of Waterford but that the struggle for home rule had become 'all-engrossing'.[47] The IPP leader did, however, exert his parliamentary influence to secure housing loans for Waterford Corporation, even if this meant occasionally overruling the LGB.[48]

Following the Municipal Corporations Act of 1840 local representation in the city had been dominated by nationalists. Redmond's advocacy in parliament ensured the passage of the Waterford Corporation Act in 1896, which tripled the area of the city and transferred the powers of the grand jury to the corporation.[49] The Local Government Act of 1898 extended the franchise but, nonetheless, Labour had failed to make any significant electoral progress. At the 1912 corporation election Labour secured just three of the forty seats. The most notable of these was Richard Keane, a local trade union activist and organizer.[50] Seven seats were won by representatives of the Ratepayers and Burgesses Association, which represented the conservative and business interests in the city. Founded by Charlie Strange and W.G.D. Goff in 1896, the association, which mainly lobbied to maintain low rates, was led by Strange, a self-proclaimed socialist and atheist. Waterford city had been and continued to be very progressive in the provision of social housing and had significant rental income. Consequently, rates were low in comparison to other urban centres in Ireland.[51] The other seats in the 1912 corporation election were won by supporters of Redmond. Though elected annually, the mayoralty, a prized position, was often filled by the same incumbent for two or three years in succession.

The Local Government Act occasioned major changes in local government structures in the county, including the creation of a county council, urban and rural district councils and boards of guardians, elected triennially (see map 3).[52] For electoral purposes Waterford county was divided into twenty electoral areas, each returning one member. This group of twenty together with the seven chairmen of the rural district councils, three members nominated by the county grand jury and two co-opted members comprised Waterford County Council. That body had significant local powers in terms of construction and administration and was funded by local taxation, the rates, and a grant from central government. From the outset some local landlords such as Sir John Keane and Gerard Villiers-Stuart took an active part in the county council, standing successfully at elections and participating in council deliberations. Most of the other seats were held by members of the UIL, who often discussed purely party matters at council meetings. The primary concerns of all the councils – city, county and urban and rural district – were housing, road maintenance, capital expenditure on piers, bridges and roads, as well as other local issues.

In the decade prior to 1912 the cause of labour in Waterford gained ground with 1908 proving a watershed year. After several failed attempts, a sustainable Trades Council was established in the city to represent the interests of organized labour.[53] Although its strength and influence subsequently waxed and waned, the Trades Council succeeded in maintaining itself as a voice for an alternative agenda to that of the merchants and factory owners. As in other cities and towns across Ireland, the initial growth in organized trade unionism was based mainly on dock and other transport workers. Waterford was represented at a meeting of disaffected National Union of Dock Labourers (NUDL) members on 28 December 1908 which decided to form an Irish union for general workers. On 4 January 1909 the Irish Transport and General Workers' Union (ITGWU) was officially launched with most of the NUDL membership in Dublin, Cork, Belfast and Waterford transferring to the new union.[54] Under the inspirational leadership of Jim Larkin, the ITGWU moved aggressively to improve the pay and conditions of its members. Larkin himself visited Waterford on 15 October 1908 to an enthusiastic welcome from the workers and much adverse comment from the business class.[55]

Reflecting both a new-found confidence in its own strength and the industrial conflicts sweeping England and Ireland, the local union movement participated in a number of national disputes and initiated local strikes. In September 1911 rail services to and from Waterford were paralyzed by a railworkers' strike called in sympathy with the actions of the Amalgamated

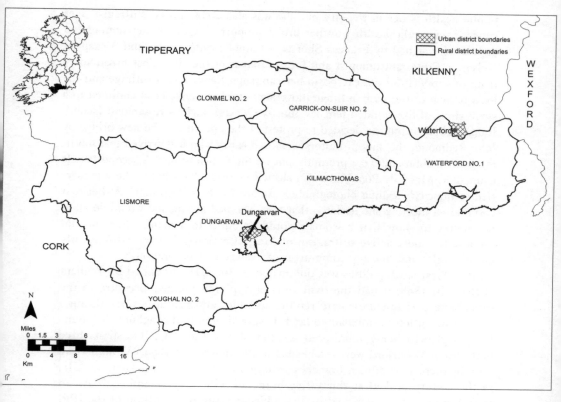

3 Local government divisions

Society of Railway Servants (ASRS) in England.[56] This action soon involved
local dockers who refused to handle 'blacked' goods. Although the strike was
not successful and the ASRS admitted defeat, labour morale remained high.
Between 1912 and 1914 four strikes in Waterford won significant wage
increases for groups such as painters, carpenters, masons and tailors.[57] However, all of these victories were for skilled workers. The great mass of the city's
working class, general labourers, saw no improvement and the union movement failed to recruit them in any significant numbers. The general strikes of
unskilled workers in Belfast (1907), Dublin (1908 and 1913), Cork (1909) and
Wexford (1911) had no counterpart in Waterford. Yet by 1913 the labour
movement had established itself in the city with a functioning Trades Council
and three representatives on Waterford Corporation. Rural labourers remained
unorganized but were a potential source of future recruits.

Dr Mary Strangman was the first woman elected to Waterford Corporation
in January 1912.[58] She probably owed her election to her crusading zeal on

public health issues in the city but she was also a committed suffragist. Her concern for public health won her broad support. A Quaker, her nomination papers were signed by Frances Shortis, a Catholic cattle dealer and Alexander Nelson, a Protestant unionist and former mayor of the city. That broad spectrum of support did not extend to her campaign for women's suffrage and the local branch of the Irish suffrage movement seems to have been confined to a small circle of like-minded females, mostly Quakers such as Rosamond Jacob.[59] Indeed when suffragists decided to protest at the opening of the new bridge by John Redmond, the only protestors were two ladies who had arrived that morning from Dublin and were promptly put on the return train.[60] A second female councillor, Mrs Lily Poole, was also elected in 1912. A Catholic, she was married to the city's leading photographer, Arthur Poole, a Protestant. At her first corporation meeting she declared that 'now she had got in, she would do all in her power to show that a woman would be equal to a man'.[61] She did not espouse the more active suffragism of Mary Strangman but served diligently on the health and housing committees of Waterford Corporation.[62]

At a local level, politics was dominated by the UIL. Founded by William O'Brien in 1898, it had the twin aims of applying popular pressure to the squabbling parliamentarians to reunite and alleviating rural poverty through the redistribution of untenanted land. It spread rapidly throughout the country, its growth being monitored assiduously by the RIC. The first three branches in Waterford were established in the summer of 1899. Within twelve months there were fifteen branches with 902 members. A year later the UIL in the county peaked at thirty-five branches with 2,333 members.[63] As an organization it soon achieved its first objective, the reunification of the IPP. Its second aim had geographical limitations as the so-called 'ranch war' was restricted to Connacht and the midland counties and had little impact on the largely dairy and tillage farms of the south-east. The national UIL convention in June 1900 sealed the reunification of the IPP and defined the relationship between party and league with UIL branches becoming the local IPP branches. In areas where the revived land war was a burning issue there was often tension between the radicalism of the local branches and the innate conservatism of the parliamentary leadership. There was no such tension in Waterford, however. The two general elections in 1910 occasioned an upsurge in interest in politics with the first contested parliamentary election in Waterford for over a decade being won decisively by O'Shee. Reflecting the upsurge in interest, the number of UIL branches in Waterford city and county grew from twenty-two to twenty-nine between December 1909 and December 1910, rising to thirty a year later.[64]

On the surface, the thirty branches and 1,306 members of the UIL in Waterford in 1912, spread over the three parliamentary constituencies, suggest a vigorous political movement in touch with the concerns of the electorate. However, scrutiny of the minute book of the UIL National Directory reveals a very different picture.[65] Each branch was required to pay an annual affiliation fee of £3 but in 1913 only twenty branches in Waterford city and county did so. While this was certainly an improvement on 1909, when just thirteen branches paid up, it reflected heightened political expectancy engendered by the introduction of the home rule bill in 1912. Yet it still suggests that a third of the branches existed on paper only. This was in part a reflection of the dominance of the UIL and the IPP. Political organizations exist to fight elections. In an era of uncontested elections it was inevitable that some branches would fall into abeyance. The death of Patrick Joseph Power in January 1913 saw a flurry of meetings of the East Waterford constituency branches, all well reported in the local newspapers, as candidates sought support.[66] Once Martin Murphy had secured the nomination, reports of meetings disappeared, suggesting a return to apathy. Would the UIL be a sleeping giant or a paper tiger in the event of a powerful electoral challenge?

There was a small but important Fenian legacy in Waterford. In the aftermath of the failed rising of 1867, the IRB had infiltrated and influenced various nationalist movements such as the Young Ireland Association, the Amnesty Association and the 1798 Centenary Celebration Committee.[67] All had been active in Waterford and all had been carefully monitored by the RIC. In 1892 the police estimated that there were 450 active Fenians or sympathizers in the city, including all of the officers of the city branch of the Young Ireland Society, namely: John Redmond, president; Charlie Strange, vice-president; John Shallow, secretary; and J.P. Walsh, treasurer.[68] Two years later a crowd of over 600 attended an Amnesty Association meeting in Waterford city addressed by Fred Allan, president of the IRB. The 1798 Centenary Celebration Committee in the city was identified by the RIC as an IRB front; Martin Arthur, president; Bryan Cunningham, treasurer; and Thomas Meagher, secretary were all suspected of IRB membership. In Dungarvan, two other IRB men controlled the local branch – John Curran, president and Thomas O'Connell, secretary.[69] However, with the release of the last of the political prisoners and the completion of the '98 centenary commemorations, the IRB lost focus. By 1906 it was virtually moribund. While some young recruits joined, they almost invariably drifted away after a year or two of fruitless theorizing and no prospect of action. To all intents and purposes it had become a social club for former revolutionaries.[70] The John O'Leary funeral in March 1907 was eloquent testimony to the IRB's reduced condition. Organizationally it was a shambles and the attendance modest at best. The annual Manchester Martyrs' commemoration was little better. A longstanding key date in the separatist calendar, it constituted the most visible demonstration of support for militancy. Yet in 1909 the RIC Crime Special Branch reported an attendance of just 300 in Waterford and 'the crowd consisted principally of the artisan, labouring and corner-boy classes'.[71] It seemed that republican Ireland, like romantic Ireland, was with O'Leary in the grave!

However, just when this last vestige of Fenianism seemed about to expire, it received a transfusion of new blood. From 1907 younger men revitalized the organization. Thomas Clarke returned from America and his idealism inspired men like Seán Mac Diarmada, Diarmuid Lynch, Bulmer Hobson and Denis McCullough. With new dynamism they set about recasting the movement.[72] The old leadership was ruthlessly purged. A few key members were appointed as organizers, among them Michael Crowe of Limerick, who later became divisional centre for Munster. Acting discreetly, he recruited likeminded individuals such as Willie (Liam) Walsh of Waterford.[73] Born in the city in 1879, Walsh was the leading figure in Waterford GAA circles. In 1909 he was sworn into the Brotherhood by Crowe and tasked with establishing an IRB circle. Over the next few years Walsh swore in thirty-one men in Waterford city, including Kilmacow native Seán Matthews, who later succeeded Walsh as head centre for Waterford.[74] Meetings took place in the house of J.D. Walsh in John Street, usually on a quarterly basis. To maintain more frequent contact and to provide a cover for their activities, Willie Walsh established the John Mitchell Hurling Club; the membership was drawn almost exclusively from the ranks of the IRB. Attached to the Survey Branch of the Post Office, P.C. O'Mahony's duties took him around the country and provided perfect cover for his work as an IRB organizer.[75] In September 1914 he was posted to Dungarvan as supervising clerk. O'Mahony was active in the local company of the Irish Volunteers. He also established an IRB circle and inducted twenty men, among them Pax Whelan, Dan Fraher and George Lennon, all were later prominent during the War of Independence.

A parallel, though open, organization was Fianna Éireann. Formed in 1909 by Countess Markievicz, who was assisted by Bulmer Hobson, it was an avowedly nationalist boy scout movement controlled by the IRB.[76] Two years later, Liam Mellows was appointed full-time organizer and instructor. He travelled the country by bicycle to organize the 'slua', as each branch was known, while at the same time operating as an IRB organizer. In 1912 he visited Waterford and stayed with Willie Walsh. At a meeting in the Gaelic League Hall in William Street, he inaugurated the 'Thomas Francis Meagher Slua' with Thomas Barry, Paddy Hearne and James Nolan, a nephew of Willie Walsh, as its officers.[77] Though never numbering more than fifty, the slua went on to fulfil its main purpose, to provide a steady stream of volunteers for the IRA during the period 1919–22. Unlike IRB circles in other parts of the country, Walsh and Matthews managed to keep their activities secret from the prying eyes of the RIC Crime Special Branch. As late as 1914 it was reported that there were 'no secret societies in Waterford city and county'.[78] A branch of the new Sinn Féin (SF) political party was formed in the city in

1906. James Upton, a prominent local journalist, presided over the inaugural meeting. James Fleming was elected chairperson of the new branch and Patrick Brazil secretary.[79] But the party failed to make any headway locally and by 1912 was moribund.

In terms of sport and cultural life, Waterford was well served by both the Gaelic Athletic Association (GAA) and the Gaelic League. The first GAA clubs were established in 1885, one year after the foundation of the association.[80] By 1912 there were thirty clubs in Waterford city and county. Football was the more popular game in the county and hurling more popular in the city. Coverage of the games in the local press was extensive and the GAA was undoubtedly growing in popularity. There were also numerous cricket and association football clubs. The first branch of the Gaelic League in Waterford was established in 1895, two years after the league was inaugurated.[81] A number of priests and teachers organized classes in Irish for local communities and the *Waterford News* began to publish an Irish column. While the local classes soon became a valuable social outlet for the members of the league, the use of Irish in the county continued to decline. In the 1911 census 29 per cent of the population of County Waterford described themselves as Irish speakers but, as in other parts of the country, the daily use of Irish was in seemingly inexorable decline.[82]

Local and national newspapers were very important in forming and reflecting local opinion. The *Munster Express*, published in the city, was owned and edited by Edward Walsh, a dedicated supporter of John Redmond. According to his son, Walsh was a 'most arduous home ruler who believed in the display of physical force rather than the use of it'.[83] The *Munster Express* consistently reflected the position of the IPP. Although strongly nationalist, the *Waterford News* gave qualified support to Redmond and was routinely monitored by the RIC for any signs of sedition. It was owned and edited by Edmund Downey, a noted local historian.[84] The *Waterford Standard* was the voice of the unionist and commercial community. Robert Whalley, its owner and editor, took a firmly unionist line on political matters and campaigned against high business rates and other taxes. The weekly *Church of Ireland Gazette* also reflected the concerns of the Protestant community in its editorials, reports and correspondence. The west of the county was served by the *Dungarvan Observer*, established in 1912 by James Lynch, a fervent nationalist and supporter of home rule.

This, then, was Waterford in 1912 and in many respects it reflected the country at large, outside of the north-east, with a falling mainly Roman Catholic population, an economy based on agriculture and a politically dominant IPP. While these were the main features of the social, economic and political landscape, there were other emerging elements, including small groups of dedicated people committed to realizing their ideal of an inde-

pendent republic or of a socialist state. Although these were minority positions, their potential was immense. At one end of the political spectrum stood
the IRB, a small band of nationalists who were committed to the physical
force ideal. At the other was the unionist community, predominantly but not
completely Protestant, who dreaded the prospect of home rule. Socially there
was an equally large divide between the landed aristocracy and the inhabitants
of the slums of the city. Cultural nationalism, as embodied in the Gaelic
League and the GAA, was making progress. For many people though, their
main focus was on gaining employment that would provide them with a living
wage and they regarded the trade union movement as their vehicle for
advancement. This book explores how the hopes and fears of these various
groups were realized during the period of the Irish Revolution, 1912–23.
Drawing on a range of sources both national and local – parliamentary
debates, local government records, newspapers, diaries, IRA sources, RIC and
British army reports – the story of Waterford and its people is charted against
a background of national and international developments in a period of
unprecedented turbulence at home and abroad.

2 'We have fought and we have won':[1] Waterford and home rule, 1912-14

On 11 April 1912 Prime Minister Herbert Asquith introduced the third home rule bill in the House of Commons.[2] While Conservative and Unionist members shouted and jeered, John Redmond sat quietly in his seat reflecting on his moment of triumph. With support from both the Liberals and the Labour Party, and with the power of veto of the House of Lords curtailed by the provisions of the Parliament Act of 1911, the passage of the bill through parliament could be delayed for two years but could not be prevented. The occasion was celebrated in nationalist circles throughout Ireland but for the unionist community it generated fear and anger. With the aggressive support of Andrew Bonar Law, leader of the Conservative Party, Unionists prepared to resist the measure by all means possible, both inside and outside parliament. The debate over home rule dominated politics in Ireland and in Britain for the next two years. Arising from the unique bond between Redmond and the nationalists of Waterford city and county, his constituents demonstrated unwavering loyalty to home rule at every opportunity. By contrast, the small unionist community in Waterford opposed the bill and awaited its enactment with apprehension. As the debate moved from parliament to extra-parliamentary methods both nationalists and unionists showed their readiness to support such means. But home rule was not the only issue facing Waterford and Ireland between 1912 and 1914. The move to extend the franchise to women received a setback in 1912 when the Franchise (Women) bill was defeated in parliament with the support of the IPP. 'Larkinism', an employer catchword for the new militant trade unionism, was spreading and the years 1913 and 1914 were marked by strikes, lock-outs and other forms of industrial action in Irish urban centres, including Waterford. The new aggressive labour tactics of the sympathetic strike or 'one out, all out' and the refusal to handle goods produced by firms involved in industrial disputes had the potential to provoke equally hard-line reactions from employers. Labour solidarity in Ireland was tested and found wanting in this period. In Waterford, as in other centres of trade unionism in Ireland, the movement was in a position of unprecedented strength in 1913 but a year later had become a demoralized and contracting force.[3] By comparison with the city, rural Waterford remained quiet. The monthly reports of the county inspector for 1913 and 1914 revealed that rural Waterford continued 'to be very peaceable' with 'no evictions, seizures for rent, notices of eviction or sales under the land acts'.[4] By summer 1914 the constitutional crisis overshadowed all other concerns as Ireland moved, seemingly inexorably, towards civil war.

Immediately after the introduction of the home rule bill, Redmond was inundated with messages of congratulations from nationalist groups at home and abroad.[5] Waterford Corporation, Waterford County Council and the district councils all moved congratulatory motions. The corporation met in special session on 25 April and agreed that the mayor, high sheriff and members of the corporation would 'attend in state on Mr Redmond to present the motion to him'.[6] Local branches of the UIL took the opportunity to launch collections for the home rule fund which was to be used to counter unionist propaganda in Britain.[7] Neither the local nor the national press carried significant analysis of the content of the home rule bill, which granted very limited powers to the proposed Irish executive.[8] According to Alan Ward, the '1912 home rule bill was one step forward and two steps back' when compared to earlier home rule bills as it invested enhanced powers of veto in the lord lieutenant.[9] While the Irish parliament would have jurisdiction over internal affairs, all matters pertaining to defence, foreign policy, initial control of the RIC, and most crucially, control over revenue, were to be reserved to Westminster.[10] The majority of nationalists accepted Redmond's assurances that this was 'a great and historic measure'.[11] Limitations on the powers of the proposed executive, which were a concern to advanced nationalists, did not mollify unionist opposition.[12] Local newspaper coverage in Waterford was cautiously optimistic. The *Munster Express* confidently predicted 'Bill sure to pass' and 'Unionists and the home rule bill – a hopeless battle'.[13] The *Waterford News* carried interviews with prominent local citizens, including the mayor and the Catholic bishop, and claimed that they had 'pinned their faith' on Redmond's acceptance of the bill.[14] In his speech to the House of Commons on 11 April 1912 the IPP leader assured his listeners that this measure would satisfy nationalist demands and sound 'the death knell of separatist sentiment in Ireland'.[15] For the next two years Irish newspapers, both local and national, reported the legislative proceedings in parliament with each stage of the bill being celebrated as a victory. From an Irish point of view, Redmond dominated the parliamentary proceedings although his leadership and tactics have been subject to recent analysis and criticism.[16] Delegates from Waterford featured prominently at meetings to support Redmond, such as the 'Great National Convention' organized by the UIL at the Mansion House in Dublin on 30 April 1912. Michael Kirwan, mayor of Waterford, and Patrick O'Gorman of Lismore, chairman of the county council, were present along with a large number of delegates, including priests.[17] The Waterford Corporation representatives took advantage of the convention to present their address to Redmond and a cheque for £100, the first instalment of their contribution to the home rule fund.[18]

If nationalist reaction to the prospect of home rule was euphoric, that of their unionist fellow citizens was a mixture of trepidation and determination to resist. Both the *Waterford Standard* and the *Church of Ireland Gazette* reflected their concerns. The main local unionist spokesmen were Sir William Goff and Bishop Henry O'Hara. Both attended a special general synod of the Church of Ireland on 16 April 1912 and a meeting of Munster unionists in Cork on 20 April.[19] The special general synod was probably the most important event in defining the Church of Ireland's position towards home rule and it endorsed a series of motions that committed the church to opposing any home rule bill.[20] In Cork over 2,000 unionists were addressed by the duke of Devonshire and Viscount Midleton, both of whom warned of the threat to the liberties and prosperity of the unionist community under a home rule parliament.[21] In Waterford Goff spoke repeatedly about the fiscal consequences of home rule which, he claimed, would result in increased taxation, reduced trade and an end to the current prosperity.[22] This economic theme was also taken up by O'Hara. On 29 June 1912 he warned the diocesan synod of Waterford and Lismore that home rule would lead inexorably to separation: 'Under settled government or anarchy, a monarch or a republic, a separate Ireland must be a very poor Ireland and a very weak Ireland'.[23]

Inspired by the success of the Cork meeting, Goff decided to organize a similar event in Waterford. He was refused the use of the city hall. The mayor was 'glad to give it for any purpose except that of holding an anti-home rule demonstration'.[24] The meeting went ahead instead in the grounds of the Goff mansion, Glenville, on 13 June 1912. According to police reports, 'a large and representative crowd', heard Goff pronounce on the economic woes that would inevitably accompany home rule.[25] He also suggested that the refusal of the city hall was a foretaste of discrimination to come.[26] The *Waterford News* tried to cast scorn on the meeting. It claimed that the attendance was less than 300 people of whom over 200 were women and that the majority were from the 'furthest reaches of the county' and that 'the muster of citizens of this city did not pass a round dozen'.[27] The list of those in attendance published in the *Waterford Standard* suggests that the RIC were more accurate in their assessment of the crowd.[28] The Solemn League and Covenant was signed on Ulster day, 28 September 1912, as a popular and determined protest against home rule. Four days later Bishop O'Hara presided over a special prayer service in Christchurch cathedral convened ostensibly to give Ulstermen resident in Waterford an opportunity to sign the covenant.[29] Of the thirty-seven men who signed, most, but not all, were from Ulster. Eighteen women signed the Ulster Declaration, the equivalent document for women.[30] No similar ceremony was held in the surrounding counties of Wexford, Kilkenny, Tipperary or Cork. The Glenville meeting and the signing of the covenant were the highpoints of unionist resistance in Waterford. No other public meetings were held, although Robert Whalley and the *Waterford Standard* continued to track the legislative passage of the home rule bill and to record the utterances of Goff and O'Hara. There is no record of prominent Waterford unionists attending any meetings in Ulster or in England. Unionist women were seemingly content to express their opposition by signing the declaration and no branch of the Women's Ulster Alliance was formed in Waterford. By mid-1914 O'Hara had decided that 'it was best for him to say as little as possible on political matters' and informed the diocesan synod that 'all they could do in this part of Ireland was to put themselves in God's hands and to turn to Him for deliverance'.[31]

The home rule bill was introduced at the expense of the Parliamentary Franchise (Women) bill of 1912, which would have given the vote to women. Redmond and the IPP had helped to vote down this measure to secure parliamentary priority for home rule. This aroused the fury of promoters of female suffrage in Ireland.[32] In an interview with the *Waterford News*, city councillor Mary Strangman stated that she would not accept any home rule bill that did not contain a clause giving women the vote. In her opinion, Redmond had 'sacrificed the suffragist cause'.[33] In a lecture to the local branch of the YMCA she criticized the stance of the local MPs on the suffrage question: 'Power was always opposed and nothing should be expected of him; Shee had previously been in favour but was now considering his position and Redmond had betrayed Irish women.'[34] A few months later, Redmond was physically assaulted in Dublin by a group of English suffragettes, one of whom threw a hatchet at him.[35] Although the Irish Women's Franchise League (IWFL) had no knowledge of the presence of the English women or of their plans, they became the object of verbal attack by outraged members of the IPP and UIL. At the July 1912 meeting of Waterford Corporation, Mary Strangman was insulted and verbally abused. One unidentified councillor called on the men of Waterford to 'take up the cudgels against Dr Strangman'.[36] It is hardly any wonder then that the local branch of the IWFL chose not to demonstrate at the opening of the new bridge a few months later. Similarly, three women who had travelled from Dublin to heckle Redmond at a major meeting in Waterford in January 1914 were prevailed upon to return to Dublin before the meeting started.[37] Securing votes for women would have to wait.

The cause of labour made little progress in Waterford between 1912 and 1914. In 1911 workers in the city had shown themselves willing to engage in sympathetic strikes in support of their trade union colleagues in other parts of the United Kingdom. They showed no such readiness to support their colleagues in Dublin who were locked out in August 1913. National trade union leaders such as P.T. Daly and Peter Larkin, brother of Jim Larkin, appealed in vain for support at meetings in Waterford.[38] Local labour councillors were strangely silent on the Dublin dispute. James Gleeson, city councillor and president of the Waterford Trades Council, was supposed to chair a meeting at which Peter Larkin spoke but he neither attended nor sent an apology.[39] His fellow labour councillor, Richard Keane, attended but did not speak.[40]

According to the local press, attendances were small and those present left after the speeches 'amused but not enthused'.[41] Catholic and Protestant clergymen spoke in the city throughout September and October, warning against the spread of socialism and condemning sympathetic strikes.[42] For example, on 21 September Bishop O'Hara preached to his congregation on the dangers of socialism. During that month the local papers carried lengthy extracts from sermons by Catholic priests around the country. Particular attention was paid to the sermons by a Fr Condon, an Augustinian priest who had been born in Dungarvan and who ministered in Dublin. 'The red hand of socialism can be found in parts of Ireland', he thundered, and called on Irish workers 'to be guided by their church'.[43] At one meeting in Waterford in November 1913, Daly found it necessary to condemn clerical interference.[44] The attempt by Mrs Dora Montefiore and others to send children from distressed families in Dublin to homes in England, where they could be properly fed and clothed, led to a confrontation between the Catholic Church and the ITGWU. Archbishop William Walsh of Dublin condemned the move as transferring the children to Protestant care. When a rumour circulated in Waterford that some of the children were to travel by rail via Waterford to the mail boat at Rosslare, Fr Thomas Furlong, administrator of the cathedral parish and a UIL activist, led a large number of clergy and lay people to Waterford North Station where all trains bound for Rosslare were searched. Vigilante action continued at the station for a number of days but no children bound for England were discovered.[45] A week later the Waterford branch of the Associated Society of Locomotive Engineers and Firemen found it necessary to pass a motion declaring that it 'placed our religion first and our trades unionism afterwards'.[46] No real support for the Dublin lockout materialized and at the end of the year the *Waterford Standard* observed that the city was not affected by the Dublin dispute. The editor mused that the experience of 1911 had been enough for the local labour leaders.[47] Indeed the port and the dock labourers benefitted from the increased traffic of ships diverted through the port.[48] A concurrent dispute in the city between masons and employers occasioned no such condemnation. Instead, it was seen as 'old-fashioned trade unionism' and was eventually settled after twelve weeks.[49]

As the home rule bill was completing its final passage through the House of Commons during the early months of 1914, nationalist Ireland celebrated each stage as a triumph. In January Redmond visited Waterford for a major rally.[50] An estimated 50,000 people thronged the city streets as he drove to Ballybricken where a banner proudly proclaimed: 'historic Ballybricken pledges allegiance to Redmond'. The IPP leader told the assembled crowd that this was 'the most remarkable nationalist demonstration ever held in Munster'.[51] A succession of speakers paid tribute to the IPP leader and thanked him 'for leading our oppressed people from political slavery to legislative freedom'.[52]

Redmond concluded the proceedings with a ringing declaration: 'we have fought and we have won. Lift up your hearts. Ireland's long travail is at an end. You are to witness the rebirth of Irish freedom, prosperity and happiness'.[53] The meeting received widespread coverage in the national press.[54] One headline in the *Irish Independent* referred to 'The eve of triumph'.[55] By contrast, the *Irish Times* suggested that the nature of the meeting illustrated 'Redmond's failure as a statesman' as his speech was 'devoted to an enthusiastic hailing of the triumph of home rule rather than confronting the political reality of Ulster resistance'.[56] Three weeks later the Protestant community of Waterford city attended a service in Christchurch cathedral to pray for guidance in their hour of danger.[57] Rosamond Jacob, Quaker, campaigner for the women's franchise, Gaelic League enthusiast and nationalist, noted that a reporter from the *Waterford News* had been sent to record the names of those present.[58] The 'marking of those opposed to home rule' was referred to in the House of Commons by Bonar Law and others, the former being quick to point out that this was done 'by constituents of the hon. member (Redmond)'.[59] This in turn prompted Waterford Corporation to meet in special session and declare that 'the people of Waterford have always respected the religious opinions of their Protestant fellow citizens with whom they have always lived in amity'.[60] To Emily Ussher, of Cappagh House near Dungarvan, the political atmosphere was 'electric' and among her friends gun-running and the prospect of home rule were the sole topics of conversation. She noted a rumour that a unit of the Ulster Volunteer Force (UVF) was being organized in west Waterford for armed resistance to any home rule government.[61] The Usshers were a prominent land owning family known to be liberal in their politics and were gradually excluded from all meetings of their landed neighbours.[62] The appointment of Sir George Richardson, a retired Indian army lieutenant-general, as commander of the UVF, gave rise to a degree of unrest in Lismore where Richardson normally lived with his brother-in-law, Colonel Charles Gordon, and the RIC felt it necessary to provide security at his house.[63]

On 25 May 1914 the home rule bill passed its third reading in the House of Commons. It now needed only the royal assent to become law. That evening and over the next few days nationalists throughout Ireland celebrated. Mass meetings were held, impassioned speeches were made, Irish Volunteers paraded and public bodies met to pass resolutions.[64] On 26 May Waterford Corporation met in special session to pass a resolution congratulating Redmond on his achievement and on his leadership which had, it seemed, at last delivered home rule, the holy grail of constitutional nationalists for more than a century. The motion concluded with the fervent wish 'that Mr Redmond may be long spared to guide the destinies of our country in the old house at College Green'.[65] That evening the city battalion of the Irish Volunteers paraded through the city to the courthouse where they were reviewed by the mayor, Richard Power, and by Martin Murphy MP.[66] Similar motions were passed at specially convened meetings of the county council and the RDCs while demonstrations by the Volunteers also took place in the towns of Dungarvan, Lismore, Tallow and Cappoquin.[67] The *Munster Express* summed up the feelings of Waterford people with its banner headline: 'The triumph of home rule'.[68] But these celebrations, premature as they turned out to be, took place against an ominous background.

Deprived of their last constitutional bulwark, the House of Lords' power of veto, Unionists resorted to the threat of force to prevent enactment of home rule. The paramilitary UVF was formed in 1913 to 'resist home rule by all means possible'. Nationalist Ireland watched with growing alarm as the Unionists organized and armed the UVF. They were able to achieve in a few months what the Supreme Council of the IRB had dreamed about for decades. In July 1913 the IRB decided to establish a similar movement but it would not be publicly led by them since it wished to attract as broad a spectrum of nationalist support as possible. The cue came from outside the movement when in November 1913 Eoin MacNeill, the distinguished historian and Irish scholar, suggested in an article in the journal of the Gaelic League that the South should follow the North's lead.[69] A group of prominent nationalists led by Bulmer Hobson approached MacNeill and his friend Michael O'Rahilly ('The O'Rahilly') and together they convened a public meeting in the Rotunda in Dublin on 25 November 1913. Some 7,000 enthusiastic nationalists attended. The Irish Volunteers were duly established and over 4,000 men enrolled on that first night.[70] None of those who were later prominent in the Volunteers in Waterford attended the Rotunda meeting, although some Waterford-born individuals resident in Dublin were present, including Richard Mulcahy, who became IRA chief of staff in 1918.[71]

The IRB infiltrated the Irish Volunteers from the outset and occupied many key positions but were content to let MacNeill lead the new force. A more open approach by the IRB might have alarmed moderate nationalists. P.C. O'Mahony recalled: 'The general line of policy in regard to it was that IRB men would not take too prominent a part or show their hands completely in the formation of the organization.'[72] After Christmas, the Volunteer executive began to organize the movement outside Dublin.[73] It spread rapidly throughout the country, often building on an existing local nucleus of IRB members or cultural nationalists.[74] In January 1914 the first steps were taken to establish the Volunteers in Waterford city. A local committee which included Willie Walsh, Seán Matthews and Patrick Brazil, all IRB men, was set up to plan a launch meeting, which took place early in March.[75] Five hundred men marched to the city hall, led by the Barrack Street Brass Band and the Erin's Hope Fife and Drum Band. A large number of local dignitaries and priests were on the platform as MacNeill and O'Rahilly addressed a sizeable crowd on the Mall. Discretely in the background on the platform were Brazil and Matthews. The

meeting concluded with the announcement that a Waterford City Battalion of
the Irish Volunteers would be established. Drilling would take place on
Tuesday and Thursday evenings and on Sunday mornings at the Butter Market
on High Street. Enrolment forms were distributed and, according to press
accounts, hundreds signed up immediately.[76] Robert A. Kelly, a prominent
businessman and president of the local branch of the Ancient Order of
Hibernians (AOH), was appointed chairman. He was subsequently elected commanding officer of the battalion with the rank of colonel. W.A. Jacob, also a
member of the AOH, was appointed secretary. In all there were twenty members of the provisional committee including Dr Vincent White, a prominent
local physician; Edmund Bolton, president of the Waterford Trades Council;
P.W. Kenny, a member of Waterford Corporation; and at least five solicitors.
Four members of the IRB sat on the committee: Matthews, Brazil, J.D. Walsh
and Patrick Woods. They were content to remain officers at company level. CI
Hetreed believed that the AOH was primarily responsible for the local
Volunteers and in April he reported that the 'Waterford AOH was very active
during the month regarding the Irish Volunteer movement which was formed
here under their auspices'.[77] Local British army reservists were engaged as
instructors. All of this was carefully monitored by the local RIC who expressed
surprise at the 'number of persons of considerable local influence who have
attended and spoken at these meetings.'[78] By the end of April the City Battalion
numbered over 700 men in eight companies.[79] Such was the growth of the
Volunteers in Waterford city that the Butter Market quickly became too small
and drilling was transferred first to the Market House and then to the grounds
of the courthouse. Route marches on Sundays became a regular feature and
proposals were drawn up for weekend camps in Tramore.

   Once the city was organized, attention turned towards the hinterland. For
villages and towns adjacent to Waterford, there was a simple but effective
method. The City Battalion paraded to the village or town, speeches followed
and then a local company was established. Tramore was organized on 24 May
and Kilmacow on 6 June.[80] In the west of the county, Dungarvan was the
scene of a mass meeting on 22 April with O'Rahilly as the main speaker; likewise Lismore in early June.[81] While some local units marked their establishment by field days, Kilrossanty chose to do so in verse. Titled the 'Comeragh
Volunteers', it began:

> Kilrossanty has joined the ranks of Erin's army bold
> Amongst those gallant heroes her sons are now enrolled.
> To make our land a nation and to wipe out past arrears
> And help guard our hard won rights – the Comeragh Volunteers.[82]

It continued in a similar vein for a further nine verses.

There was broad support for the establishment of the Volunteers. On 15 June Waterford County Council passed a motion welcoming them 'as a necessary reply to the threat to deprive Ireland by force of the parliament now on the point of being won back'.[83] Sir John Keane and Gerard Villiers Stuart dissented from the motion. With the exception of the *Waterford Standard*, all the local newspapers welcomed the setting up of the Irish Volunteers, none more than the *Dungarvan Observer* whose proprietor, James Lynch, presided at the Dungarvan inaugural meeting. By May the CI reported that the Irish Volunteer movement had made very considerable progress. There were four branches in the county with 365 members and one in the city with 710 members. Again he commented on the respectable class of people who had joined and noted that the 'force was drawn largely from members of the GAA, the Gaelic League and the AOH, especially the latter.'[84]

Although a number of women attended the inaugural meeting of the Irish Volunteers in Dublin, they had been escorted to a small side gallery and their active participation in the movement was not encouraged. Not content with a passive role, they established their own militant organization, Cumann na mBan. The inaugural meeting of the new body, with the declared aim of advancing the cause of Irish liberty, was held in Wynn's Hotel, Dublin, on 5 April 1914.[85] Branches were established throughout the country, the first in Cork in June and another in Waterford city in July 1914. The first local officers included Alice Colfer, a teacher and secretary of the city branch of the Gaelic League, as president, and Rosamond Jacob as secretary.[86] Although Cumann na mBan boasted an impressive rate of expansion, claiming thirty branches by the end of July, this was not reflected in police reports or in other sources. Many of these may have been 'paper' branches without the necessary number of enthusiasts to keep the branch active.[87] The Waterford branch never numbered more than a dozen members.[88]

Redmond and the IPP watched the growth of the Irish Volunteers with some dismay as it seemed to threaten their hegemony in nationalist Ireland. In June 1914 the IPP leader demanded that the provisional committee of the Irish Volunteers accept the admission of twenty-five of his nominees, thus giving him control; if they failed to do so, he would publicly and vigorously oppose them. Anxious not to split the movement, the Volunteer executive reluctantly agreed.[89] Among Redmond's nominees was P.A. Murphy, his key local activist in Waterford, who placed himself 'wholeheartedly' at his leader's disposal.[90] Redmond's assumption of control of the Volunteers was seen as endorsing the movement and in the words of the RIC inspector-general caused it to progress by 'leaps and bounds'.[91] Nowhere was this more evident than in Waterford, where Hetreed had previously commented that many local nationalists were non-committal because they believed that Redmond was not in favour of the movement.[92]

Throughout the spring and summer of 1914 the constitutional crisis deep-
ened as various schemes excluding parts of Ulster were mooted. Several compromise proposals, all involving some form of partition, were rejected by the
Ulster Unionists whose resolve was strengthened by the support of Bonar
Law. The country appeared to be heading towards civil war and nationalist
fervour intensified. More and more moderate nationalists gave their open support to the Volunteer movement. Armed action now appeared acceptable to
many people who would have recoiled from the prospect with horror a few
months previously.[93]

By August 1914 it was conservatively estimated that there were more than
180,000 men enrolled in the Irish Volunteers. Such numbers required a more
formal military structure and the returns for Waterford to Volunteer headquarters on 28 July show for the first time a brigade structure with two brigades in
Waterford, each with four battalions (the standard British army structure). The
East Waterford Brigade had a total of 2,349 volunteers with battalions in the
city, in Gaultier and two in the Comeragh Mountains. Its western counterpart
had two battalions in the Dungarvan area and one each in the Blackwater Valley
and in the Knockmealdown Mountains with a total strength of 1,385. A note on
the return mentioned that the City Battalion had an enrolled strength of over
1,000 men but that approximately 50 per cent did 'not attend drills regularly'
and were therefore not included. The active strength of the combined brigades
was 3,734.[94] The issue of absenteeism from parades and drills was not confined
to Waterford or to the Irish Volunteers; the UVF had similar problems.[95] The
RIC estimate of the strength of the Volunteers in Waterford city and county was
3,994 – quite an accurate figure.[96] In comparison with its neighbouring counties,
Volunteer density (that is, the number of Volunteers per 1,000 of the Catholic
population) at fifty was slightly below Kilkenny and Tipperary, similar to
Wexford and substantially ahead of Cork.[97]

While there was no shortage of willing manpower, the supply of arms was
wholly inadequate. Each Volunteer was required to pay 2*d*. a week to an arms
fund. From June onwards, regular 'collections for arms' were taken up
throughout the city and county and were well supported. Some wealthy members purchased their own rifles but generally what arms the Waterford
Volunteers possessed came from headquarters and slowly at that. It is estimated that by August 1914 there were only 275 rifles plus an unknown
number of revolvers and shotguns in the hands of the Waterford Volunteers.[98]
Of this total, the City Battalion had over 200 rifles. An elaborate diversion
focused the attention of the authorities on the Waterford coast on the weekend of 26 July, when Erskine Childers and his accomplices landed 1,500
Mauser rifles at Howth, County Dublin, and at Kilcoole, County Wicklow.[99]
Only about two or three of the famous 'Howth' rifles found their way to
Waterford.[100]

The killing of innocent bystanders at Bachelor's Walk in Dublin on 26 July by British troops as they returned from a futile attempt to seize the rifles caused outrage throughout nationalist Ireland. On 28 July the Volunteers paraded through Waterford city to a mass meeting on Ballybricken Hill. P.A. Murphy delivered a rousing address to the thousands present and ended with a call for more men to enrol in the Volunteers: 'After Sunday's business any Irishman not in the ranks of the Volunteers was not for but against Ireland'. Contrasting the treatment of the Irish Volunteers and the UVF, he warned that 'any attempt made to take from the city of Waterford Volunteers, any rifle or ammunition while the Ulster Volunteers were allowed to retain their arms would be resisted to the bitter end'.[101] Other speakers included the mayor, Richard Power, Colonel Kelly and Fr Flood from the nearby Dominican community.[102] Similar meetings took place that week throughout the country and the political temperature rose even further. In the last days of July 1914, like the rest of nationalist Ireland, the Waterford Volunteers, enthusiastic but largely untrained and badly equipped, prepared for what seemed to be inevitable civil war to defend the home rule bill.

From April 1912 to July 1914 the people of Waterford watched as the home rule crisis unfolded. For nationalists it proved a series of triumphs; for unionists it was a time for resistance. As the focus of the crisis shifted from parliament to extra-parliamentary means, both sides organized themselves into Volunteer units and sought arms. It was also a time of changing strategy for the Ulster Unionist leadership. When it became clear that their opposition would not block home rule for all of Ireland, their attention shifted to exclusion for all or part of the historic province of Ulster. This left unionist communities in Waterford and other parts of the south feeling isolated and resigned to their fate. In June Bishop O'Hara told his flock that 'all they can do in this part of Ireland was to put themselves in God's hands and seek his guidance and help'.[103] In July 1914 the leaders of all the political parties gathered at a conference in Buckingham Palace at the invitation of King George V in a final bid to agree a compromise. However, after three days of talks the conference collapsed on 24 July over the exclusion of Ulster.[104] At that point it seemed inevitable that home rule would be imposed, Ulster would resist with force and Ireland would be plunged into civil war. For some, in the aftermath of the Bachelor's Walk killings, it appeared that civil war had already begun and that the British army had fired the first shots. In Waterford, as elsewhere throughout the island, people waited anxiously for what would happen next.

3 'Waterford has done its duty magnificently':[1] war, rebellion and Waterford, 1914–16

As the crowds dispersed from Ballybricken on the evening of 28 July 1914, they could not have known that a few hours earlier Austria-Hungary had declared war on Serbia. On 4 August, having received no answer to its ultimatum, Britain declared war on Germany and Austria-Hungary.[2] Within days some of those who had cheered the rousing words of P.A. Murphy were wearing khaki and preparing to embark for France. As in the rest of the country, enthusiasm for the war swept Waterford city and county.[3] About 140,000 men enlisted in Ireland in the British armed forces during the war.[4] When added to serving soldiers and reservists, over 200,000 men domiciled in Ireland served. At least 10,000 of these came from Waterford city and county, and the adjoining counties of Kilkenny, Wexford and Tipperary.[5] The home front too was mobilized to provide support for the troops and a range of voluntary committees was formed. During the war agriculture benefitted greatly from increased demand and a reduction of foreign competition in the British market.[6] The resultant boom brought prosperity to Waterford's farmers and processors of farm goods. Non-agricultural industries also benefitted from increased demand for their products. The outbreak of war changed the balance of power between labourers and employers, an opportunity that trade union leaders were not slow to exploit. Full employment and the flow of army allowances resulted in a major cash injection into the economy, although much of this gain was eroded by increased prices for foodstuffs. Redmond committed himself fully to the war and the public representatives, clergy and newspapers of the city and county wholeheartedly endorsed his stance. Given the expectation that the war would be short, this was probably the only viable policy for Redmond and the IPP. However, as the war dragged on, an increasing number of people began to doubt the wisdom of this policy, following the failure of the British government to respond to Redmond's generous gesture and the postponement of home rule. Nonetheless, Redmond continued to support recruitment. At a national level between 1914 and 1916 there was a sharp decline in support for the IPP and its leader, though this was less pronounced in Waterford than in the rest of the country.[7] During the same period a tiny minority of nationalists in Waterford regarded the war as an opportunity for armed rebellion.

Waterford witnessed significant activity once the War Office started the mobilization process on 1 August. An important rail junction, Waterford North Station, like other major rail centres, saw heavy traffic and for nearly a week it was the scene of great excitement. Reservists often marched to the station accompanied by the Volunteers and a band, while cheering spectators lined the quays and the bridge as fathers, sons and brothers went off to war. Naval reservists were processed at the Custom House in Waterford city. The *Waterford Standard* estimated that 300 of them were processed on 4 August alone.[8] An army recruiting office was opened on Parnell Street in the city. The response was initially very positive and during the first four days 251 recruits were accepted.[9] Regular British army units stationed in Ireland, their ranks filled with reservists, began to move to France. Special trains from all over Ireland conveyed men and equipment to the embarkation ports of Dublin, Belfast, Cork and Rosslare. Troop trains often stopped for refreshment at Waterford North Station where a feeding point had been set up. The South Irish Horse, a special reserve cavalry unit, was the first to leave Waterford, entraining for Limerick, the regimental depot, on the morning of 5 August.[10] Later that day a special train left Waterford for Clonmel carrying members of the Royal Irish Regiment. Reservists who had served with the Royal Munster Fusiliers made their way to Ballymullen Barracks in Tralee, County Kerry, while others travelled to Dublin, the Curragh in County Kildare, or further afield. The speeches delivered a week before on Ballybricken Hill were clearly forgotten. On 14 August the regular army unit in the city, the 72nd Battery, RFA, embarked for France amid cheering crowds.[11] Their barracks served as a training base for signallers attached to the Royal Engineers for the duration of the war.[12] Meanwhile veterinary teams toured the county requisitioning horses for the army. A temporary holding area was set up in the People's Park in Waterford city where the animals were assessed and compensation paid to their owners.[13]

The outbreak of war immediately transformed the political situation in Ireland by relegating the issue of home rule from the forefront of British politics. On 3 August Redmond reassured the government that it could withdraw troops from Ireland because the coast could be 'defended from foreign invasion by her armed sons, and for this purpose armed Nationalist Catholics in the South will be only too glad to join arms with the armed Protestant Ulstermen in the North'.[14] This speech took Ireland and the Irish Volunteer executive by surprise, yet it could not be criticized; even John Dillon and Joseph Devlin, who had reservations about Redmond's stance, thought it prudent to remain silent.[15] Although Asquith and the British cabinet welcomed Redmond's assurance, during the next month they misled him on a number of critical political and military issues.[16]

The response to Redmond's position throughout Ireland was remarkably positive. The sentiment was endorsed by local Volunteer committees and local newspapers. They had called for vengeance following Bachelor's Walk but now wholeheartedly supported the war effort.[17] While Ulster unionists withheld comment, nationalists throughout Ireland and southern unionists endorsed Redmond's call with zeal.[18] In Waterford political, clerical and press support for Redmond's policy was both unanimous and enthusiastic.[19] Hearne & Co., a furniture manufacturer, together with other prominent employers in the city, showed their support for recruiting by promising to keep their employees' jobs open for them and to make up any difference in wages for those who enlisted.[20] Local unionists such as Sir John Keane and Sir William Goff wrote to the *Waterford Standard* commending Redmond and urging support for the Volunteers.[21] Others pledged practical help. Colonel Charles Gordon of Lismore, a retired Indian army officer and brother-in-law of Richardson, the commander of the UVF, wrote to Maurice Moore, inspector general of the Irish Volunteers, to offer his services as an inspecting officer for County Waterford.[22] In the event the offer was not accepted and Gordon later commanded the Belfast district of the UVF.[23] CI Hetreed claimed that 'the Irish Volunteers can be depended upon to a man to fight any foreign foe and the unionists here are of the same opinion'.[24] Although Redmond's speech had been made without any consultation with the Volunteer executive, the executive had little option but to support it.[25] Outside of Ulster it seemed that an Irish equivalent of *l'union sacrée* had been formed as Protestant and Catholic, unionist and nationalist, rallied behind Redmond and his support for the war effort.[26]

This unity was soon fractured, however. On 18 September the home rule bill received the royal assent and was placed on the statute book but along with a measure that suspended its operation for the duration of the war. This was greeted by the usual flurry of congratulatory motions and newspaper headlines in nationalist Ireland. A meeting of Waterford Corporation on 6 October declared: ''Tis done – our freedom's won'.[27] Although the *Freeman's Journal* carried the headline: 'Ireland's day of triumph', public reaction was notably muted. There were no marches, bonfires or public meetings.[28] The IPP MPs returned to Ireland, euphoric at the final enactment of home rule. As Redmond travelled to his home in Aughavanagh, County Wicklow, on Sunday 20 September, he heard about a Volunteer parade that was taking place at Woodenbridge nearby. He interrupted his journey and in an unscripted but widely reported speech he called on the Volunteers to 'Go on drilling and make yourselves efficient for the work, and then account your-selves as men, not only in Ireland itself, but wherever the firing line extends, in defence of right, of freedom, and of religion in this war.'[29] It has been sug-gested that Redmond was looking for a suitable reply to the government's enactment of home rule two days earlier – the realization of his life's ambi-tion.[30] Typically, he had not consulted anybody about this speech and pre-dictably it caused consternation.

A special meeting of the original provisional committee of the Irish Volunteers (without Redmond's nominees) was held on 24 September and

twenty of its twenty-seven members, including MacNeill, Patrick Pearse and
O'Rahilly, issued a statement repudiating Redmond's policy. They declared
that 'Mr Redmond was no longer entitled through his nominees to any place
in the administration and guidance of the Irish Volunteers'.[31] The split in the
Volunteers at national level was replicated at a local level. When the
Waterford Volunteer committee met, it appealed for calm and urged that no
action be taken that might cause division.[32] Such appeals proved futile, how-
ever, as companies and battalions decided which side to take. Throughout the
country the majority backed Redmond and joined the 'Irish National
Volunteers', whereas only a small number withdrew and gave allegiance to
MacNeill's group, which retained the name 'Irish Volunteers'. Redmond's
force kept the arms, the drill halls, the funds and the support of the public.
Laurence Kettle and J.T. Donovan were appointed national secretaries of the
National Volunteers and Colonel Maurice Moore was given the post of
inspector general with full control over all military aspects.

There are varying estimates of the relative strengths of the two forces.
The police believed that there were 156,500 National Volunteers with 10,117
rifles throughout the country compared to about 9,700 Irish Volunteers who
held 1,435 rifles.[33] Bulmer Hobson claimed there were 3,000 Irish Volunteers
in November 1914, a figure which grew to about 10,000 by the end of 1915.[34]
The RIC estimates for Waterford and neighbouring counties indicated that
about 95 per cent of the Volunteers followed Redmond. A table in the
Redmond papers suggested that 3,423 Volunteers in Waterford did so while
only 190 sided with the Irish Volunteers, a figure similar to the rest of the
country.[35] According to Thomas Cleary, a Waterford city Volunteer, only
about twenty-five men stayed with the Irish Volunteers. In Dungarvan
Michael Mansfield recalled that only six of his company did likewise.[36] This
included the cadre of IRB men – Matthews, Walsh, O'Mahony, Brazil and
Woods – but they had few followers.

In Waterford the local press welcomed the secession of the minority and
suggested that it left Redmond's leadership of the Volunteers more secure:

> The Irish Volunteer movement has now been placed on a satisfactory
> footing and can proceed uninterruptedly with the work before it.
> Having rid itself of the small and insignificant element which all along
> had been seeking to create trouble and foment strife.[37]

On 11 October Redmond visited the city to present regimental colours to the
local National Volunteers. Augmented by contingents from Kilkenny and
Wexford, over 5,000 men paraded through the city to a meeting in the sports
field, where Redmond made the formal presentation and listened as various
motions supporting his policy were passed with acclamation.[38] This meeting

was undoubtedly the apogee of the National Volunteers in Waterford but the seeds of decline had already been sown. The calling up in August of 150 British army reservists, who were members of the Volunteers in Waterford, removed a vital core of instructors and trained men. Recruitment from the ranks of the Volunteers had a further debilitating effect on the Waterford city corps as those who went to war were not replaced. No parades were held and, at times, it seemed that the only activity engaged in by the local National Volunteers was to escort their comrades to the railway station to give them a good send-off when they joined the army. This merely associated the National Volunteers with the war effort and discouraged potential new members. Redmond visited Waterford again in January 1915. On this occasion his visit was somewhat overshadowed when, during preparations for the parade, Volunteer William Hartery was accidentally shot and fatally wounded by a colleague, John Lonergan.[39]

After an early surge the rate of enlistment declined and by November 1914 it was less than twenty per week.[40] The *Waterford Standard* observed with disapproval how too many young men 'were idly parading the streets and participating in dances and other amusements'.[41] Even at this stage there was a marked contrast between recruitment rates in city and county. In September CI Hetreed noted that 'very few men are joining from the county. There have been some bad characters from this city among those who have joined the army.'[42] A year later he similarly remarked how 'a great number have joined principally from the towns and villages but the rural population are not joining the army except in isolated cases.'[43] Occasional intensive recruiting campaigns provided a short-lived stimulus but the overall rate continued to decline.[44] That trend was in line with the rest of Ireland and the UK.[45] About half of those who enlisted were members of the National Volunteers. When Colonel Maurice Moore inspected the City Battalion in May 1915, he was informed that the low turnout of 450 was due to the number who had enlisted.[46]

In the city enlistment affected two classes disproportionately. The unionist community responded enthusiastically to the call to serve king and country. Of the 193 names on the roll of honour in Christchurch, the Church of Ireland cathedral, twenty-three were killed in action. For many unskilled labourers enlistment presented an opportunity to escape from poverty. The wife and family of a serving soldier were better off financially than the wife and family of an unskilled labourer even if he had been able to secure employment six days a week.[47] Separation money and other allowances could give a wife with four children 23s. 6d. per week while labouring would have provided between 15s. and 18s. Even wartime increases secured by workers did not eliminate this differential.[48] However, recruiting among the unskilled was limited as a result of the high rejection rate. In March 1915 the city and its hinterland were the target of a major recruiting campaign orchestrated by

Hedley Le Bas, advisor to the War Office.[49] A highlight of the campaign was a carefully staged public meeting in city hall on 24 March. Local MPs, Murphy and O'Shee, were present and spoke. Murphy told the packed attendance that of thirty-two caddies at Tramore Golf Club, no less than twenty-eight had already enlisted. Unable to attend, Bishop Sheehan, the Catholic prelate, sent a letter of apology and expressed strong support for Redmond's policy, declaring that 'the war is an Irish war to save our people from ruin and misery'.[50] According to Stephen Gwynn, Sheehan was 'strong for the war' and represented a force 'which was not often active on our side'.[51] A number of priests also addressed the meeting and all urged enlistment. Some used very emotional language. Fr William O'Donnell, parish priest of St Patrick's, told the assembled crowd of his anger when he thought about 'the savagery that had been carried out in the convents of Belgium by these brutes, the Germans', while Fr O'Cogley of the local Dominican community believed that 'England had confessed its past misdeeds' and should now be supported.[52] Maurice Day, Church of Ireland dean of Waterford, spoke about the need for sacrifice for king and country. Both his sons had enlisted; one had already been killed in action while the other died in 1917.[53] According to the *Waterford Standard*, 450 men 'of all classes' presented themselves to the recruiting officers during the two-week campaign but 260 were rejected on medical grounds.[54] In Britain authorities expressed concern at a rejection rate of just under 25 per cent but the Waterford rate was almost 60 per cent – an indictment of the poor state of public health in the city's tenements. Not all recruits were driven by a sense of duty or by hunger. Paddy Paul, who enlisted in March 1915 and later commanded the East Waterford Brigade IRA, accepted 'unquestioningly the catch cries raised at the time by the Irish Party in support of the recruiting campaign – "the fight for small nations" and "by fighting in France we were fighting for Ireland."'[55]

Although Redmond's visit and the high-powered recruiting campaign in March 1915 gave a temporary boost to recruitment, from May onwards the number enlisting once again declined.[56] Bishop Sheehan continued his strong support for recruiting. In July he circularized the 110 priests of his diocese seeking volunteers to serve as chaplains but only four came forward.[57] Despite growing disillusionment with the war and the failure to implement home rule, Redmond retained the overwhelming support of the people of Waterford. Later that year he again visited Waterford as part of a recruiting campaign, accompanied by Lord Wimborne, the lord lieutenant. At a conference for local representatives from Waterford, Wexford, Kilkenny and Tipperary, Redmond declared:

> Waterford city has done its duty magnificently. I don't think that there is a city in the United Kingdom which for its population has sent a

larger number of its men to the front, and I am certain of this, that there is not a city in the United Kingdom less likely to leave her boys in the lurch.[58]

Redmond's rhetoric to his loyal followers and devoted constituents could not hide the fact that voluntary enlistment in Waterford, as in the rest of the UK, was no longer sufficient to fill the gaps left by the dead and the wounded. By the end of 1915 about 1,756 Waterford men, approximately 35 per cent of the male population of military age in the city, had enlisted.[59] There was very little overt opposition to recruitment in Waterford. The local newspapers 'were all in sympathy with Mr Redmond's policy'.[60] Between the outbreak of war and Easter 1916 there were only two prosecutions for anti-recruitment activities, one for tearing down posters and the other for interrupting a meeting. In both cases alcohol was pleaded in mitigation and both defendants were let off with warnings.[61] O'Shee and Murphy strongly supported recruiting and regularly spoke on platforms or joined local recruitment committees.[62] Notably, they were not among 'the great majority of nationalist MPs who seem to have been intimidated by local anti-war protests or (more commonly) espoused "mental neutrality" and ignored recruitment'.[63] By the end of 1915 the vast majority of those set to go to war had already departed. As early as July the police suggested that 'as far as voluntary enlistment is concerned the resources of the county have been practically exhausted'.[64]

The course of the war and Waterford fatalities, in particular, were extensively reported in the local press. Among the dead following the battle of Mons, the first major action of the British Expeditionary Force on 23 August, were two members of the Royal Irish Regiment from Waterford. Sergeant Denis Walsh was a 39-year-old native of Cappoquin with over twenty years of service while 42-year-old Private John Connolly came from Ferrybank in the city.[65] News of their deaths reached Waterford a week later. All classes in the city and county were affected by wartime fatalities during the next four years. The story of Agnes Collins, a widow who lived on Philip Street, was particularly poignant. Her six sons enlisted, some before the war. Four died in action; Stephen, the youngest, was only sixteen when he was killed at Le Pilly on 19 October 1914 while serving with the Royal Irish Regiment.[66] Thirty-two other Waterford men were killed that day and over 300 members of the regiment were taken prisoner, about seventy of whom were from Waterford. James Shine of Abbeyside, a retired colonel in the British Army Medical Service, had three sons commissioned in Irish regiments; all were killed in action. The youngest, John, was wounded at Mons and died the next day.[67] During 1915 the death toll on the Western Front continued to rise. Among the dead was John Condon, believed to have been just 14 years old and the youngest known British fatality of the war, who was killed on 24 May at Ypres.

Sailors and merchant seamen were also lost. In the first naval engagement of the war on 22 September, three British cruisers were sunk by a German submarine. Thomas Foley from Dungarvan, a crewman on HMS *Aboukir*, was among the dead.[68] When HMS *Monmouth* was sunk at the battle of Coronel on 1 November 1914 Arthur Bellman, a stoker from Lismore, was killed.[69] On 13 May 1915 the Turkish destroyer *Muvanet-I-Milet* torpedoed the British battleship HMS *Goliath*, killing 570 of her 700 crew. Ten of the dead were from the coastal towns and villages of Waterford. According to Tom Burnell, 1,138 Waterford men and women, soldiers, sailors, airmen and civilians were killed in the war. While the Waterford connection of some of those listed may be tenuous, it is certain that over 800 men from the city and the county died, many buried in Palestine, Gallipoli, Salonika, France and Belgium; others were lost at sea or their bodies never found on the battlefields.

Soon after the outbreak of the war various committees were set up in Waterford city and county, as happened throughout Britain and Ireland, to provide comforts for the troops.[70] On 2 September the *Waterford Standard* reported that wealthy citizens of the city had provided a fully equipped ambulance named 'The Waterford car' for use at the front.[71] Six months later three similar vehicles were provided by a committee under the patronage of the duke of Devonshire and the marchioness of Waterford. There were also regular public appeals for clothing, cigarettes and other comforts for the troops. Among the officers and men of the Royal Irish Regiment captured at the battle of Le Pilly in October 1914 were a large number of Waterford men.[72] Their plight as prisoners of war soon came to the attention of their friends and relatives and they too were assisted by Waterford relief committees.[73] In March 1915 a flag day was held throughout the city and county to raise funds for them. After Private J. Casey from Waterford city, a wounded prisoner, was exchanged in August 1915, he gave an interview to the *Waterford News* in which he claimed that the prisoners were living solely on the contents of the relief parcels they received from home.[74] This had an immediate and positive impact on collections. When news broke later that month that six Waterford-born prisoners of war had joined Roger Casement's Irish Brigade, the local newspapers responded with a mixture of outrage and anger.[75] In January 1915 German men living in Waterford were detained by police as part of the nationwide detention of enemy aliens and were sent to an internment camp in County Meath.[76] While the men were interned some Austrian or German-born women living in Waterford were deported.[77] In November 1914 preparations began for the reception of Belgian refugees. Numerous public appeals for funds and clothing were made and elicited a generous response. In February 1915 three Belgian families arrived in Waterford and were accommodated in Tramore, Portlaw and in the city.[78] Membership of various fund-raising committees comprised a cross-section of

Waterford society, usually including Protestant and Catholic clergy, members of the landed ascendancy and businessmen as well as local politicians and supporters of Redmond.

Sometimes misunderstandings around the purpose of emerging groups could give rise to farce. On 10 August 1914 the organizers of the inaugural public meeting of Cumann na mBan were surprised at the large turnout in city hall. However, most of those in attendance had come under the impression that the Cumann was a voluntary ambulance corps founded to nurse wounded British soldiers. When asked whether they were prepared to treat wounded Germans, Ms Colfer, presiding, replied that she would rather tend to wounded Germans than to wounded British soldiers and the meeting broke up in disorder.[79]

By the spring of 1915 the decline of the National Volunteers was being commented on in the local press. Appeals for recruits and parades such as on St Patrick's Day had little effect. This was confirmed by Captain A.P. O'Brien, who, in a report to Colonel Moore, described drill attendance as 'wretched'.[80] W.J. Smith, second-in-command of the City Battalion, attributed the fall-off to the recall of 160 reservists and enlistment of 450 recruits from the City Battalion.[81] During the summer all volunteer activity in Waterford was suspended. A general muster was called for 5 October after the '6-week furlough' but the response was poor. Robert Kelly resigned his position as colonel and was replaced by Smith. Various schemes to reorganize the corps were considered and discarded as the decline continued. This mirrored a national trend. The force existed only nominally with no drills or parades being organized.[82]

The UIL was also in decline. In January 1915 the national executive recorded that only twelve Waterford branches were paid up, one of the lowest returns in the country.[83] Fr William O'Donnell, a prominent UIL activist and supporter of recruiting, warned a meeting of the UIL in March 1915 that the organization needed to be made 'stronger and better' to meet post-war challenges.[84] In August 1915 Redmond, O'Shee and Murphy attended a UIL convention in Waterford city, part of a nationwide campaign to revitalize the organization which ultimately failed.[85] Redmond made an impassioned plea for new UIL members and also for more recruits to enlist.[86] This was an unfortunate linkage as it seemed to suggest that the UIL had been reduced to a recruiting agency. For the remainder of the year O'Shee tried to reinvigorate the UIL in Waterford but without success.[87]

Despite his unambiguous support for the war, Redmond retained the unquestioning support of his Waterford constituents. His refusal to take the seat offered to him in Asquith's new coalition government in May 1915 was supported uncritically by the local nationalist press.[88] By contrast, the *Waterford Standard* hailed the inclusion of Carson and declared that home rule was dead.[89]

Many commentators have seen Redmond's refusal as a fatal error that yielded power and influence to his opponents and contributed significantly to the decline of the IPP.[90] According to Stephen Gwynn, the formation of the coalition cabinet marked 'the first stage in the history of Redmond's defeat and the victory of Sir Edward Carson and Sinn Féin'.[91] But this was not immediately evident because on a national level Redmond and the IPP retained the support of the overwhelming majority of nationalists as shown by the contested by-elections of the period.[92] However, the historian Michael Wheatley's analysis of the IPP suggests that these electoral victories masked a declining level of political involvement at grass-roots level by UIL activists.[93]

In the words of F.S.L. Lyons, 'the war brought to Ireland an unprecedented prosperity ... Up and down the country, in industry and in agriculture, all the signs were that prosperity was both more solid and more widely diffused than at any time in living memory.'[94] Waterford shared in this prosperity in a number of ways. First, 'separation money' injected significant cash into the local economy. As the CI noted in April 1915, there was 'no acute distress as there is a good deal of money in circulation from the allowances paid to dependents of the considerable number who have joined the army from the county and city'.[95] At the same time concern was expressed at social problems arising from access to this money. In May Bishop Sheehan accused some women of not learning 'thrift and care' and of abusing the allowances by spending the money on drink.[96] Second, the recall to service of reservists and the embodiment of the part-time soldiers of the Special Reserve created many vacancies in the workforce that were quickly filled from the pool of unemployed. Other men, most of them middle-aged, found work in English munitions factories.[97] Third, the war greatly restricted the ability of food exporters to access the British markets and created a boom for Irish farmers. In early 1915 Waterford farmers complained about a 'great scarcity of male labour' and suggested organizing female workers to take the men's place.[98] Later that year, Hetreed remarked that farmers were 'rather glad that the war is in progress as they are getting increased prices for their stock and agricultural produce'.[99] Fourth, some Waterford firms gained War Office contracts. For example, in January 1915 Hearne & Co., the furniture manufacturers, won a lucrative contract for the manufacture of ammunition boxes.[100] In February the old Neptune Ship Works was taken over by Thompsons engineering firm for the manufacture of shell cases and soon employed over 200.[101] In March Waterford Corporation unanimously passed the first of several motions demanding the establishment of more war industries in the city.[102] Waterford Chamber of Commerce lobbied Redmond to this end and when this did not produce immediate results wrote directly to the prime minister to press Waterford's claim for a munitions factory, but without effect.[103]

At home the war led to a steep rise in prices for basic commodities. Within days of the outbreak it was reported that sugar, meat, flour and coal prices in Waterford were subject to 'abnormal rises' as a result of panic buying.[104] The alarm soon subsided but an inexorable increase in food prices had begun. The Board of Trade's retail price index rose by 10 per cent in the last five months of 1914 and by a further 22 per cent in 1915.[105] These price increases were not evenly spread and the cost of some basic staples rose by even more: tea increased by 49%, eggs by 45% and bread by 26%.[106] The cost of bread in Waterford was the subject of much discussion at meetings of Waterford Corporation. In March 1915 P.W. Kenny, claimed that a loaf of bread cost between 8*d.* and 10*d.* compared to 7*d.* in the rest of the UK.[107] His call for price controls went unheeded. In mid-1914 the price of coal in the city was 22*s.* per ton but by early 1915 it has increased to 40*s.*[108] Such steep rises put additional pressure on households, especially on the poorest and it was inevitable that workers would seek pay increases to compensate.

The wartime demand for labour altered the balance of power between employers and workers throughout Britain and Ireland. Waterford was no exception to this. In February 1915 the Clyde Shipping Company gave its workers a 'war allowance' of 5*s.* a week following a strike that lasted only five days.[109] Other groups of workers followed suit. Within a month Waterford Corporation workers had secured a war bonus of 4*s.* per week. A pattern of short strikes followed by concessions was set and by the spring of 1916 most workers in the city and county had benefitted. In November 1915 dock workers went on strike for an increase in the rate for unloading coal. Short of money since the 1913 lockout, their union, the ITGWU, was reluctant to support them so the men formed a branch of the NUDL and secured an increase. A few years later the NUDL merged with the Amalgamated Transport and General Workers Union, giving the latter a foothold in Waterford, a move that would have far-reaching implications for trade-unionism in the city.[110] Trade unionism prospered as the employed workforce grew. Even the as yet unorganized agricultural labourers experienced improvements. By 1915 agricultural wages were on average between 1*s.* 6*d.* and 2*s.* per week higher than in 1914.[111] This marked the beginning of a wage spiral in agriculture although the RIC Inspector General observed that while farmers were flourishing, they 'did not appear disposed to share increased profits with their labourers'.[112] These increases did nothing to improve recruiting in rural Waterford.

It was against this backdrop of war-related mortality and prosperity that Seán Matthews and P.C. O'Mahony set about reorganizing the Irish Volunteers in the city and in Dungarvan in October 1914.[113] With just a few like-minded individuals in isolated groups and without premises, funds, arms or public support, the first priority was to keep the organization intact. Public drilling was not possible in Redmond's stronghold and, for the moment at least, meetings could only take place in private houses. In November 1914 J.J. ('Ginger') O'Connell joined the Irish Volunteers. A veteran of the American army, he was appointed by MacNeill as an organizer and played a major part in rebuilding the movement. Close to MacNeill with whom he shared views on the role of the Volunteers, O'Connell wrote an unpublished history that offers a unique insight into the rebuilding work following the split.[114] In April 1915 he visited Waterford. This did not go unnoticed by the RIC who believed that he was unsuccessful in establishing a branch of the Irish Volunteers.[115] It was not until December that the police first referred to a Volunteer branch in the city; they noted an average attendance of thirty at drilling.[116] The following March the local company took part in the St Patrick's Day procession but were unarmed.[117]

In August 1915 the funeral of Jeremiah O'Donovan Rossa, the veteran Fenian, was the occasion for the first national public display by the revitalized Irish Volunteers. A group of Waterford Volunteers joined contingents from all over the country in the funeral procession to Glasnevin cemetery.[118] Two weeks later the Waterford city company organized a solemn requiem mass for Rossa in Waterford cathedral. The mayor and some members of the corporation attended while the Volunteers paraded in uniform to the cathedral.[119] The next public show of force by the local Irish Volunteers was the Manchester Martyrs' commemoration in November at which Pearse and O'Connell were present.[120] The latter recalled:

> It was significant of the change coming over the feeling of the country that an Irish Volunteer meeting could be held in public in Waterford – John Redmond's own constituency. And it was a complete success, too. On this occasion I took command of the Volunteers separating the sheep – or the compact, well-formed Volunteers – from the goats, or the more numerous body of recruits that flocked in the enthusiasm of the moment.[121]

Pearse briefly addressed those in attendance and afterwards had a private meeting with Matthews and J.D. Walsh. He was informed that there were approximately thirty sworn men in Waterford city with two Howth rifles, a couple of revolvers and a few shotguns. Pearse then confided in them that there would be a rising in spring 1916 and gave them a code word. According to Matthews, he then said

> ye have nothing; ye can put up no fight, the best thing ye can do is to go to the GPO (Waterford) when you get word of the Rising, break up everything you can especially the telegraph and telephone installations and then go into Wexford, join up with the Wexford Volunteers, but only bring with you such men as are armed.[122]

In January 1916 P.C. O'Mahony received a similar visit from Liam Mellows, a Volunteer organizer. The Dungarvan Company of twenty-one men was relatively well armed with six rifles, twelve revolvers and eighteen shotguns. It was to proceed to Waterford city to assist Matthews' men.

As Easter 1916 approached preparations for the Rising gathered pace. On Wednesday 19 April both Matthews and O'Mahony received detailed instructions from Pearse and James Connolly via couriers, Maeve Cavanagh-McDowell and Marie Perolz. Cavanagh-McDowell recalled how nervous Matthews was and when he read the note said: 'Tell Connolly that we have a few rifles but we'll do what we can'.[123] In Dungarvan O'Mahony simply responded: 'Thank God, at last'.[124] On Good Friday, 21 April, O'Mahony called his men together and issued orders for general mobilization at 6.30 p.m. on Sunday with arms and rations. He then prepared a message for Matthews and confirmed details of the planned link-up. The next morning his wife delivered the despatch to Matthews in the Metropole Hotel. On reading it he said: 'tell P.C. it is all off. Ginger (J.J.) O'Connell is in town and he has come from a meeting in Dublin where it was decided.'[125] Surprised at the news, Mrs O'Mahony rushed to the railway station where she met O'Connell, who was about to board the train to Wexford to call off the Rising there. He confirmed the order and requested she tell her husband 'to disregard any notes'.[126] Matthews called a meeting of the officers of the city Volunteers. They faced a dilemma. As sworn members of the IRB should they follow instructions from the Military Council or as Volunteers should they obey O'Connell's orders? They agreed that Willie Walsh, who was due to attend the Annual GAA Congress in Dublin the following day, should ascertain the real situation and communicate with them using coded telegrams. Walsh travelled to Dublin on the evening train but, even though a member of the IRB, did not seek out Pearse or Mac Diarmada when he reached the capital. Instead, early on Sunday morning, he took a taxi to Rathfarnham where MacNeill told him categorically that there would not be an outbreak.[127] Walsh then went to the GAA Congress where he detected an air of uncertainty. When he asked Harry Boland about the planned Rising, Boland gave him no information. The next day, certain that there would be no Rising, Walsh telegraphed Matthews and O'Mahony.[128] As far as his comrades in Waterford were concerned, this confirmed MacNeill's newspaper notice and the orders from O'Connell that there would be no Rising. Walsh was, of course, mistaken. The IRB Military Council decided to proceed with the Rising in Dublin on Monday and dispatched couriers with fresh orders. For a second time, Cavanagh-McDowell travelled to Waterford and met an upset Matthews before attempting to return to Dublin to join the Rising.[129]

Matthews pondered the content of the despatch, signed by Pearse, which read simply: 'Carry out orders. Dublin strikes at noon.' He assembled a few of his IRB comrades and, armed with revolvers, they approached Waterford GPO only to find it occupied by RIC and British troops. By 3 p.m. it was clear to Matthews that owing to their very limited supply of arms and ammunition, any action was out of the question and they returned to the Metropole Hotel, where Cavanagh-McDowell was waiting having missed her train. After some discussion, Matthews suggested that they contact the Kilkenny Volunteers to ascertain if a joint action might be possible.[130] Cavanagh-McDowell offered to bring a message to Kilkenny, which she reached only on Wednesday as all trains had been cancelled. There she met J.J. O'Connell who was staying with Peter DeLoughrey, IRB centre in Kilkenny. O'Connell was clearly under severe strain. Cavanagh-McDowell recalled how he said '"They should have waited till there was conscription. Look at that – it is all over already" he said showing me an English newspaper.' Cavanagh-McDowell returned to Waterford with a despatch to that effect; Matthews was 'disgusted' when he read it.[131] Any possibility of armed action in Waterford city during Easter 1916 had vanished.

No attempt appears to have been made to send a despatch to O'Mahony in Dungarvan. On Easter Monday morning he received Walsh's telegram and spent the day reflecting on the recent events – command, countermand and confusion. At 8 p.m. he went on duty at Dungarvan Post Office where he found a note which read 'All communication with Dublin broken down'. O'Mahony also decoded a police telegram from the CI in Waterford to the district inspector in Dungarvan which advised that an ammunition train with a small military guard would be passing through Dungarvan that night en route to Cork. He immediately mobilized his twelve IRB men and set up an ambush about two miles outside Dungarvan. They blocked the line and, armed only with revolvers, waited for the train. However, the only train to pass was the ordinary goods train, which they stopped, searched and then allowed to continue. Having waited in vain all night, O'Mahony dispersed his men.[132] On Wednesday he was arrested by the RIC along with Dan Fraher, Phil Walsh and Peter Raftis. It was not until Monday 1 May that O'Mahony's wife managed to make contact with Matthews. When she asked him why he had not been in touch he replied: 'I got Pearse's message on Monday that Dublin was rising at noon but all my men were out of town and there was nothing I could do about it'.[133] In Dublin Walsh and James Nowlan, a GAA colleague from Kilkenny, made a number of unsuccessful attempts to reach the GPO. On returning to Waterford on 1 May, Walsh was arrested and detained for three weeks before being released without charge as were O'Mahony and the other Dungarvan men.[134]

Four Waterford men took part in the Rising. Seán Ó Gríobhtháin and Liam Ó Reagáin from the Ring Gaeltacht were employed as shop assistants in Dónal Ó Buachalla's hardware store in Maynooth, County Kildare. They

were members of the Maynooth Volunteer Company that reached the GPO
on Tuesday morning and fought for the rest of the week. After the surrender Ó Reagáin was among the first batch of prisoners to be deported to
England for internment while Ó Gríobhtháin was court-martialled and sentenced to two years imprisonment with hard labour.[135] Liam Raftis, a native
of Waterford city and an employee of the Great Southern & Western
Railway, was in the Boland's Mills garrison but slipped away during the confusion of the surrender, thereby avoiding arrest, deportation and internment.
Unable to explain his activities during Easter week to his employers, he was
suspended without pay indefinitely.[136] Lastly, Richard Mulcahy, who was
born in Manor Street in Waterford city, was second in command to Thomas
Ashe in the Fingal Battalion of the Volunteers in north County Dublin. This
unit carried out a number of successful arms raids culminating in the battle
of Ashbourne.[137] Far more Waterford men were engaged in the suppression
of the Rising. The first British army unit to react in Dublin was a reserve
battalion of the Royal Irish Regiment stationed at Richmond Barracks,
Inchicore, in the west of the city. Throughout the week it was engaged in
heavy fighting at the South Dublin Union and in the O'Connell Street
area.[138] The unit recruited from Tipperary, Waterford, Kilkenny and
Wexford and at least three Waterford-born soldiers were wounded during the
fighting.[139] Dublin Metropolitan Police Constable John McGrath, a native of
Modeligo in west Waterford, was badly wounded by a sniper and invalided
from the force a few months later.[140]

    The National Volunteers received news of the Rising with alarm, regard-
ing it as a pro-German plot that would undermine all that Redmond had
achieved. Colonel Smith, O/C Waterford Battalion, contacted the military
and police in Waterford to offer them the services of 180 armed men to
maintain order in the city. The authorities declined this offer but gratefully
accepted the loan of 198 rifles, 193 bayonets and 10,000 rounds of ammunition, which were delivered to the military barracks on Wednesday. On 17
May, on behalf of the (British) GOC South of Ireland, Lieutenant-Colonel
Buckley thanked Smith for 'his offer of assistance ... to the officer commanding troops, Waterford, during the recent crisis as well as the loan of
arms and ammunition'.[141] Despite repeated requests from Smith and other
officers of the National Volunteers, the arms were not returned.[142] A mobile
column of 26 officers and 558 other ranks of the 3rd Battalion, Connaught
Rangers, accompanied by a battery of the RFA arrived in Waterford on 10
May. For a week it traversed the county searching houses for arms. The battalion war diary noted that the RIC in all towns throughout the county were
opposed to arrests and to house-to-house searches since they claimed that
the vast majority of the people were not in sympathy with the Sinn Féin
movement.[143]

Initially nationalist public opinion was strongly opposed to the rebellion.[144] Newspapers strongly denounced the Easter Rising especially the *Irish Independent*, the most popular nationalist newspaper in the country.[145] The Catholic hierarchy was at first equally condemnatory but many of the bishops soon became more sympathetic.[146] At a political level branch after branch of the UIL passed motions of support for Redmond. The Fenor, County Waterford branch, for example, expressed 'wholehearted confidence in the policy of Mr John Redmond'.[147] Local representative bodies such as Waterford County Council passed motions condemning the Rising and denouncing the participants as 'German dupes'. As the executions continued, however, the original motions were often amended to plead for an end to the killings and to pay tribute to the 'misguided patriotism' of the participants.[148] The Waterford Board of Guardians strongly condemned 'the foolish and mis-guided conduct of the persons in Dublin whose insurrectionary activity has brought such discredit on our country'.[149] At the Church of Ireland diocesan synod in June Bishop Henry O'Hara thanked God 'for a very great deliver-ance'.[150] CI Hetreed earned considerable praise for his management of the sit-uation in Waterford. Bishop Hackett commended 'the responsible officer of the constabulary whose intimate knowledge of the people for some years enabled him to feel the true pulse of the people and ensured a line of policy was followed that had not caused friction'.[151] Waterford County Council like-wise praised the CI's 'level handed' approach and noted 'that not one man was arrested in the county on a warrant issued by him'.[152] Gauging the public mood in May 1916, Hetreed observed that 'public feeling is altogether against the rebellion but there are signs that the public desire that clemency may be exercised towards the rank and file of the movement'.[153] That month Lismore District Council passed a motion of sympathy with the relatives and friends of the executed rebels, the first such motion in the county. Significantly, this motion was passed in west Waterford rather than in the Redmondite heart-land in the east. The changing mood of the people reflected a similar trans-formation throughout the country.[154]

In an impassioned speech to his Waterford constituents in November 1915 Redmond said: 'we have sent our Waterford men to the front and now we are sending our Waterford shells to the front'.[155] He encapsulated the impact of the war in Waterford – large-scale recruiting and significant economic spin-offs. In all its military and economic aspects the war dominated life in Waterford as it did throughout the rest of Ireland. Between August 1914 and Easter 1916 over 300 men from Waterford city and county died in the ranks of the British army or the Royal Navy. An unknown number of others were wounded while over eighty became prisoners of war. Army allowances, war contracts and increased demand for a variety of goods, both foodstuffs and consumer items, created an economic boom in Waterford. Unemployment virtually disappeared in both city and county. Farmers benefitted from the increased demand for their produce while labourers gained from the need for their labour. There were also other, more sombre, signs of the war with an increasing number of disabled servicemen returning home. The Barry brothers, John (who lost an arm) and Michael (who lost a leg), could be seen almost every day sitting together on Ballybricken Hill, a reminder to all of the cost of war. Support for Redmond and his policies remained steadfast and he was supported by the other local MPs, O'Shee and Murphy, by the churches and by the local press. The Easter Rising in Dublin had no immediate impact on Waterford. The small number of committed Volunteers, the confusion surrounding the orders and counter-orders and the indecision shown by the leadership, all contributed to the absence of insurrectionary activity in Waterford in 1916. In this Waterford was like most of the country. As Deaglán Ó Reagáin, a Volunteer from Ring, put it: 'We took no part in the Easter Rising. For one thing, we knew nothing about it until it was well on and in any case there were no arms worth talking about.'[156] Little wonder then that the RIC recorded in their confidential review of the year that

The general condition of the county [Waterford] was very peaceable and orderly during the year. There was some excitement during the period of the rebellion, but with the exception of an attempt to wreck a goods train in which ammunition was being conveyed on Easter Monday night near Dungarvan, no overt acts were committed or attempted.[157]

4 'An oasis in the political desert of Ireland':[1] the resistible rise of Sinn Féin, 1916–18

The 1916 Rising was a watershed in Irish political history. Within two-and-a-half years the IPP was swept to political oblivion by the rise of Sinn Féin (SF).[2] However, in Waterford, especially in the city, the rise of SF was bitterly contested. Not for the first time the difference between the east and west of the county was starkly demonstrated. In two hard-fought electoral contests, the city and its hinterland remained loyal to Redmond but the west of the county was swept along in the rising SF tide. This change was not immediate and it was aided by British government blunders such as the failure of the Irish Convention in 1917 and the decision to extend conscription to Ireland in 1918. As the political landscape changed, the First World War continued with its grim toll of dead and wounded. The resumption of unrestricted submarine warfare by the German navy in 1917 brought further grief to the families of the coastal communities of Waterford. Although the establishment of a munitions factory in Waterford brought economic gain to the city, workers found that inflation eroded the value of their new wage and strikes became frequent. The introduction of compulsory tillage orders under the Corn Production Act (1917) generated further demand for agricultural labourers. Trade union organization now spread rapidly among the rural work force and the ground was laid for major class conflict in rural Waterford.

While the Irish political landscape was changing, the war had degenerated into a bloody stalemate. In 1916 the battle of Jutland in which the giant fleets of Britain and Germany clashed inconclusively and the four-month-long battle of the Somme added to the ever-lengthening list of Waterford war dead. At Jutland on 31 May 1916 the Royal Navy lost over 6,000 men. HMS *Warrior* was sunk with the loss of all of her 903-man crew, including five from Waterford. On 1 July 1916 the British army launched its much anticipated offensive on the Somme in France. Before the day was over it had suffered almost 60,000 casualties of which 19,600 were fatal. Waterford men Maurice Grant and Frank Phelan went over the top with the Tyneside Irish and were killed.[3] Joseph Butler from the city was with the 36th Ulster Division and died in the assault on the Thiepval redoubt.[4] Fourteen Waterford men were killed on the first day of the Somme and another thirty-six during the remainder of July. The Somme offensive continued until October with ever-mounting casualties. The 16th Irish Division joined the attack in September and stormed the village of Guillemont. Drawn from the southern Irish regiments, the division had more than 1,000 men killed that month, including over fifty from Waterford.

The killing continued throughout 1917. On land Passchendaele replaced the Somme as the killing ground and at sea merchant seamen bore the brunt of German submarine warfare. On 7 June 1917 Major Willie Redmond, brother of John, was killed fighting with the 6th Royal Irish Regiment.[5] He was MP for East Clare and his death precipitated the by-election won by de Valera. Waterford Corporation expressed its sympathy to Redmond and attended a solemn requiem mass in their robes of office.[6] The battle of Passchendaele started in July and finally ended in November with little ground captured but at enormous cost. At least seventy Waterford men died in the mud of Flanders during those months. The greatest single wartime tragedy for Waterford city occurred in December when the *Formby* and *Coningbeg*, two small vessels belonging to the Clyde Shipping Company on the Waterford–Liverpool route, were lost. The *Formby* was torpedoed by U-62 on 14 December and three days later the *Coningbeg* met the same fate. There were no survivors. Eighty-three people died, of whom sixty-seven were from the city and its hinterland.[7] The week before Christmas was marked with grief as families gathered daily on the quays in the hope of some news of their missing relatives. A public relief fund, chaired by Bishops Hackett and O'Hara, raised £7,970 within two weeks. While this helped alleviate economic hardship, it could not compensate for the loss of so many fathers, brothers and sons.[8] By the end of 1917 over 700 men from the city and county had lost their lives and by the end of the war the number of Waterford-born fatalities was over 800. The last to die was William Hales of Brown Street, Portlaw, who was killed on 10 November, less than a day before the guns fell silent.[9]

Recruiting continued for the British forces but at an ever declining rate. By March 1918 an average of just two recruits a week enlisted.[10] In January 1917 CI Hetreed reported that

> Recruiting is not very brisk in the county. The farmers who are making high prices for agricultural produce and stock are very prosperous and likewise apathetic towards recruiting. Those likely to join the forces have already done so and others are employed at remunerative labour. A good many are employed at munitions or other work in this city or in Great Britain.[11]

In February 1917 the army attempted to repeat the success of the March 1915 recruiting campaign. The band of the Irish Guards toured the city and county while a series of public meetings was held. This yielded a mere twenty-three recruits, most 'would have joined under ordinary circumstances anyway.'[12] Occasional improvements in recruitment numbers were usually due to economic factors. For example, in October 1916 Hearne & Co. completed their War Office contract for ammunition boxes and dismissed a number of temporary employees, many of whom then enlisted.[13] An improvement in the allowances paid to soldiers in December 1917 had a similar short-term effect. In March 1918, faced with a critical shortage of military manpower, the British government decided to extend conscription to Ireland. In June the government launched a revitalized recruiting campaign and announced that conscription would not be imposed if 50,000 volunteers came forward instead. Each recruiting area was given a quota. That for the Waterford area which comprised Waterford, Tipperary, Kilkenny and Wexford was 5,200.[14] Between June and the end of the war, only 748 joined, 14 per cent of the target.[15] Most of the new recruits came from urban areas, especially Waterford city.[16] To the end unemployed urban labourers rather than the sons of farmers went to war.

The Waterford economy continued to flourish. In June 1916 it was announced that Waterford South Station, a disused railway terminus, was to be converted into a munitions plant. The conversion contract was awarded to a local building firm, Hearne and Company.[17] By Christmas hiring and training of workers was under way and by April 1917 almost 500 people were employed there making cartridges. Like similar firms in Britain, most of the workforce was female.[18] Other firms such as MacDonnell's margarine factory also expanded. Furthermore, in November 1916 Austin Motors recruited men for their Birmingham plant through the Waterford Labour Exchange.[19] In 1916 and again in 1917 the harvests were excellent and the CI noted that farmers were 'very prosperous'.[20]

Although the initial reaction to the Easter Rising was negative, the public mood changed as sympathy for the rebels became widespread and openly expressed. In May the CI observed that 'generally Sinn Féin ideas are spreading. The German origin of the rebellion is forgotten and sentimental sympathy for the executed rebels is spreading.'[21] On 24 June 1916 an immense congregation, many wearing SF rosettes, attended a solemn requiem mass in the cathedral. The principal celebrant was Fr Michael Dowley, secretary of the local branch of the Gaelic League. His sermon was not reported but some soldiers apparently took exception to remarks about the Rising and walked out.[22] The RIC also noted that 'Sinn Féin Irish Volunteers' organized a demonstration outside the cathedral.[23] Sympathy with the rebels was given more practical expression when a branch of the Irish National Aid Association was established in June.[24] Set up to support the dependants of those killed and imprisoned, it was led by their widows and wives. Patrick Woods and Seán Matthews, both members of the Irish Volunteers, were elected to the committee but were content to remain in the background. Among the officers elected was Dr Vincent White who had previously been prominent in the National Volunteers. A sum of £53 17s. 6d. was collected on the night and White headed the subscription list with a donation of £5.[25] This was followed by a house-to-house collection which, within a month, brought the total for the city to £242 6s. 0d.[26] Collections were also organized throughout the county on a parish basis. By February 1917 Waterford city and county raised £647 12s. 2d. or 2 per cent of the national total. As in the rest of the country, collections for the fund helped to radicalize public opinion and promote the cause of separatism.[27]

Throughout 1916 Willie Walsh, Seán Matthews and others strove to keep the Irish Volunteers together. As Walsh put it, 'in 1916 we were just marking time'.[28] Attendance at the Volunteer hall fell away in May but revived as sympathy for the executed rebels grew. The strength of the Irish Volunteers was estimated at sixty, with eight members of Cumann na mBan and eighteen in the Fianna.[29] Though few in number, this was a cadre of activists, centred on the IRB circle and led by Walsh, Matthews and Brazil who were ready to play their part in future developments. By contrast, Redmond's National Volunteers became completely dormant.

Despite the almost immediate labelling of the Easter Rising as the 'Sinn Féin Rebellion', there was no political party associated with the Irish Volunteers. As sympathy for the rebels and their actions grew, various political movements tried to capitalize on the growth in republican sentiment. Ultimately, they were subsumed into SF but not before they had tried to harness support throughout the country. All these organizations were resisted bitterly by the UIL as a threat to its hegemony. The most significant of these developments was the Irish Nation League (INL). Formed in July 1916 to rally northern nationalist opinion against the proposed exclusion of the 'six counties' from home rule, its declared aim was to replace Redmondism and to give constitutional politics one last chance.[30] It was greatly inhibited by having its head office in Omagh and lacking professional organizers throughout the country. The first mass meeting outside Ulster took place on 10 September 1916 in the Phoenix Park.[31] It attracted a large crowd largely because it was the first public nationalist gathering in Dublin since the Rising. The main speaker was George Murnaghan, a leading Tyrone nationalist.[32] The meeting was chaired by P.W. Kenny, a veteran member of Waterford Corporation with a reputation for independent thinking. In 1914 he had been a staunch supporter of Redmond's pro-war policy. But as the war continued he grew critical of aspects of that policy, though his was often a lone voice at meetings of the corporation. In early 1917 CI Hetreed identified 'a clique headed by Kenny and backed by the *Waterford News*' that was increasingly critical of the IPP leader.[33] That group also included Alderman Maurice Quinlan, a prominent member of the Ballybricken Pig Buyers' Association and Richard Power, an old Fenian sympathizer and former mayor.[34] On 28 May 1917 Murnaghan and Kenny presided at a private meeting in the Granville Hotel to set up a branch of the INL in Waterford. Among those

elected to the committee was Vincent White.[35] The INL did not prosper in
Waterford and merged with SF in 1918. Thus, after a journey from the
National Volunteers via the Irish Nation League and an even briefer dalliance
with Count Plunkett's Liberty League, White joined SF and represented the
party in future electoral battles in Waterford city.[36]

Conscious, perhaps, of the still nascent but potentially major challenge to
his position, Redmond visited his constituency on 6 October 1916 and
addressed a capacity crowd at city hall. Rumours of planned disruption had
been rife and his traditional supporters, the Ballybricken Pig Buyers'
Association, turned out in strength. As expected, when Redmond rose to
speak, there were jeers and hostile questions from a minority who shouted
'who fears to speak of Easter week' and attempted to unfurl a tricolour. The
objectors, including Alderman Kenny, were speedily removed by the stewards
in a fashion that subsequently drew criticism from both newspapers and
clergy.[37] Most of Redmond's speech dealt with the need to put their trust in
constitutional means despite the failure of the Lloyd George negotiations in
June–July 1916 on home rule. The IPP leader closed with a fighting appeal to
his faithful supporters:

> I was told I dare not come to Waterford. I have come to Waterford. I
> will come to Waterford where and when I please and in Waterford I
> will speak as I choose. I will not be dictated to by anyone. I hope the
> day will never come when I will be afraid to come here to Waterford
> to speak my mind.[38]

Although the meeting closed to rousing cheers for Redmond, Emily Ussher
perceptively saw 'a broken man, come to make his last appeal to his "own
people of Waterford who had never failed him". Redmond pale, eyes fixed
afar on some dread horizon, contemplating doom, tragedy incarnate.'[39] That
Redmond was heckled in Waterford was symptomatic of the decline of the
IPP and UIL; that the hecklers were dealt with as they were was a foretaste
of politics in Waterford over the next few years.[40] In Waterford, at least,
Redmondism would not fade quietly away. Redmond also took the opportunity to visit the newly completed munitions factory at Bilberry – the clearest
proof to his constituents that his support for the war effort was yielding local
economic benefit.

During 1917 SF emerged as the political wing of militant Irish nationalism with a series of spectacular by-election victories, each of which boosted
the morale of SF workers nationally and greatly aided the spread of the party
and the Irish Volunteers.[41] The first success was in North Roscommon where
Count George Plunkett, father of the 1916 leader, Joseph, was elected. He
was not a SF candidate even though his candidature was endorsed by the

party. After his triumph Plunkett saw himself as the leader of Irish nationalism. He called a national convention at the Mansion House on 19 April at
which Waterford was represented by Maurice Quinlan and Richard Power.
Plunkett's Liberty League floundered. Only thirteen people attended a meeting to establish a branch in Waterford and the League was soon subsumed
into SF.[42] Another by-election victory followed in Longford in May. Just
before the Longford contest, the Catholic bishop of Derry, Charles McHugh,
had called on all Catholic and Church of Ireland prelates to sign a letter
against partition. This move was seen as highly critical of Redmond who had
accepted the principle of partition if only on a temporary basis. Eighteen
Catholic and three Anglican bishops signed, including Dr Hackett of
Waterford and Lismore – an indication that another pillar of traditional support for the UIL and IPP, the Catholic clergy, was crumbling.[43] In July 1917
O'Shee was one of a number of MPs who put their names to a letter to
Redmond urging him to take a harder line with the British government, an
action which was roundly condemned in Waterford. While SF went from
strength to strength, the IPP nationally seemed content to let things drift.
Subscriptions and membership fell sharply as the party held virtually no
meetings, few speeches were made by the leadership and even the UIL
national directory did not meet between July 1916 and April 1918.[44]

   The release of the last of the Easter Week prisoners from Lewes Prison in
June 1917 and the triumph of Éamon de Valera in the East Clare by-election
in July were celebrated throughout nationalist Ireland.[45] Waterford shared in
these celebrations with parades and public meetings but there were no triumphant homecomings as no Waterford resident had been interned after the
Rising. The celebrations in Kilmacthomas to mark 'Dev's' election led to a
mini-riot and the arrest of four prominent members of SF: Frank Drohan,
George Kiely, Patrick Lawlor and Dan Cooney. They were sentenced to fourteen days' imprisonment.[46]

   The roll of SF electoral successes was completed that year with the election of W.T. Cosgrave in Kilkenny. The growth of SF in Waterford was
tracked assiduously by the RIC. By December 1917 SF had grown dramatically from one club with sixty members to twelve with 703 members.[47] The
CI's monthly reports repeatedly indicated that SF was 'the only political
organisations showing activity'.[48] Despite the efforts of O'Shee, the UIL
branch network continued to atrophy. As Hetreed noted, 'local farmers are
not inclined to pay up for the affiliation of the UIL branches'.[49] In December
P.C. O'Mahony was dismissed from his position in Dungarvan Post Office
for his nationalist activities. This action proved counterproductive as he subsequently became a full-time SF organizer and established a branch in every
parish in Waterford.[50] The dominance of nationalist Ireland by SF was confirmed at its convention in October 1917, which was attended by a Waterford

delegation led by P.W. Kenny and Richard Power. Arthur Griffith stood aside in favour of de Valera as president.[51] Wide-ranging policies were adopted. Rosamond Jacob, one of the Waterford delegates, was instrumental in obtaining a commitment to gender equality and women's suffrage.[52]

Although SF had developed strongly in the county, it was not as successful in Waterford city, even though Kenny, Quinlan and Power, by then members of SF, gave it a strong voice at corporation meetings.[53] The hosting of the Gaelic League oireachtas in August gave a much-needed boost to SF morale in the city.[54] On 11 November de Valera and Griffith were to address a meeting on the Mall. On their arrival the previous night they were met by Irish Volunteers and paraded across the bridge but were stopped at the city end by a large contingent of Redmondites.[55] The RIC interposed themselves between the rival factions and the situation was defused. DI George Maxwell then proclaimed the meeting and sent for reinforcements.[56] Three hundred soldiers were sent by special train from Fermoy and 250 extra policemen were drafted in from adjoining counties. The troops sealed off the Mall with barbed wire and mounted machine-guns on the roof of city hall. There was a minor riot when de Valera emerged from 11 a.m. mass in the cathedral and was confronted by Redmondites. Further confrontation was avoided when SF moved their meeting to Ballinaneeshagh, just outside the city limits. De Valera and Griffith spoke in the teeming rain to a crowd estimated at several thousand. The meeting dispersed peacefully. A counter-demonstration by Redmondites on Ballybricken Hill was held that night.[57] Although violence had been narrowly avoided, it was clear that both sides were preparing for a major confrontation and they did not have long to wait.

In early 1918 SF suffered by-election defeat in South Armagh by a margin of almost two to one. This was the first of three hard-fought victories for the IPP with further successes in Waterford and East Tyrone. John Redmond died in London of heart failure on 6 March 1918 following an operation for gallstones. Worn out by over thirty years of public life and seeing his life's work slipping away, it seemed to many that the IPP leader died of a broken heart.[58] News of his death evoked memories throughout Ireland of his great service to his country, nowhere more so than in Waterford city, the constituency he had represented for twenty-six years. National and local newspapers, parliamentary leaders and local bodies paid fulsome tribute to the man who had finally put a home rule act on the statute book but had seen that great prize taken by the machinations of the Unionists and the Conservatives and the chicanery of Lloyd George and the Liberals.[59] He was interred in the family vault in Wexford. In a final tribute the coffin was carried from the church by eight of his Ballybricken supporters.[60]

The IPP moved the by-election writ quickly, with polling day set for Friday 22 March. Determined to hold the seat, the party fielded their strongest possible candidate, Captain William Redmond, the 36-year-old son of the late IPP leader, lawyer, MP for East Tyrone, and a serving officer with the Irish Guards. He resigned East Tyrone to fight his father's constituency. Throughout the campaign he wore his uniform, a move which de Valera commended as a shrewd political ploy in a city that had a greater than normal interest in the war.[61] SF nominated Vincent White. Redmond stood firmly on the achievements of his father and of the IPP, while White offered a new vision of a free Ireland. Socio-economic issues were not raised by either candidate.

SF's first public meeting was held on the Mall on the night of 11 March. White and Seán Milroy, a member of the party standing committee and the SF candidate in the East Tyrone by-election, addressed a crowd of several hundred Volunteers and supporters but struggled to make themselves heard above the Redmondite crowd's shouting and singing. The songs were followed by a shower of stones and the police had to intervene to keep the factions apart.[62] Two days later de Valera arrived in Waterford with leading members of SF, an indication of how seriously they took the contest. That afternoon he had his first taste of 'electioneering, Waterford-style' when he attempted to canvas voters in the centre of the city but was soon surrounded by a mob of Redmondite supporters. With great difficulty an escort of Volunteers managed to rescue him. A dishevelled de Valera, his clothes torn and covered with mud, was taken to SF election headquarters, which was then besieged by the mob for over an hour before the RIC cleared the streets.[63] In response, Dan McCarthy, SF director of elections, sent for Volunteer reinforcements from neighbouring counties and from Dublin. Soon between 800 and 1,000 men were on hand to assist the local Volunteers. De Valera and his fellow leaders stayed in the Metropole Hotel which was run by a staunch republican, Ms Power.[64]

For the IPP and the UIL the Waterford by-election was of critical importance. A loss there would spell the end of the party. The Metropolitan Branch of the UIL appealed to the electors of Waterford 'to carry Capt. Redmond at the head of the poll by a thumping majority'.[65] The IPP campaign was launched with a monster meeting on Ballybricken on 13 March when a crowd of over 5,000 heard speeches from Mayor John J. O'Sullivan and others.[66] The next day Captain Redmond arrived in the city to a tumultuous reception.[67] A parade through the city culminated in a meeting on Ballybricken, where the mayor declared that Ballybricken-men would stand on their home ground supporting Redmond and would never yield it. In response Redmond declared:

There is one thing of which Ireland can be certain, that Ballybricken is there every time to support the patriotic policy, the sane policy, the policy that had brought prosperity to Waterford ... The invasion of

Waterford had started but like other invasions would be repelled by the men of Waterford.[68]

He also referred to SF's German connections. In a city still mourning the loss of sixty-seven of its citizens aboard the *Formby* and *Coningbeg*, this was an emotional and powerful appeal. The election campaign continued with nightly meetings followed by riots. On 15 March Patrick Walsh, a Redmondite, was shot in the leg as the crowd attempted to storm the Volunteer hall on Thomas Street. A Dublin Volunteer, Owen Passan, was later charged but acquitted.[69] At this stage, the RIC apparently resolved to stand by and observe proceedings unless SF appeared to be winning in which case they would intervene vigorously. St Patrick's Day was marked by a truce. Both sides took part in the customary parade but were kept well apart. From then until polling day hostilities resumed and troops and extra police were drafted into the city to keep order.[70] Rosamond Jacob took a very active part in the canvas and flew a republican flag from her parent's house in the wealthy Newtown district. According to the *Irish Independent*, a lighted torch was thrown into the house.[71] Tension was increased further when Joe Devlin, backed by a large contingent of his Belfast supporters, arrived in the city to lend muscular support to Redmond. Devlin himself took charge of the closing days of the campaign.[72]

Polling day was marred by continuous rioting.[73] Between fifty and sixty Volunteers were deployed at each of the ten polling stations. They were matched by at least the same number of Redmondites. Consequently, the situation was extremely volatile. Dr White was struck on the head as he made his way to Mount Sion school to vote. After treatment he returned, escorted by a large contingent of Volunteers. The RIC cleared a path through the mob and he was finally able to vote.[74] Other SF supporters had similar experiences. The closing of the polling stations that evening did not end the violence. Approximately 400 Volunteers paraded to the Volunteer hall where they were besieged by about twice that number of Redmondites, confident that they had won the electoral contest and spoiling for a fight. The police sealed off the street but declined to intervene. They did, however, prevent other Volunteers from reaching the hall. When both sides produced firearms it appeared that bloodshed could not be avoided. De Valera intervened and following negotiations with the RIC the crowd was ordered to disperse on the assurance that the Volunteers would leave Waterford the following morning.

The result was declared at the city courthouse on the morning of 23 March. Redmond received 1,242 votes to 764 for White. Amid scenes of wild jubilation, Redmond told his supporters: 'We defeated our opponents in South Armagh. We have snowed them under in Waterford and we have them on the run'. In an allusion to his father's victory in 1891, won then with the support of the Fenian movement, he said: 'This was not a fight won by old men. It was a fight by the young men of Waterford who were with them today just as the young men of Waterford were with my father twenty-seven years ago'.[75] John Dillon, leader of the IPP, telegraphed Redmond: 'Waterford has struck a blow for Ireland and splendidly vindicated your father's name'.[76] Similarly, the *Freeman's Journal* proclaimed a 'splendid Nationalist victory over Sinn Féin'.[77] Many local bodies in neighbouring counties, still dominated by UIL members, passed motions congratulating Redmond.[78] Michael Collins accepted that SF's 'complaisance received a rude shock' and that the result was a setback.[79] Nonetheless, the police were impressed that SF received so many votes in Waterford and concluded that 'Sinn Féinism would appear to be progressing.'[80] On learning the election result a crowd outside the SF headquarters on Harcourt Street, Dublin, groaned about 'another British victory'.[81] The same theme was taken up by an *Irish Independent* editorial which suggested that most of Redmond's majority came from unionist voters who were prospering from the war.[82] When the IPP recorded a third by-election victory by retaining Redmond's former seat in East Tyrone, it must have seemed as if the political tide was turning in its favour.[83]

If there was any truth in John Dillon's assertion that 'Sinn Féin was on the rapid down grade, in fact a slump had set in' then the party was saved by the actions of the British government.[84] Faced with a crisis on the Western Front as the German army launched a major offensive and with the army crying out for reinforcements, Lloyd George and his government turned to the last untapped pool of manpower and decided to introduce conscription in Ireland in March 1918.[85] The response of nationalist Ireland was immediate. The IPP opposed the bill relentlessly in the House of Commons. During the debate Redmond claimed that 'If they persist in this proposal of conscription, there will be no Irish Party in the House of Commons but then you will have a very much harder nut to crack in Ireland.'[86] His statement was seized on by SF and used in the East Cavan by-election in May with the slogan 'vote for Sinn Féin and give England a hard nut to crack'.[87] Dillon led his party out of parliament and back to Ireland only to find that the leadership of the anti-conscription movement had been seized by SF.[88] Although the IPP joined forces with SF and Labour in an impressive display of national unity against the threat of conscription, the IPP, tainted by its previous support for the war, was forced to play only a supporting role. Following a cross-party nationalist meeting in the Mansion House on 17 April the Catholic hierarchy endorsed opposition to conscription.[89] On the following Sunday a national pledge – reminiscent of the signing of the Ulster Covenant six years previously – was signed at church doors. This was followed by a one-day general strike that paralyzed the country. Throughout Waterford long queues formed to sign the pledge. The general strike was fully observed with the closure of all factories, shops and commercial premises. The day was marked by a multitude of meetings and parades organized by SF and the local trades' union council.[90] The IPP seemed to deem it politic to keep a low profile during the conscription crisis – a symptom of the party's decline. Bishop Hackett used the occasion of a confirmation ceremony to urge the congregation 'to resist conscription by all lawful means'.[91] The crisis gave an immediate boost to SF and the Irish Volunteers as new members joined throughout the county. In August the reported strength of SF in the city and county peaked at thirty clubs (cumainn) and 2,478 members.[92] That month the conscription crisis eased as the tide of war turned in favour of the Allies and it became clear that Germany would be defeated. Although many of the new recruits dropped out as soon as the crisis passed, the organizational framework for both SF and the Volunteers was in place for future challenges.

By the autumn of 1918 a general election was long overdue. There had been none since 1910, and all parties expected one before the end of the year. The Representation of the People Act (1918) introduced universal suffrage for men over 21 years of age and for the first time gave the vote to women, although only to those over 30 who were either householders themselves or married to householders. This more than doubled the electorate and SF was confident of capturing a majority of new voters. The act also changed the electoral boundaries in Waterford, reducing from three to two the number of constituencies. As discussed in chapter one, Waterford city was combined with its immediate hinterland while the rest of the county became the new Waterford County constituency. Martin Murphy, the outgoing MP for Waterford East, stood down and gave his support to Captain Redmond. From August to November SF was busy selecting candidates. Although the local organization could put forward names, the party standing committee, dominated by Collins and Boland, had to approve them and in some cases reject prospective candidates.[93] Ironically, Boland himself fell foul of one of its rules which decreed that only candidates with a command of Irish could be nominated for constituencies with a Gaeltacht population.[94] This, of course, included Waterford and Boland had to decline his nomination for Waterford County as he was not an Irish speaker.[95] Cathal Brugha, wounded hero of the South Dublin Union garrison of 1916, was nominated instead.[96] His opponent was J.J. O'Shee, the sitting MP. In the Waterford city constituency White again faced Redmond. With the expanded electorate and the national mood strongly in favour of SF, the local organization was confident it could win both Waterford seats.

On 25 November Lloyd George dissolved parliament and called a general election. Polling day was set for 14 December. Constituencies were given the option of counting the votes on 21 or 28 December – the delay being necessary to allow the return of postal votes from serving soldiers overseas. A confident SF was ready to contest every constituency in Ireland while a despondent IPP was fighting for its political existence.[97] The RIC Inspector General observed that

> For some time past it has been obvious that the Irish Parliamentary Party had outlived their popularity even with the R.C. clergy. The chief complaint now urged against them is that on the outbreak of war they failed to obtain from [the] Government satisfactory guarantees with regard to Home Rule. Their organisation has been singularly apathetic with regard to the new register of voters. Thirty-two members of the party did not seek re-election, allowing twenty-five Sinn Féiners to be elected on nomination day unopposed and it is not improbable that many more nationalist seats will be lost.[98]

SF started its election campaign early in Waterford County. On 18 November Dan Fraher, O'Mahony and other speakers addressed a large crowd in Dungarvan under a banner which read 'For Cathal Brugha and Independence'. The dominant theme in the speeches was Brugha's 1916 experience.[99] From 4 December until polling day Brugha, escorted by Volunteers, spoke in every town and village. By contrast, O'Shee had difficulty in mounting a proper campaign due to lack of both money and a network of functioning UIL branches. The *Dungarvan Observer* urged support for Brugha.[100] On the eve of the poll, a despondent O'Shee conceded that SF might win but would do so with a very small majority.[101] In the event Brugha secured 12,890 votes, 75 per cent of the vote and one of the biggest winning margins in the country, to 4,217 votes for O'Shee.[102]

It was a different story in Waterford city. There SF had opened its campaign with a rally on the Mall on Sunday 17 November. Despite being warned by the police to avoid any 'military-like' display, several hundred Volunteers marched to the meeting behind their band. White and Rosamond Jacob were the main speakers with the latter urging female voters to support SF as the party offered women a full part in public life. She also criticized the IPP's 'record of failure for a dubious measure of Home Rule while SF would appeal to the Peace Conference and the world for the status of Ireland as a free nation.'[103] In scenes reminiscent of the by-election in March, the meeting was attacked by the wives of absent soldiers, the so-called 'separation women' and other supporters of Redmond.[104] White later recalled that these separation women had been most grateful to him for his efforts during the influenza epidemic that had swept the city a few months previously.[105] A riot ensued as the police tried to keep order. On 19 November Redmond launched his campaign with a mass meeting on Ballybricken. He attacked the SF policy of abstention and pointed out the economic benefits that the war had brought to the city. He also emphasized the benefits and continuity of parliamentary resistance to England as shown by O'Connell, Parnell and his late father.[106]

Although the RIC noted that 'the leaders on both sides are making honest efforts to guard against collisions with good results', the reality was a repeat, though not as severe, of the clashes that had marred the March by-election.[107] Volunteers were drafted in from Cork, Kerry and Clare, where SF was unopposed. They guarded meetings, escorted canvassers and met the Redmondites' sticks with sticks and stones with stones. Redmond made the outside invasion of Waterford a theme in his speeches. Polling day saw violent scenes around the polling stations and the police were forced to fix bayonets to separate the rival factions on Francis Street. The day ended with the almost customary attack on the Volunteer hall. The count did not take place until 28 December. Redmond triumphed once again with 4,915 votes to 4,421 votes for White.[108] Conscious of the SF landslide elsewhere, he declared that Waterford city was 'an oasis in the political desert of Ireland'. After the count Redmond's supporters paraded from the courthouse to Ballybricken where they burned an effigy of Dr White. The same local newspapers that acclaimed his triumph also carried an announcement from the ministry of munitions in London that the cartridge factory at Bilberry was to close and that all the employees would lose their jobs.[109]

Demobilized soldiers began to return home from 1919 onwards to a much changed Waterford city and county. They did so in a low key way, attracting little or no attention. Even a function held in city hall on 16 January to welcome home 100 released prisoners of war attracted little interest.[110] It was a far cry from the parades and bands that had marked their departure in 1914 or 1915. Large firms such as the banks, the railways or Graves, the building contractors, honoured their promises to keep open the jobs of those who had enlisted. They quickly and quietly resumed their pre-war occupations while many others returned to their pre-war lives of unemployment, poverty and occasional casual labour. They formed a large and cohesive pressure group in the city, strongly supportive of Captain Redmond.

SF was not the only movement to make dramatic progress in Waterford during this period. The insatiable demands of a war economy for food and manufactured goods had brought a boom to the city and county and it was not just farmers, traders and industrialists who had benefitted. Recruitment and increased demand for workers in the factories and on the farms had tilted the balance of power towards labour. In Waterford the land under tillage had increased by 31 per cent from 52,966 acres in 1911 to 69,360 in 1918. With excess labour absorbed by the army and the munitions factories, the war presented an opportunity for agricultural labourers and for the ITGWU, both nationally and locally, which the union was quick to exploit.[111] In Waterford the first sign of growing militancy among the labourers was the establishment of a 'Land and Labour Union' in Clonea-Power in late 1917. Like other similar local unions it was quickly absorbed by the ITGWU.[112] In January 1918 the ITGWU had only two branches in Waterford, one in the city and the other in Dungarvan, both catering for dockers, carters and industrial workers. As their numbers increased the ITGWU launched a recruitment drive. Laurence Veale and W.P. Coates were appointed organizers and from a low base of only one branch in the county in Dungarvan there were twenty-four by the end of the year, almost one per parish. The new branches catered almost exclusively for agricultural labourers.[113] Of the 544 members in the new Kilmacthomas branch, 453 were agricultural labourers. The Dungarvan branch doubled its membership to 582 in 1918, the increase due to farm labourers from the surrounding countryside. Much of the expansion was due to Nicholas Phelan, who had been appointed a full-time organizer for the county. From its new position of strength the union campaigned vigorously and successfully for wage increases and against the use of non-union labour. The growth in trade union membership among agricultural labourers was not confined to Waterford.[114] Across the country, but especially in the south-east, the ITGWU experienced rapid expansion and to some it seemed that in rural Ireland there was a climate conducive to revolutionary action.[115]

Before 1919 the agricultural labourers were not organized on a county-wide basis. This meant that strikes and other confrontations tended to be localized, short and often violent. One such confrontation took place in Fenor near Tramore in November 1919 when some farmers refused to pay the traditional harvest bonus. The resultant affray involved about 300 labourers and 120 police. The *Munster Express* reported a pitched battle 'in which revolver shots, batons, and bayonets, were freely used' and injuries on both sides.[116] Phelan was one of several protestors sentenced to short terms of imprisonment for breach of the peace. In addition to winning improvements in wages and conditions, the union enforced a ban on non-union labour. On 9 August Phelan placed a notice in all local newspapers that union members had 'the right to refuse to work for supervisors that employ non-union labour.'[117]

The spread of trade unionism was not just a rural phenomenon. The war had led to the establishment of new industries in the city, most notably the National Cartridge Factory (540 workers) and McDonnell's Margarine Plant (200 workers) and to the expansion of existing ones. The ITGWU repeated their rural success with a recruiting drive in the city. In February 1918 the union had one city branch with 102 members. By June that branch had 903 members and it was necessary to establish a second branch. As Tommy Dunne, full-time secretary of the city branch, recalled every firm of size joined up. At first there was much talk of resistance and talk of forming an employers' federation. But the only opposition came from the building employers led by John Hearne. A strike notice made him change his mind within a week.[118]

Other unions were also active in the city. The Irish Women Workers' Union and the craft unions either established branches or increased their membership, sometimes in the face of opposition from the ITGWU. Politically, trade unionism in Waterford moved to the left, something reflected in the change of name from 'Waterford City Trades Council' to 'Waterford and District Workers' Council'. Between 1918 and 1920 the unions won substantial wage increases for their members but not without resistance from the employers. Excluding general strikes, such as the one against conscription, or unofficial industrial action, there were twenty-six strikes in the city in this three-year period, involving well over a third of the workforce.[119] The strikes lasted an average of seventeen days. The gains were hard won but as the wartime boom ended, the question now became: could the workers hold on to them?

Despite the growth in the trade union movement in Waterford during this period there was no similar rise in the political organization of the workers. In August 1918 the Labour Party held its annual congress in Waterford and decided to contest the forthcoming general election. This decision was endorsed unanimously at a meeting of the party's executive the following month. Almost immediately practical difficulties emerged. There was insufficient money, candidates and electoral organization. Even in constituencies such as Waterford city, Cork, Kilkenny and Wexford – centres of trade union membership – no candidates were put forward. In addition some labour leaders believed that union members would 'not support the nominees of Labour' preferring to vote for SF in an election which would be fought as a plebiscite on the future of the country. In the end the Labour Party convened a special conference and decided not to put forward any candidates – a decision that was greeted with gratitude by SF and with rage by the IPP.[120] The ITGWU delegation from Waterford criticized the decision but its own failure to select a candidate at a local meeting in Waterford in October reflected poorly on it.[121]

Between Easter 1916 and December 1918 nationalist politics in Ireland shifted dramatically from the old constitutionalist home rule policy of the IPP to the more radical republican ideal of SF that would be achieved, if necessary, by force of arms. This seismic shift engulfed the once-dominant IPP throughout southern Ireland except in Waterford city. Uniquely, Waterford stood alone against the seemingly irresistible rise of SF and twice demonstrated its loyalty to Redmondism at the ballot box. Now that loyalty faced new challenges in a dramatically changed environment. On 21 January the newly elected SF MPs met in the Mansion House as the first Dáil. There were only twenty-seven present since many of the elected members were in prison and others, including Collins, were in England arranging the escape of de Valera from Lincoln Jail. Captain Redmond, although invited, did not attend. His fellow representative from Waterford, Cathal Brugha, was elected chairman. The same day Volunteers of Tipperary No. 3 Brigade shot dead two RIC men who were escorting a cart-load of gelignite near Soloheadbeg, generally accepted as the first shots in the War of Independence. How peace in Europe and war in Ireland affected Waterford is the focus of the next chapter.

5 'Waterford has not done much'?: the War of Independence, 1919–21

On 21 January 1919, in line with their policy of abstention from Westminster, the newly-elected SF MPs met in the Mansion House in Dublin and created their own assembly – Dáil Éireann. By coincidence, on the same day a group of Volunteers ambushed and killed two RIC constables at Soloheadbeg in County Tipperary. From that date until the truce in July 1921 political activism was accompanied by steadily escalating violence. The rate and the extent to which the War of Independence developed differed not only from county to county but also within counties. The armed struggle in Waterford was slow to develop when compared to its neighbours to the west and north, Counties Cork and Tipperary. But activity in Waterford was far in advance of Wexford and Kilkenny. Within Waterford the intensity of the conflict differed sharply. In the west of the county, buoyed by SF's impressive electoral victory, the West Waterford Brigade (Waterford No. 2 Brigade) engaged Crown forces from January 1920 onwards. The east of the county and Waterford city were different because the strength of Redmondism provided a nationalist alternative to SF. The East Waterford (Waterford No. 1 Brigade) did not become an effective fighting force and in 1921 was riven by internal strife. Dissatisfaction with this state of affairs led IRA General Headquarters (GHQ) to amalgamate both brigades in July 1921. Politically, local elections in 1920 and the election for the proposed parliament of Southern Ireland in May 1921 gave SF opportunities to consolidate its dominance in the county and to make progress in the city. While the IRA and SF focused their attention on the conflict with Crown forces, workers in both city and county fought to keep the gains they had made during the years of wartime prosperity as the balance of power in the labour market swung towards the employers.

A dividing line from Clonmel through Kilmacthomas and along the River Mahon to the sea demarcated the area of the West Waterford Brigade from that of the East Waterford Brigade (see map 6). Under the command of Pax Whelan, the western brigade, with a nominal strength of about 1,800 men, comprised four battalions centred on Dungarvan (1st), Kilrossanty (2nd), Ardmore-Old Parish (3rd) and Lismore (4th).[1] The East Waterford Brigade, with Seán Matthews as O/C, contained three battalions: Waterford city (1st), Dunhill-Ballyduff (2nd) and Gaultier (3rd). It was much weaker than its western counterpart and could muster only about 500 men, making it one of the weakest brigades in the country.[2] Within battalion areas companies were organized on a parish basis, as were SF clubs. The strength of companies and battalions varied. A strong company might have between sixty and eighty

62

Waterford, 1912–23
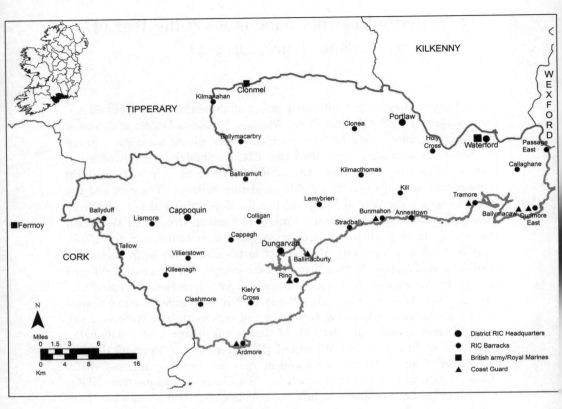

4 Distribution of the Crown forces in January 1919

members, while some of the city companies had as few as twenty Volunteers.
The strength of the City Battalion never exceeded 150 men. Ranged against the
two IRA brigades were 240 members of the RIC who were dispersed throughout the city and county in small barracks (see map 4).[3] They were later reinforced by detachments of the British army and Royal Marines (see map 5).

While there was no shortage of manpower, as with every brigade in the
country, arms were in short supply. The Waterford IRA conducted extensive
arms raids during 1919 and early 1920, many as Jeremiah Cronin, a city
Volunteer, recalled on private houses.[4] These yielded a plentiful supply of
shotguns, which were of limited military use. A number of Volunteers had
acquired revolvers but there were few modern as opposed to obsolete rifles.
The variety of weapons made the supply of ammunition a logistical night-
mare. There was also a change in emphasis as open training drills and route
marches were frowned upon in favour of clandestine meetings, the acquisition
of arms and, where possible, firing practice.

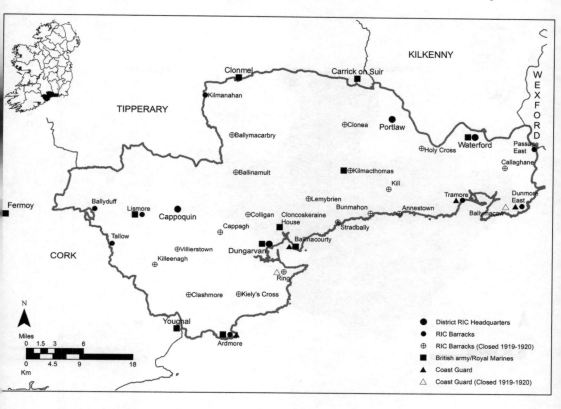

5 Distribution of the Crown forces in July 1921

The RIC responded to the growing level of crime by arresting, whenever possible, known IRA leaders. In February the police were prevented from entering a churchyard in Fenor during the burial of Volunteer Michael O'Gorman. The following month Seán Matthews, who refused to recognize the court, was sentenced to three months' imprisonment for obstructing the police.[5] Many Volunteers were similarly arrested and served short sentences during 1919 for low grade offences such as drilling or wearing a military uniform. This approach did not restrict the growth of the Volunteers. Funerals continued to offer opportunities for the IRA to demonstrate its strength and organizational abilities. The funeral of Michael Walsh, a Ring Volunteer, in May was the scene of a major demonstration by the IRA and SF but passed off peacefully. On 29 April Walsh approached Ballinagoul RIC Barracks to seek help to stop a fight in a nearby public house between local republicans and the crew of a British gunboat. The lone policeman on duty, thinking he was under attack, fired through the door, fatally wounding Walsh who died

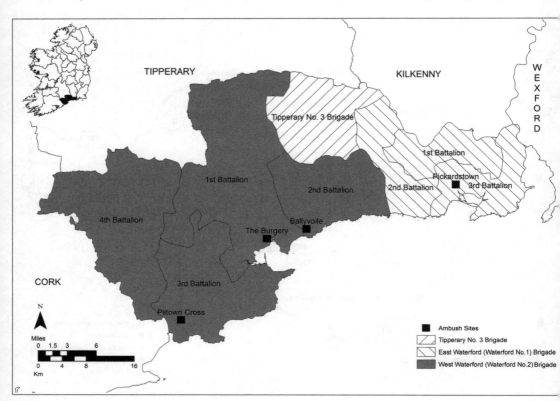

6 Waterford brigades and battalion areas, January 1919 to June 1921;
and ambush sites

two weeks later.[6] His was the only death attributable to political violence in
Waterford in 1919.

From September 1919 Volunteers nationwide were given the new but
equally important task of raising the Dáil loan.[7] The Dáil authorized Michael
Collins, as minister for finance, to 'issue Republican bonds to the value of
£250,000'.[8] Unable to use the national press to publicize the loan, Collins
relied on the IRA to distribute the prospectus, canvass potential subscribers
and collect and remit monies. He appointed a full-time organizer for each
province, including P.C. O'Mahony for Munster.[9] The police did all in their
power to hinder the drive. They noted the number of times that O'Mahony
visited Waterford, raided houses, seized literature and tried in vain to locate
the money. Collins kept a black list of constituencies that were underper-
forming. When the loan was closed in July 1920, just over £370,000 had been
raised.[10] O'Mahony could be proud of his efforts. Of the total raised in

Ireland, Munster contributed over £171,000 or 48 per cent. The money was raised and audited on a constituency basis. The average contribution of the twenty-three constituencies in Munster was £7,440. Limerick West (£17,385), Clare East (£13,609) and Cork city (£12,067) headed the subscriptions. Waterford County raised £4,550 which though below the Munster average was in line with adjoining constituencies which ranged from £3,787 in Cork North East to £5,281 in Kilkenny South. Waterford city presented a different picture, however, as only £636 was collected – the lowest of any constituency outside the unionist heartland of east Ulster. Even the strongholds of southern Unionism, the Dublin constituencies of Rathmines (£1,235) and Pembroke (£2,580), raised more.[11] As an indicator of IRA and SF organization, the Dáil loan collection showed how weak republicanism was in Waterford city. The county, by contrast, was on a par with its neighbours and ready for the next phase in the War of Independence.

During the first six months of 1919 there was relatively little revolutionary activity in Ireland beyond a few isolated attacks on police. Much attention was paid to the futile efforts of a SF delegation to raise the case of Ireland at the Versailles Peace Conference. SF membership in Waterford was concentrated in the west of the county. David Fitzpatrick calculated SF membership per 10,000 of the population and with 285 Waterford was ahead of Wexford (249) but significantly behind Kilkenny (483), Tipperary (467) and Cork (333).[12] SF in west Waterford supported the West Waterford Brigade as it began to engage in armed conflict with Crown forces. As ever, Waterford city was different. Two hard-fought elections had shown that the name Redmond retained the allegiance of a large number of nationalists. Sporadic violence between Redmondites and SF came to a head on St Patrick's Day 1919 in what the *Munster Express* described as 'minor scuffles' but the strongly pro-SF *Waterford News* termed an 'orgy of hooliganism'.[13] Many of the participants had to be treated for injuries in the city infirmary. The following month William Grant, a labourer who lived on Harrington's Lane and a supporter of Redmond, was killed in a brawl that started following the trading of rival political slogans, 'Up Redmond' and 'Up White'. No one was convicted.[14] Intra-nationalist faction fighting persisted into 1920. This situation was unparalleled in nationalist Ireland outside Ulster.[15]

Local elections in 1920, which had been repeatedly delayed since 1917, gave SF a means of consolidating its political dominance in the country. They also offered Labour an opportunity to translate its success in organizing workers, as discussed in the previous chapter, into electoral gain. In January 1920 elections, under the new proportional representation (PR) system, were held for city and urban district councils. SF put a major effort into these contests even though no candidates stood under the UIL banner. In Waterford city supporters of Captain Redmond stood either for the Ratepayers' Association or as Independents. In the city SF won twenty-two of the forty seats on the corporation. The result for the Labour Party was a grave disappointment. It won only three seats, although three of the successful SF candidates and one Independent were noted trade union activists. Only six declared Redmond supporters were returned; they had held twenty-eight seats on the outgoing corporation.[16] Mary Strangman did not contest the election but campaigned for Sarah Holmes-White of the Women's National Health Association who won a seat and continued Strangman's work on health and housing issues.[17] Lily Poole stood for re-election but polled poorly and lost her seat.[18] Labour was more successful in the UDC elections. In Dungarvan it won three out of fifteen seats and in Lismore two out of nine.[19] All other seats were won by SF. Elections for the county council were held in June. Twenty members were elected in four electoral districts. All were members of SF but at least three were identified with Labour.[20]

A further electoral contest scheduled for May 1921 for seats in the new Southern Ireland parliament did not take place. John Dillon announced that the IPP would not contest the election since the oppressive policy of the British government made it impossible for any nationalist to oppose SF.[21] Hence Captain Redmond did not stand in Waterford. SF used the opportunity to elect members to the second Dáil. Waterford city and county had been joined with East Tipperary to form a new five-seat constituency under PR. The five SF nominees – Vincent White, Cathal Brugha, Éamon Dee, Séamus Robinson and Frank Drohan – were returned unopposed.[22] Membership of SF in Waterford continued to grow and in 1921 it was estimated at 2,186 men and 259 women. This was equivalent to 290 per 10,000 of the population, comparable to Wexford but significantly below the figures for Kilkenny, Tipperary or Cork which ranged from 340 to 510.[23]

Once in power in the various local authorities, SF indulged in dramatic gestures and passive resistance while being careful not to jeopardize the payment of the LGB grant, which was vital for the financing of the local authorities. When the new Waterford Corporation first convened in February 1920 Vincent White was elected mayor. He immediately demanded that the mace and other symbols of the city's royal charters, which he described as 'imperial baubles', be removed from the chamber.[24] When Waterford County Council met in July 1920 it passed a resolution acknowledging the authority of Dáil Éireann and also expunged from the official minute book a motion that had condemned the Easter Rising.[25] For the next twelve months both local authorities sought to obstruct the British government by measures such as refusing to pay the gas bill for courthouses.[26] Both the city and the county authorities refused to pay awards in malicious injuries cases, which had been made a local authority charge in October 1919. The LGB responded by withholding part of the central government funding. On the advice of Captain

Redmond, Waterford Corporation applied unsuccessfully to Westminster for a supplementary housing grant.[27] Both the county council and the corporation faced a financial crisis, a situation not resolved until after the Treaty.[28]

If 1919 was relatively quiet in terms of politically motivated violence, events changed dramatically countrywide in January 1920 when IRA GHQ authorized a campaign against police barracks.[29] Fourteen were attacked, including Ardmore in Waterford on 29 January. James Mansfield, commandant of the local battalion, was in charge of the operation in which about fifty Volunteers took part. All roads leading to the village were blocked with felled trees to prevent the arrival of reinforcements. An improvised mine was placed against the barracks wall but failed to explode, a sustained round of shotgun fire proved totally ineffective and no casualties were sustained on either side.[30] The CI noted 'careful preparation and good discipline' on the part of the IRA.[31] Although the attack failed in its primary purpose of capturing the barracks and its arms, it, nonetheless, afforded local Volunteers invaluable experience under fire without any loss. It also exposed the vulnerability of the smaller, rural police barracks and accelerated the withdrawal of the RIC from such stations. The fourth anniversary of the Easter Rising in April 1920 was marked by a series of arson attacks on over 300 vacated police stations and twenty-two income tax offices across the country.[32] In Waterford the unoccupied police barracks at Clashmore, Colligan, Cappagh, Villierstown, Kiely's Cross, Kilmacthomas, Callaghane, Clonea and Holy Cross, as well as the income tax offices in Dungarvan and Lismore, were destroyed.[33]

The following month members of the West Waterford Brigade attacked two occupied barracks at Stradbally and Ardmore but in both cases failed to capture the buildings.[34] In these attacks key activists such as the Mansfield brothers, Mick and James, Pat Keating and George Lennon, all from Dungarvan, came to the fore. They provided leadership as the conflict intensified. While overall membership of the IRA tended to be rural-based, many of those involved in the use of force came from urban areas. This was similar to a pattern observed in Tipperary and Cork by historians Joost Augusteijn and Peter Hart.[35] The police remained vulnerable when on patrol. The IRA disarmed RIC patrols at Kinsalebeg in May, at Clashmore in July and at Dungarvan railway station in August 1920.[36]

The British government responded to this surge in violence by reinforcing the RIC with additional personnel and detachments of the army and marines. The 1st Battalion, the Royal East Kent Regiment (The Buffs), was stationed in Fermoy. One company of 150 officers and men under the command of Captain Donald Thomas was sent to Dungarvan in June 1920.[37] Most of the company was billeted in the castle with the RIC but about fifty were detached to Cloncoskraine House, the home of Sir Nugent Humble, a JP and prominent and outspoken unionist. In September another detachment was sent to Lismore where it was billeted in the local hotel. In addition, 47 officers and 981 men of the 1st Battalion, Devonshire Regiment, under the command of Colonel E.D. Young, arrived in Waterford in June.[38] Battalion headquarters and B Company, approximately 350 men, were stationed at the Infantry Barracks, Waterford, while the remainder was dispersed in small detachments in Kilkenny and Wexford.[10] A number of local ex-servicemen enlisted in the Devonshire Regiment during its stay in Waterford. The CI reported 'a small but fairly steady number of recruits trickling in at Waterford city. They are mostly men who already served in the army and failed to get any employment after demobilization.'[39] These men appear to have been used for barrack fatigue and guard duties only and not for patrolling or raiding. Both The Buffs and the Devons were part of the 16th Brigade, which had its headquarters in Fermoy and was part of the 6th Division. Two detachments of Royal Marines, each about thirty strong, were deployed in the coastguard stations at Ardmore and Ballinacourty.

From the beginning of 1920 the RIC had been weakened as members, often under family pressure, resigned from the force. The first to do so in Waterford were Constables Shanahan and Treacy, both stationed in the city.[40] These were replaced by ex-servicemen recruited in England as temporary constables, the so-called 'Black-and-Tans'. The nationwide boycott of the RIC, instigated by the Dáil on 10 April 1919, appears to have been applied only intermittently in Waterford. Constable Ernest Brookes, who was stationed in Ballyduff Upper, dismissed its effect as minimal.[41] In 1920 depleted manpower posed a dilemma for the CI in Waterford who recommended a minimum strength of ten in any occupied police station. To achieve this he would have to close five smaller stations lest the RIC presence be 'weak everywhere and strong nowhere. Police are of little use in barracks unless they have control of their area'.[42] In the event only Kill station was closed. In October 1920 the CI described west Waterford as 'a Sinn Féin land. We have lost not only control but even touch with large areas with the result that … West Waterford is practically un-policed'.[43]

The void in terms of the administration of justice and policing was filled by the Dáil courts and the republican police. One of the most remarkable achievements of SF was to make the administration of justice through the Crown courts unworkable and instigate a parallel mechanism in the form of Dáil courts. Although the Dáil had decreed in August 1919 that a national system of arbitration courts was to be set up, it was left to individual constituencies to make their own arrangements. As a result progress was slow and depended on local initiative.[44] In May 1920 Austin Stack, the Dáil minister for home affairs, issued a circular specifying the format of the new court system and instructing all constituencies to establish the courts. SF representatives for Waterford met in Dungarvan on 8 July to establish the Dáil courts. Waterford was one of the last counties in Ireland to adopt the new system and in August SF announced the establishment of parish courts and a district court.[45] In many parts of the country land disputes had been the driving force behind the setting up of the courts but this was not the case in Waterford.[46] The disputes adjudicated on ranged from ownership of property to theft and minor assault and were reported in the Waterford press from September onwards.[47] The sanctions imposed included fines, being bound to the peace, and banishment from the district or county. An isolated cottage near Kilrossanty was used as an improvised prison where short sentences were served. From the beginning the use of solicitors was common. The officers of the court were not identified in newspaper reports but frequent references to 'the reverend president' suggest the involvement of local clerics as presiding officers. These courts won widespread acceptance, especially in rural areas, and proved a major victory for SF.[48] At the same time, the Crown court system was disrupted through the intimidation of JPs, many of whom resigned. Prospective jurors were also threatened. Those due to attend the 1921 spring quarter sessions in Waterford city were advised that to do so would be 'considered an act of treason against the Irish Republic, and you are hereby warned that you will do it at your peril'.[49] The hearings were abandoned when few jurors turned up. At a later sitting the judge fined the jurors and chided them for allowing themselves to be intimidated by a piece of paper. One juror retorted that the piece of paper had been delivered by three armed and masked men.[50]

To support the Dáil courts, SF set up the republican police.[51] According to a Dáil order of 1 November 1920, this force was a separate body although under the control of the IRA. This created problems as there was no effective separation of function in practice. Active Volunteers preferred to serve in an Active Service Unit (ASU) rather than in the republican police. In most parts of the country this police force was not properly organized until the truce when it could and did function openly. Patrick Ormond, O/C republican police, West Waterford, recalled:

> My job was to organise a Volunteer police force to take the place of the RIC who dared not carry out their ordinary duties as they did formerly. Unfortunately, I never got down to the job properly. I did effect some arrests for larceny, but my time was mostly occupied with other Volunteer activities, and I acted only on cases reported to me.[52]

In some instances the republican police were asked to fill the vacuum left by the retreat of the RIC. Tom Kelleher of Cappoquin recalled being asked by the curate of Ballinameela to enforce the closing time of the local public houses.[53]

The contraction of the RIC presence greatly weakened intelligence gathering as there was nobody to watch, observe and report on IRA activities.

Furthermore, the resignation of experienced policemen meant a loss of vital local knowledge. Temporary constables, who were mostly English-born, could make little useful contribution to the intelligence war. In Waterford there was no occupied police station between Portlaw and Dungarvan (see map 5), leaving that large stretch of countryside un-policed except for the occasional motor patrol. From the summer of 1920 diminishing RIC intelligence was supplemented by army intelligence. Each army unit was required to designate one officer to collate all information. The designated officer in the Devonshire Regiment was Lieutenant Frederick Charles Yeo, who, like his IRA counterparts, was young and inexperienced but quickly established himself as a capable officer. One of his main duties was to interrogate prisoners and he was awarded an MBE for his intelligence work in July 1921.[54]

From October 1920 as director of intelligence, Collins sought to improve IRA intelligence gathering outside Dublin. Each IRA brigade was ordered to appoint an intelligence officer. Denis Madden performed this role in the East Waterford Brigade and Michael Desmond was his western counterpart.[55] Each had a network of agents especially in the post offices. Madden also had a well-placed police informant in Sergeant John Greene, who was stationed in Peter Street Barracks in the city.[56] The IRA put great effort into the interception of mails as their primary source of information. Trains using the Waterford to Tramore and the Waterford–Dungarvan–Fermoy lines were frequently stopped and the mails removed for scrutiny.[57] Postmen, especially on rural delivery routes, were routinely held up and all letters taken away for examination. Raids on post offices, often for money as well as mail, were a weekly occurrence. Letters when later delivered were stamped 'censored by the IRA'. This helped to create a sense of IRA ubiquity. Over time raids on the mails yielded less and less information as the authorities became more circumspect in their use of the post office. In addition, the withdrawal of the RIC to the main centres of population made it easier for them to communicate with each other securely. From August 1920 the military used aircraft to deliver despatches. Mail was taken from 6th Division HQ in Cork by heavily armed convoy to Fermoy, the base of No. 2 Squadron, RAF. A typical flight dropped mail at Dungarvan, Waterford, Kilkenny and Clonmel before returning to Fermoy.[58] These flights were not, however, without risk to crew and aircraft. On 21 August 1920 a Bristol Fighter experienced engine failure and was forced to land near Lismore. The crew were unharmed but had to watch helplessly as the local IRA piled hay around the aircraft and set it alight. The crew were then released and made their way to Fermoy.[59] On 17 November another Bristol Fighter crashed into the rooftops opposite the military barracks in Waterford while dropping the mails.[60] The two crew members were injured. The sight of the aircraft embedded in the roof of Aspel's public house created a lasting visual image of the War of Independence for many

Waterford people (see plate 19). Of much more benefit to the IRA than intercepted letters was the steady flow of information provided by Sergeant Greene. His timely warnings of raids ensured that most of the officers of the East Waterford Brigade escaped capture during the War of Independence.

The retreat of the RIC into just a few heavily defended posts changed the nature of the conflict. Henceforth, the policemen themselves became the IRA's target. In January 1920 IRA GHQ reluctantly endorsed a policy of armed confrontation with the Crown forces but later encouraged a general offensive against the police. There was a dramatic escalation of violence nationally in the early months of 1920, especially the number of attacks on individual policemen and small patrols.[61] They were often the result of local IRA initiative retrospectively sanctioned by brigade headquarters. As in other aspects of the War of Independence, the frequency and effectiveness of such attacks varied from county to county and from brigade to brigade.

The first such action in the West Waterford Brigade area took place in July 1920 when Michael Shalloe of the 3rd Battalion shot Head Constable Ruddick as he left a religious service in Youghal; although wounded, Ruddick survived.[62] The next policeman was not so fortunate. Having observed a weekly pay patrol of two RIC that cycled between Kilmacthomas and Lemybrien, Pat Keating led an ambush in September 1920. According to one of the IRA participants, the police were unarmed.[63] Sergeant Martin Morgan was seriously wounded and died a few days later.[64] Two policemen were killed in separate opportunistic attacks in Cappoquin: Constable Isaac Rea on 21 November and Constable Maurice Quirke eight days later.[65] The shooting of Quirke, who was very popular in Cappoquin, provoked much resentment in the district. Vincent O'Donoghue, a local Volunteer, later claimed that if a policeman needed to be shot local Volunteers were capable of doing it without assistance from Dungarvan men.[66] The last RIC man to be killed by the West Waterford Brigade in this phase was Constable Maurice Prendiville. He was fatally wounded on 3 December while a member of a three-man patrol from Youghal which delivered pension money to a retired constable who lived on the Waterford side of the River Blackwater. This attack was led by James Mansfield, O/C 3rd Battalion.[67] The killing of these policemen undoubtedly contributed to an increased edginess and tendency to shoot first by the police and military. On 11 December James Lawlor, a 35-year-old train driver, was shot by a sentry in Lismore for allegedly refusing to halt when challenged.[68] Another civilian, Hyde Marmion, son of Thomas Marmion, a Lismore JP, was killed in similar circumstances near Salterbridge Lodge, Cappoquin, on 28 January 1921. A court of inquiry attached no blame to the RIC.[69] This pattern of misfortunate civilian fatalities continued in 1921. Mary Foley, an elderly woman, was shot by a military patrol near Dungarvan on 28 May while gathering firewood. She was deaf and could not have heard the challenge to halt.[70] Patrick Walsh, a 65-year-old labourer, was shot dead near Rathgormac on 19 June.[71]

The first IRA ASUs (or flying columns) developed spontaneously in the more active counties such as Limerick, Cork and Tipperary during the first half of 1920.[72] They were composed of Volunteers who had been forced to go on the run. This development was later endorsed by GHQ, which recognized the value of small mobile 'standing troops of a well-trained and thoroughly reliable stamp' whose actions could be 'far more systematic and effective' than regular IRA units.[73] It was envisaged that the ASUs would attack enemy posts and patrols, generally harass Crown forces and interrupt communications.[74] An ASU was to consist of twenty-six men divided into four squads. They could both instigate independent action and form an effective auxiliary to local battalion or brigade actions. Notably, the O/C was not elected, as most IRA officers were, but was appointed by the brigade commander. The West Waterford ASU of twenty men was formed in September 1920. George Lennon was appointed O/C, George Kiely vice O/C and Andrew Kirwan transport officer.[75] The ASU was trained by John Riordan of Dungarvan, a British army war veteran. The training was made more realistic by occasional sniping attacks on army or police patrols.[76] Despatch riders were used to communicate with the brigade O/C and the four battalions in the brigade. A full-scale engagement was avoided until the men gained sufficient experience. The IRA imposed a levy to support the full-time members of the ASU, to purchase arms and to help the families of prisoners. This levy was collected throughout the county. Most people paid up whether through conviction or fear.[77]

By the end of October Lennon believed his unit was ready and he began to plan a major ambush. Ardmore RIC Barracks had been attacked unsuccessfully a number of times in 1920. On each occasion the police had signalled to Youghal for military reinforcements. Pax Whelan and Lennon decided to use this pattern to draw troops into a carefully prepared ambush on 1 November at Piltown Cross, three miles west of Ardmore on the main Dungarvan to Youghal road. About 100 Volunteers were involved, mostly from the local 3rd Battalion. They blocked roads, acted as scouts and kept both the RIC barracks and the marine detachment in the coastguard station under fire. As expected the police sought assistance and at about 11 p.m. a military lorry from Youghal crashed into a trench cut across the road at Piltown Cross and was fired on by the IRA. Private Anthony Leigh of the Hampshire Regiment, the driver, was killed and the commanding officer was wounded before the remaining eighteen soldiers and two policemen surrendered. The Piltown ambush was a major boost to the West Waterford Brigade. A well-planned and executed operation had inflicted casualties on the enemy but none on the IRA.[78] The capture of twenty rifles and several thousand rounds of ammunition transformed the ASU into a well-armed unit with high morale. Unsurprisingly, at the end of

October the RIC Inspector General wrote that, with the exception of the city, Waterford was 'in a most unsatisfactory condition'.[79] By the end of 1920 the War of Independence in west Waterford had evolved according to the model outlined by historian Charles Townshend.[80] Low-level violence had escalated into attacks on RIC barracks and individual policemen. The resulting crackdown by Crown forces in turn led to the creation of an ASU which was capable of relatively large-scale operations.

By contrast the East Waterford Brigade was notably inactive. In the first half of 1920 the two most significant contributions to the national struggle in Waterford city came not from the IRA but from the trade union movement. According to Frank Edwards there was considerable crossover between the republican and labour traditions in the city, especially among railway workers.[81] In April 1920 the Irish Trade Union Congress called a general strike in support of republican prisoners on hunger strike. This included three Waterford men: Pat Dalton in Belfast Jail, and Richard Whelan and Patrick Brazil in Wormwood Scrubs.[82] In Waterford the Workers' Council coordinated a strike that shut down all business activity and effectively took over the running of the city. Their actions made newspaper headlines all over Britain. For three days the city was in a state of revolutionary fervour. Newspapers reported 'large bodies of pickets, many armed with sticks marching through the city in military formation, enforcing the strike'.[83] The government quickly capitulated and released the hunger strikers. The Workers' Council then handed control of the city back to the mayor who congratulated the 'Soviet Government of Waterford on a very effective, masterly and successful administration'.[84] A few days later the Waterford hunger strikers returned home to a triumphant welcome. There were elements of stage-management about the 'Waterford Soviet' but it demonstrated the power of organized labour in the city and its hinterland.[85]

The second intervention occurred in May 1920 when dockers in Dublin port refused to unload military supplies. When they were unloaded by the military, railwaymen also refused to handle the material.[86] The action spread throughout the country and adopted a new form when on 14 June John Condon of Ferrybank refused to drive a train with 120 men of the Devonshire Regiment on board. He was dismissed but other railway workers followed his example.[87] By 9 July twenty drivers and thirty-four guards, porters and firemen had been sacked. The Waterford Workers' Council organized weekly collections for the men and their families. By 26 November almost £6,000 had been collected.[88] The railwaymen's strike had a major impact on British army communications.[89] The authorities quickly relented and announced that the railways would no longer be used for transporting arms, ammunitions, explosives or fuel. They also declared that only small parties of troops on non-operational duties, such as leave parties, would use rail transport. As a major rail centre, the commercial life of Waterford city was heavily disrupted by the dispute. By September there was only one daily passenger service to Dublin. By the winter the transport situation had returned to normal, but not all the dismissed men were reinstated.

By the spring of 1920 the vast majority of agricultural workers in the county were members of the ITGWU and in May the union negotiated weekly pay rates for agricultural workers of up to 38*s.* with a nine-hour working day.[90] Farmers were willing to accept higher wage costs and a 'closed-shop' only as long as demand for their produce was strong and prices remained high. In response to the growing militancy of the farm labourers the farmers formed the Irish Farmers' Union to take on labour in a cohesive and united way.[91] The local branch, the Waterford Farmers' Association (WFA), was to the fore in countering the union. As the agricultural boom petered out during the summer of 1920, food prices fell and this led to a dramatic slump in agriculture and related industries. Farmers and factory owners alike sought a return to pre-war wage rates. In May 1921, at the peak of the War of Independence, the 1920 wage rates were renewed for a further year. Although some farmers pressed for a reduction, the WFA wisely decided to avoid confrontation given the turmoil in the city and county, the absence of the RIC in the countryside and the as yet unknown position of the IRA in such a conflict. Some farmers near Kilmacthomas tried to enforce wage reductions but their resolve collapsed in the face of strong trade union resistance.[92] While the ITGWU was aware that further improvements in the agricultural wage rates were impossible, it was determined to resist any reduction. With the labourers well organized and with the backing, or so it believed, of the majority of the IRA, the union was confident of victory in any struggle.[93] The farmers continued to organize but recognized that they would need government support, whether British or Irish, to defeat the labourers. The end of compulsory tillage removed a further obstacle to an all-out struggle. To both sides it was clear that conflict could be delayed but not avoided.

The first military operation by the East Waterford Brigade took place in September 1920 when it attacked Kill RIC Barracks. Paddy Paul sought the assistance of the more experienced west Waterford men. The two brigades mobilized about eighty men and isolated the village by blocking all approach roads. About fifty men took up firing positions. The plan was to break a hole in the roof, pump in petrol to set the barracks alight, and force the police to surrender. But it quickly unravelled. No handle had been brought for the pump and a premature shot at a policeman in the village pub alerted the other RIC who opened fire from within the barracks. The IRA returned fire but withdrew when scouts reported the approach of British army reinforcements.[94] There were no casualties on either side. The IRA claimed a hollow victory when the barracks was evacuated a week later but the police authorities had decided this course before the attack. The East Waterford Brigade had shown that it could mobilize men for an attack but the implementation displayed serious weaknesses in terms of proper reconnaissance and basic preparation. To overlook a pump handle was inexcusable. Furthermore, no reinforcements approached the village. Although a useful baptism of fire for the men, the action failed in its two key objectives: destruction of a defended post and capture of arms and ammunition. There was one related episode following the withdrawal of the RIC from Kill to Portlaw. The local IRA decided to attack Constable Cullinane whose family continued to live in Kill. But this did not go according to plan either. Cullinane defended himself by throwing a grenade and firing his revolver. James Power, a Volunteer, was wounded and died three days later. This incident is not referred to in the BMH statements perhaps because Power was a newly enrolled Volunteer.[95]

After the failed attack on Kill, the East Waterford Brigade changed tactics. Paul and a few of his men prioritized opportunistic attacks by lying in wait at various locations and firing on military lorries travelling between Waterford and Fermoy. The most notable incident took place on 5 December when Paul and five Volunteers fired on a lorry at Ballyduff glen, near Kilmeaden. A couple of soldiers were slightly wounded but Paul broke off the engagement when he realized that the lorry contained IRA prisoners, including Willie Walsh, who were being conveyed to Kilworth Camp. These actions, though small, were important for the East Waterford Brigade and helped to maintain morale.[96]

Clashes with Crown forces intensified in 1921. In west Waterford a confident and well-armed ASU sought to engage Crown forces. The few remaining occupied rural police posts, such as Kilmanahan, were attacked by local Volunteers supported by members of the ASU. Although none were captured it increased the sense of the RIC being under siege.[97] The other police stations in the brigade area such as Tallow, Lismore, Cappoquin and Dungarvan were too strongly fortified and garrisoned to be attacked successfully by the ASU. The other IRA tactic was to lie in wait, mostly in vain, in the hope of ambushing a passing military convoy. It was dangerous for the ASU to remain too long in any location and there was insufficient intelligence to predict the day-to-day movement of the Crown forces.

In east Waterford Paul planned to replicate the success of the Piltown ambush by staging a similar type of operation. He again sought the assistance of the West Waterford ASU and a combined force of about sixty was involved. In January 1921 only four rural police stations were still occupied in the brigade area. Paul decided to attack Tramore Barracks as a feint to lure a relieving force into an ambush on the Tramore side of the railway bridge, at Pickardstown Cross, about a mile from the town, which would be covered by the IRA from four positions (see plate 20). It was anticipated that the first lorry of the relieving force would crash into a barricade and then come under heavy rifle fire from the West Waterford men. Paul stressed the necessity of holding fire until the military party was completely within the ambush position. He emphasized, wisely as events transpired, retreat routes for the men but apparently left it up to each section to decide when to retreat in the event of the plan going wrong.[98]

At about 11 p.m. Paul and five others entered Tramore to mount the feint attack. The garrison replied with rifle fire and grenades, and summoned help from Waterford city. After an exchange lasting about fifteen minutes, Paul led his men back towards the ambush position. As he did so, he heard a single shot followed by sustained firing from the Waterford side of the railway bridge and knew that something had clearly gone very wrong. The military dispatched a strong force of about seventy troops in four lorries, which travelled along the old Tramore Road. Just after the second lorry had passed Ballynattin Crossroads at about 11.45 p.m. a shot was fired prematurely by a member of the Ferrybank Company (it was later alleged that he had been drinking). The Dunhill Company on the railway embankment then opened fire as ordered. The convoy immediately halted with the first lorry under the railway bridge and the last two stopping on the old Tramore Road, outside the ambush position. This meant that the West Waterford ASU took little part in the action and could only fire single shots at the muzzle flashes of the enemy rifles lest they hit their own men on the other side of the ambush site. After about twenty minutes of such firing and fearful that more troops might cut them off from the west, Whelan and Lennon decided to withdraw the ASU and marched cross-country towards their base near Kilrossanty. Similarly, the men from Dunhill in position number three also withdrew to the west. Neither of these groups had suffered or inflicted any casualties.

The four riflemen in position two fired one volley before withdrawing towards Waterford. Their comrades in position one on the Ballynattin Road were now trapped by the military and subjected to heavy fire. Michael McGrath, a member of the City Battalion, and Thomas O'Brien, a member of the 2nd Battalion, East Waterford Brigade, were killed; Michael Wyley and Nicholas Whittle were wounded. William Keane, who, in the absence of Paul, was in command, had no option but to order a retreat. The Volunteers dispersed in the dark and individually made their way back to the city. The military made little effort to pursue the retreating IRA. As the troops combed the Ballynattin Road they came across Whittle's blood-stained body and presumed him dead. He had been shot in the face, neck and chest. Despite being kicked and prodded with bayonets, he lay silently in the ditch until the military withdrew. Whittle then crawled for about three miles until he found refuge in a cottage. The following day he and Wyley were taken to the Mental Hospital for treatment. One policeman had been wounded during the feint attack and one soldier was slightly wounded during the exchange at the ambush site. The IRA discovered this when the wounded man went to a solicitor's office to register a claim for compensation. The clerk who took the details and discussed the ambush at length with him was none other than Denis Madden – the East Waterford Brigade intelligence officer![99] In its first major operation, the East Waterford Brigade suffered two fatalities and two men seriously wounded.[100]

Waterford city was rife with rumours the following day that three Volunteers had been killed and up to ten wounded, whereas the Crown forces suffered only minor casualties. Many people travelled to Tramore to view the ambush scene and the railway company had to put on extra railway carriages.[101] Two bodies had been brought to the military barracks and it was believed that a third had been removed from the ambush site by the IRA. Michael McGrath's body was identified by a union card found in his pocket.[102] An enquiry found that death was caused by a single gunshot to the head. His body was released to his brother and brought to St John's church in the city. The next day a large crowd turned out for the funeral. As hundreds of people followed the hearse to Carbally cemetery, the military intervened and announced that only forty mourners were permitted.[103] There were no identifying papers on Thomas O'Brien and nobody came forward to claim the body. This was not uncommon as relatives often feared that they would be the target of reprisals. O'Brien's body was released to the town clerk and buried in Ballygunner. The military again limited the cortège to forty.[104] There were intensive raids by the Crown forces in an effort to find the wounded Volunteers. But this was hampered by insufficient intelligence. A tip-off from Sergeant Greene ensured that Whittle and Wyley were moved from the Mental Hospital before it was raided.[105] Later that week Whittle's death was announced and masses were said for the repose of his soul. But when no burial took place the authorities saw through the ruse. He was smuggled out of the country to England where he recuperated.[106]

In an important, though unrelated, development, martial law was extended to Waterford, Kilkenny, Wexford and Clare on 8 January 1921.[107] This helped to negate the collapse of the Crown court system by giving the military power to try a range of offences by court-martial and impose severe penalties. It also introduced a curfew and extensive restrictions on all movements by car or bicycle. Householders were obliged to pin to their doors a list of all occupants. The authorities had the power to use internment since January 1920 but only began to do so extensively after the introduction of martial law. Sentences handed down by the courts martial sitting in Waterford included two weeks' imprisonment for being out after curfew, six months' imprisonment with hard labour for possession of a Dáil loan application, and three years' imprisonment with hard labour for possession of a single cartridge (the

defendant claimed it was a souvenir).[108] Those suspected of IRA membership
were interned. Two Waterford Volunteers died in Ballykinlar Camp in
County Down. Maurice Galvin, an apprentice draper in Tallow, died on 9
April 1921 following injuries sustained on Belfast docks while being conveyed
to Ballykinlar. He was struck by a rivet flung by loyalists in the nearby shipyards.[109] Edward Landers of Lismore died of illness in Ballykinlar on 23 June
1921.[110] Although a steady stream of arrests and internment orders followed,
the authorities lacked the intelligence network to capture key IRA activists
who remained on the run.

    While the Crown forces sought to capitalize on their success, the East
Waterford Brigade practically disintegrated in a welter of blame and recrimination. Several officers blamed Paul for the débâcle. He was criticized for the
selection of the ambush position and for leading the feint attack on the RIC
station instead of remaining at the command post on the Ballynattin Road. It
was also alleged that Paul had not clearly briefed the men in number one and
two positions. Personal spleen was also vented. Paul's British army background and support for Redmond in 1918 were held against him. Pax Whelan
later claimed that this was 'the root of all the trouble'.[111] The situation was so
poisonous that IRA GHQ was compelled to conduct a formal enquiry into
what had transpired at Pickardstown. The investigation concluded that the
East Waterford Brigade should not have undertaken such a large and elaborate operation due to the men's inexperience and their lack of 'discipline,
morale or arms for such a fight, especially night fighting'.[112] In the event no
disciplinary action was taken. The small Ballyduff glen ambush was far more
suited to the capacity of the East Waterford Brigade. In other brigade areas
there had been a progression in the scale of attacks undertaken, graduating
from the killing of single policemen to attacks on barracks to large-scale operations such as Tramore. The East Waterford Brigade paid the price for
moving too far ahead of its limited capacity. Simmering discontent among the
brigade officers came to a head when Paul planned another, even more elaborate, three-part operation on the night of 7 March 1921. One party would
attack Dunmore RIC station with support groups blocking all roads. Another
group would ensure that the Redmond Bridge would be raised just before the
arrival of the Cork train which frequently conveyed soldiers. The Ferrybank
Company was to fire on these troops from the slopes of Mount Misery. The
centrepiece of the operation was an ambush of the nightly military patrol.[113]
At about 11 p.m. six men, led by Jeremiah Cronin, fired on Dunmore RIC
Barracks with the twelve-man garrison replying in an exchange which lasted
half an hour before the IRA party withdrew as instructed.[114] Another IRA
party forced the operator to raise the bridge as planned before the arrival of
the train. To Paul's chagrin the soldiers waiting at the bridge were not fired
on and the routine military patrol was not ambushed. Paul later recounted

how William Keane, the vice-brigadier, countermanded his instructions and asked the men: 'Why should you get shot for Paddy Paul?'[115] Paul relieved Keane of his rank and appointed Michael Bishop in his place. In protest at a special meeting on 22 May, the brigade officers voted no confidence in Paul and elected Michael Power, vice-O/C 2nd Battalion, brigadier instead. Three days later the officers notified IRA GHQ of the new East Waterford Brigade staff and pledged the 'full co-operation of this Brigade in [the] great fight at present being waged by the gallant men of other Brigades throughout the country.'[116] They made it quite clear that if Paul remained in command they would not cooperate.

At a time when GHQ was intent on introducing a more professional organization and better discipline, such an action was at best gross insubordination and at worst mutiny. The response was swift. Paul was confirmed as brigadier and all officers were instructed to obey him.[117] He received strong support from Richard Mulcahy, IRA chief of staff, who revealed that before Paul's appointment it had been impossible to get 'any scrap of organization' in the East Waterford Brigade. He believed that Paul had 'put the brigade on something like a satisfactory footing' and suggested that the chief criticism against him was his desire to make his officers 'do definite fighting work, and that he [Paul] will not agree that talking about work, or even planning work, is work.'[118] An enquiry was conducted by Seán Hyde of Cork No. 4 Brigade and Pax Whelan, who believed that the problem was actually one of leadership.[119] Given the split in the brigade, unsurprisingly no operations were mounted in the following months. Low-level harassment of the authorities such as raids on mails, destruction of army stores and road-blocking did continue. In one such operation on 25 May Seán O'Rourke of D Company, 1st Battalion, was fatally wounded by two British officers in mufti while covering an entrenching party at Holy Cross. O'Rourke's comrades took him to Butlerstown Castle but he died a short time later.[120] In a report to GHQ Paul disclaimed any responsibility for this operation, further underlining the deep division within the brigade.[121]

In west Waterford Lennon and his ASU tired of waiting in vain in ambush positions and sought to lure the Crown forces into a trap. In early February he made it known to the authorities that Cathal Brugha, Dáil minister for defence and Waterford TD, was staying in Ring College.[122] However, two military lorries reached the ambush site at Robert's Cross before all the IRA units had moved into position. In a confused exchange of fire, one Volunteer was wounded before the IRA withdrew.[123] A further attempt was made near Durrow railway tunnel on 3 March. The plan was to hold up the 7.30 a.m. train from Dungarvan to Waterford at Millarstown and take jurors bound for the spring assizes in Waterford prisoner before allowing the train to continue its journey. The ASU intended to ambush the expected convoy of troops sent from Dungarvan to investigate at a sharp bend on the road near the Ballyvoile viaduct. The operation did not go according to plan because in addition to the military patrol, extra troops were deployed on a special train that stopped at Durrow railway tunnel. The engagement lasted for most of the day before the IRA withdrew under cover of darkness. One soldier was seriously wounded and two others suffered minor wounds.[124] The ASU had performed well against superior numbers but had used up a significant portion of its precious rifle ammunition.

The blocking of roads by destroying bridges, digging trenches and erecting barricades was a key part of the IRA strategy. This disrupted communications and forced Crown forces' patrols to use a small number of predictable routes, which left them vulnerable to ambush. On the evening of 18 March 1921 the IRA planned to block the main Dungarvan to Waterford road by destroying Tarr's Bridge just east of the town at the Burgery.[125] The task was entrusted to the local company under Seán Tobin who asked the ASU to provide covering parties because the Burgery was within just two miles of three British army posts: Dungarvan, Ballinacourty and Cloncoskeraine House. The demolition work was very slow. It had to be done by pick and crowbar as the brigade had no explosives. Lennon deployed the twenty-two members of the ASU in small parties at distances of about half-a-mile. He nominated the priest's house in Kilgobnet as a rendezvous point in the event of unforeseen trouble. Also present were Pax Whelan and George Plunkett, a brother of the 1916 leader, Joseph, and a GHQ organizer on a tour of inspection of the Tipperary and Waterford Brigades.

Just after 11 p.m. the IRA noticed the lights of a small military convoy of a car and a lorry that left Dungarvan by the coast road. The party consisted of Captain Thomas, Lieutenant Griffith and twelve soldiers accompanied by RIC Sergeant Michael Hickey. Having arrested a man in Clonea, Thomas decided to inspect the military detachment at Cloncoskeraine. Just after 1 a.m. the patrol departed and returned to Dungarvan along the main road. In the intervening period the IRA hurriedly decided to ambush the convoy on its return journey and positions were selected to cover the two possible routes back to Dungarvan. Eleven men under Lennon lined the hedge at the Burgery to cover the main road while the other group, led by Whelan and Plunkett, covered the Cappoquin and Ballycoe roads. Both sections waited while the local men continued their efforts to demolish the bridge. The two vehicles stayed on the main road and made towards the Burgery. The car sped through the ambush position but the lorry, about 400 yards behind, came under sustained fire and halted. The soldiers dismounted. Some fled in the darkness while others took cover and exchanged rifle-fire with the IRA. The Volunteers at work on the bridge dispersed without any casualties. Captain Thomas, who was in the car, ordered Griffith and the driver to continue to Dungarvan to get reinforcements. He, Hickey and Private E.W. Colyer returned to the ambush site but ran into the second IRA section; Thomas and Hickey were taken prisoner.

The West Waterford ASU had done well under the circumstances. An enemy patrol had been scattered, prisoners taken and some weapons captured without loss to themselves. The IRA broke off the engagement on the approach of military reinforcements and retreated to the pre-arranged rendezvous with the prisoners. Thomas was released but Hickey was marched away. After a 'council of war', the policeman was given the sacraments and executed on the morning of 19 March.[126] Hickey's body was found on a bog at Castlequarter, about two miles from the ambush site, two days later.

The ASU and the brigade officers wished to withdraw to the sanctuary of the Comeragh Mountains. However, Plunkett prevailed on them to return to the scene of the ambush to collect any disgarded weapons or ammunition. Plunkett led six men to search the area while Whelan and six others acted as a covering party. Disastrously, they did not reconnoitre the area. Had they done so they would have learned that every available soldier and policeman was preparing to search for the missing men and to recover the abandoned lorry. The IRA and Crown forces converged on the Burgery and another unplanned encounter took place. In the exchange of fire there were fatalities on both sides. Volunteer John Fitzgerald and Constable Sidney Redman, a recent RIC recruit, were killed.[127] Pat Keating was seriously wounded and died a few hours later. After the engagement a tired and dispirited ASU withdrew to the Comeragh Mountains to regroup, angry at what many regarded as an unnecessary fiasco that had cost the lives of two comrades. The bodies of Fitzgerald and Redman were taken to the barracks in Dungarvan. Fitzgerald's remains were held there until after Hickey's funeral during which the authorities enforced a complete closure of all businesses in the town. An order restricting the number of mourners at Fitzgerald's funeral to twenty was defied and a large crowd assembled for the interment in the republican plot in Kilrossanty churchyard. Keating's body was buried secretly in Newtown churchyard but he was re-interred in Kilrossanty on 18 May 1921.

Hickey and Redman were not the only police fatalities in Waterford in March 1921. Constable Joseph Duddy, a native of Armagh, married with two children and stationed in Ballyduff Upper, was shot dead on the morning of 3 March. He was a member of a patrol sent to investigate felled trees across the Ballyduff to Fermoy road which was ambushed at Scartacrooka by members of the Cork No. 2 Brigade ASU.[128] In his report for March 1921 the RIC Inspector General described Waterford as being 'in a state of grave disorder'. Thirty outrages had been recorded which included three members of the Crown forces killed, three barracks attacked, three ambushes and five raids on the mails.[129]

In the aftermath of the Burgery the people of Dungarvan and Abbeyside waited in fear of inevitable reprisals. Unofficial reprisals by Crown forces in the aftermath of ambushes occurred in 1919 and 1920. Police and military authorities, fearful of the impact on the discipline of their forces of such unauthorized actions, pushed the cabinet to institute a policy of official reprisals, which was granted in December 1920.[130] The method of punishment involved the selection of certain houses. The occupants were given one hour to remove foodstuffs and clothing but not furniture before the buildings were blown up with explosives. People living near the scene of an ambush were especially vulnerable since the authorities believed that they must have known about the operation, should have notified the authorities but did not and were therefore complicit. Dungarvan was quiet for a few days after the fighting at the Burgery while Constable Redman's remains were returned to England and Sergeant Hickey's body was recovered and handed over to his relatives. Reprisals took place on 25 March. Ballycoe House, the substantial home of Mrs Dunlea at Abbeyside, was destroyed but not before the soldiers had painted on the walls: 'Hickey and Redman. Up The Buffs. God save the King'. The process was repeated at the Burgery where the cottage of Mrs Morrissey was blown up. Nearer Dungarvan, the house of Miss English, a suspected republican sympathizer, was also wrecked. Throughout the day other bands of soldiers and police roamed the town breaking windows and doors and removing furniture to burn it. A few weeks later the process was repeated when the Strand Hotel, Abbeyside, and the house of Mrs Fahey, whose husband was interned as a republican sympathizer, were burned to the ground. No lives were lost during these reprisals.

For much of April and May 1921 the ASU was billeted in or near Kilrossanty. At this stage, Whelan and the brigade officers were given another task. IRA GHQ planned a large-scale importation of arms. Union Hall in Cork had originally been selected as the landing point but in April 1921, Liam Lynch, O/C 1st Southern Division, decided to use Helvick instead.[131] Planning and preparation for this project occupied a large portion of the West Waterford Brigade's time. While the brigade and battalion staff focused their attention on the planned importation of arms, the men of the ASU interspersed training with occasional attacks on the Crown forces. On 20 April the military detachment at Cloncoskeraine House was subjected to intense sniping. The garrison returned fire but there were no casualties.[132] Trains carrying troops between Fermoy and Waterford were also open to attack. The RIC recorded three such attacks on 28 and 29 April near Kilmacthomas and during the third incident three soldiers were wounded.[133] There was no respite for the beleaguered police and much of Waterford remained 'in state of serious disturbance' with forty-seven outrages in April alone, 'some of a very serious nature'.[134]

One of those was the shooting on the night of 14 April of William Moran, a 65-year-old ex-soldier who lived in Lord George Lane, Dungarvan. He was taken from his home and his body was later found at the end of the lane with a label: 'Spies beware! Shot by the IRA'. The police file noted only that Moran was friendly with the Crown forces.[135] The authorities certainly relied on information from loyal citizens but captured documents proved more beneficial. When Tom Brennan, an officer of the City Battalion, was arrested in February 1921 he had a list of the names and locations of all the East Waterford Brigade officers as well as the date and location of the next brigade meeting. A timely warning from Sergeant Greene enabled the IRA officers to avoid capture.[136] Despite such information the authorities did not score any intelligence-led successes. Although the shooting of spies in Waterford was very rare, the IRA did keep an eye on suspects. In a survey of all the brigades in the 1st Southern Division, Florrie O'Donoghue asked each brigade to list suspected enemy agents. About twenty were listed for west Waterford but the East Waterford Brigade responded: 'too numerous to mention'.[137] The regimental diary of The Buffs contained one reference to 'an Anti-Sinn Féin Society' operating in the town of Tallow but there were no references in other sources to such a group.[138] The social activities of army and police officers were noted by the IRA but no attempt was made to kill them with the exception of Lieutenant Yeo. On a few occasions Volunteers waited for him at the Imperial Hotel, which he was known to frequent, but without success.[139] On 12 September 1921 Sergeant Greene's body was found in a lane in the city. He had been killed by a single shot to the head and his service revolver lay beside the body.[140] An inquest returned a verdict of suicide but IRA officers in the city believed that he had been shot by Black and Tans when his clandestine work for the IRA was discovered.[141] There is no evidence to support this and it seems that the strain of his double life contributed to Greene's decision to take his own life.

During May the ASU rested and trained in the comparative safety of the Comeragh Mountains. Patrick Ryan of Ballymacarberry recalled that training focused on 'field manoeuvres, advancing and retiring under cover and general tactics in guerrilla fighting'.[142] At the same time local IRA units continued to snipe at the Crown forces. The marines at Ardmore responded by strengthening patrols on the road between Ardmore and Youghal. During a running fight with one such patrol on 10 May, Volunteer James Quaine of Main Street, Youghal, a 19-year-old draughtsman, was killed at Piltown Cross.[143] The RIC monthly report in May noted the receipt of better quality intelligence.[144] This contributed to the capture in Kilrossanty on 18 May 1921 of five members of the ASU and two sisters named Cullinane, where they had been attending the re-burial of Pat Keating. Lennon and Mansfield were fortunate to escape across a boggy field.[145] Due to carelessness or overconfidence both the commandant and his deputy had travelled together. The captured men were each sentenced to five years' penal servitude and the women to six months.

The presence of the military showed an increased willingness to send strong patrols into an area once considered a sanctuary for the ASU. It reflected new and more aggressive tactics by the Crown forces. Heretofore, they had depended on large motorized patrols to police the rural areas vacated by the RIC. These were too big, too obvious, too noisy and too dependent on roads to surprise the IRA. From May 1921 the emphasis changed to smaller, more mobile units which operated on foot or by bicycle and tried to counter the IRA at their own game. Patrols would often establish themselves in concealed positions from which they could observe or ambush Volunteers.[146] The military presence in Waterford was also reinforced. In May and June new units arrived in Ireland at the rate of two battalions a week. On 2 July the 1st Battalion, the York and Lancashire Regiment, arrived in Clonmel and a company was despatched to Kilmacthomas to meet the repeated requests of the CI for additional manpower. By June 1921 the strength of the RIC stood at about 270 but they were concentrated in twelve barracks. In Dungarvan Captain Thomas and his men were particularly active in patrolling the countryside. This made a clash with the IRA inevitable. In an exchange at Ballyvoile on 6 June Volunteer John Cummins was killed and John Mansfield was wounded.[147] On 7 June a military court of enquiry ruled that Cummins was shot in the act of offering armed resistance to the Crown forces in the execution of their duties.[148]

Another example of more ruthless tactics by the Crown forces was the use of mines. In July this led to the greatest loss of life in a single incident during the War of Independence in Waterford. As previously stated, the trenching of roads to inhibit the movement of the Crown forces was widespread. At the request of local people, the IRA partially filled in such a trench to facilitate a funeral in Kilgobnet on 7 July. When the trench was reopened the following day, a mine, planted by The Buffs as a booby trap for the IRA, exploded killing Volunteer John Quinn and five helpers: Thomas Burke, Thomas Dahill, James Dunford, William Dunford and Richard Lynch.[149]

At the beginning of June fourteen men from the East Waterford Brigade, including Paddy Paul and Jeremiah Cronin, linked up with the ASU. Paul had originally intended that after a period of training the East Waterford men would operate as an independent unit under Cronin.[150] This was overtaken by the GHQ report on the East Waterford Brigade which questioned the calibre of its officers by recommending that the two Waterford brigades be amalgamated and that key command positions be filled by West Waterford officers.[151] The amalgamation came into force on 6 July 1921 with Pax Whelan as brigadier (see map 7). Paul was relegated to training officer. As part of its training, the enlarged ASU planned various unsuccessful actions such as seeking specific RIC targets in Cappoquin and Lismore, and ambushing trains believed to be conveying troops. Following these attacks the British army carried out a series of large-scale sweeps through the mountains but failed to find the ASU. The last offensive action by the ASU was a train ambush on 4 July. It then spent a week on the move to evade strong military patrols. On

1 John Redmond opening the new bridge in Waterford city in 1913.

2 (*above*) John Redmond
and his second wife, Ada.

3 Richard Sheehan,
Roman Catholic bishop of
Waterford and Lismore
(1892–1915).

4 Henry Stewart O'Hara, Church of Ireland bishop of the united dioceses of Cashel, Emly, Waterford and Lismore (1900–19).

5 Sir John Keane.

6 Sir William G.D. Goff (on left).

7 The nomination of Martin Murphy as IPP candidate in East Waterford in 1913. Murphy is fourth from the right in the second row.

8 Waterford city Volunteers celebrating the passing of the home rule bill, May 1914.

9 Dungarvan Cycle Corps, National Volunteers, 1914.

10 The city garrison goes to war, August 1914.

11 John Redmond presenting colours to the National Volunteers in Waterford, October 1914.

12 From left: P.A. Murphy, Martin Murphy MP (East Waterford), Pat O'Brien MP (Kilkenny City), Richard Power (mayor), John Redmond, P. Higgins (assistant town clerk), Waterford, October 1914.

13 Construction of the munitions factory at Bilberry in 1916.

14 *Formby.*

15 *Coningbeg.*

16 Dr Vincent White in 1920.

17 Captain William Redmond in 1918.

18 (*above*) Sinn Féin members of Waterford Corporation in 1920.

19 An RAF Bristol fighter embedded in the roof of Aspel's public house on Barrack Street, Waterford, in November 1920.

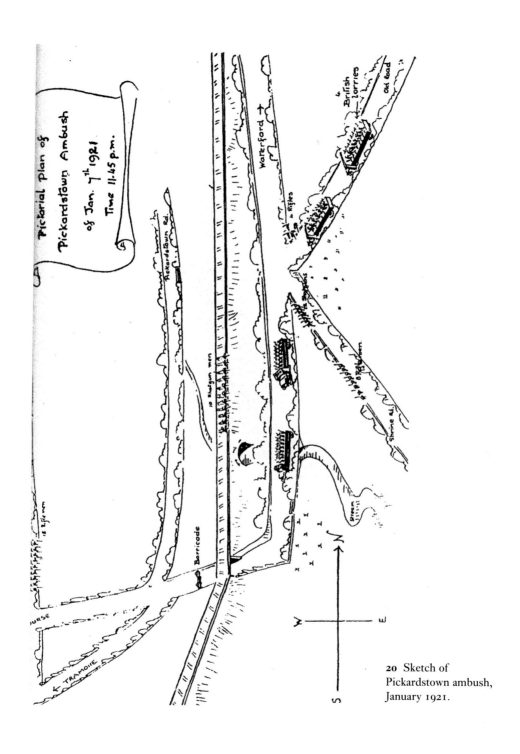

20 Sketch of Pickardstown ambush, January 1921.

21 Pat Keating IRA.

22 John Cummins IRA.

23 IRA at Waterford Military Barracks, 1922. Paddy Paul is seated second from the left.

24 Michael Collins addressing a crowd in Dungarvan, March 1922.

25 Waterford General Post Office after the siege of Waterford, July 1922.

26 National army roadblock at Cappoquin, 1922.

27 National army soldiers outside the Granville Hotel, July 1922.

28 Caitlín Brugha, Sinn Féin TD, in 1923.

29 Farmers unloading a ship at Dungarvan during the Waterford farm labourers' strike, June 1923. They are protected by National army troops.

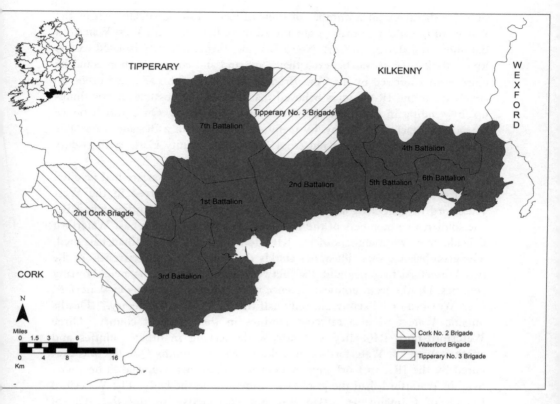

7 Waterford brigade and battalion areas in July 1921

9 July the ASU moved from the Ballinamult area to the Nire Valley when, to the men's surprise, a truce was announced.[152]

Although the Waterford IRA had failed to inflict any casualties on the Crown forces since the Burgery ambush in March, two RIC were killed in County Waterford by members of Tipperary No. 3 Brigade and one by Cork No. 2 Brigade. On 26 April DI Gilbert Potter was executed and buried near the Clodiagh River at Clonea.[153] He had been captured by the ASU of the Tipperary No. 3 Brigade near Ballyporeen. The IRA offered to release Potter in exchange for a reprieve for Thomas Traynor, who had been sentenced to be hanged in Mountjoy on 25 April, but this was refused by authorities. Traynor was duly hanged and Potter was executed the following day. The second killing took place on 8 June when Constable Denis O'Leary, who was stationed in Carrick-on-Suir, returned to his home on Main Street, Carrickbeg, and was shot dead by two members of Tipperary No. 3 Brigade.[154] The local IRA battalion had singled out O'Leary because they believed that he had been respon-

sible for the arrest of a number of their officers. Tshe amalgamation of the
Waterford brigades (see map 7) saw the Lismore Battalion (4th West Waterford
Battalion) transferred to Cork No. 2 Brigade. Geographically isolated by the
River Blackwater, it was believed that command and communication could be
more easily exercised by the Cork Brigade. In addition, this area had been relatively quiet and IRA leaders believed that it would be possible to 'stir things
up' by sending in experienced fighting men from Cork. On 2 July a police
patrol was attacked in Tallow by members of Cork No. 2 Brigade. Constable
Francis Creedon, a 41-year-old from Millstreet, County Cork, with twenty
years' police service, was shot dead.[155]

Between 1919 and the truce on 11 July 1921 guerrilla warfare had resulted
in thirty-one fatalities in Waterford. The majority occurred in the West
Waterford Brigade area where twenty-four people died violently: eight RIC,
one soldier, five members of the IRA and ten civilians. In the East Waterford
Brigade area two members of the RIC, four IRA and one civilian had died.
The grim balance sheet illustrates starkly the difference in effectiveness of the
two Waterford brigades and also between Waterford and its neighbouring
counties. Deaths from political violence were twice as numerous in Waterford
as in Wexford or Kilkenny but only half that of Cork or Tipperary.[156] Deaths
outside Waterford also affected families in the city and county. Three
Waterford-born RIC died violently while serving in other counties and
another three left Waterford-born widows. When Timothy Quinlisk was executed by the IRA in Cork city in February 1920, his widowed father, who
lived in Waterford, had the grim task of identifying the body. The Waterford
branch of Cumann na mBan was not very active during the War of
Independence but individual members in the city gave invaluable communications and logistical support.[157] As in the rest of the country outside Dublin,
there was, according to Rosamond Jacob, a 'lack of feminism among the
members' as they focused on supporting the IRA and SF.[158]

Ernie O'Malley's throwaway remark that 'Waterford has not done much'
can be applied to the East Waterford Brigade but not to its western counterpart as the War of Independence there evolved along conventional lines.[159]
Attacks on police barracks were instrumental in forcing the RIC to retreat
from the countryside. This phase was followed by the targeting and killing of
individual policemen. The subsequent police crackdown led to the formation
of an ASU which was able to maintain itself in the field and undertake more
ambitious operations, most notably at Piltown. The relative inactivity of the
ASU after the engagement at the Burgery in March 1921 is difficult to
explain. It failed to inflict any casualties on the Crown forces or to engage the
enemy until the Cappagh train ambush in July. This may have been due to
the desire of the 1st Southern Division to avoid operations in west Waterford
while preparing for a major gun-running operation into Helvick, which is dis-

cussed in the next chapter. The need to train and integrate the men from the East Waterford Brigade offers another possible explanation. A third reason was the death of Pat Keating who had been involved in every brigade operation until his death at the Burgery. He was arguably the key activist most committed to fighting.[160] A similar situation occurred in east Tipperary. Led by Thomas O'Donovan, the Mullinahone Battalion, Tipperary No. 3 Brigade, had major successes against the police and the military, and was one of the most active units in the country. But O'Donovan's death in October 1920, during a shootout with police, transformed the situation and subsequently there was very little fighting in the area.[161] One man could make a difference. Even when the West Waterford ASU was inactive it remained a challenge to the Crown forces. The East Waterford Brigade never evolved into an effective fighting force. It planned elaborate but disastrous operations such as Pickardstown, which led to the deaths of two Volunteers. The brigade officers failed to engage with the dynamic of guerrilla warfare and to start with the killing of lone policemen. Riven by strife and indiscipline and with most of its officers in a state of mutiny, unsurprisingly, the brigade proved a military failure. IRA GHQ had no option but to amalgamate it with its western counterpart. Politically, SF had made great progress in the city and county. It had become the dominant force in the local authorities which transferred their allegiance to the Dáil. SF had also been successful, especially in rural Waterford, in establishing the Dáil courts, the most visible manifestation of the republican counter-state. In the summer of 1921 the agricultural boom, on which both rural and urban prosperity depended, collapsed.[162] It remained to be seen how the people of Waterford would react to the new economic and political challenges.

6 'I cannot shake off a dread premonition':[1] truce and gun-running, July–December 1921

In the immediate aftermath of the truce IRA morale was high. In Cork Frank O'Connor deemed it a 'perfect summer' when 'you were saluted and cheered in the streets, work could be put to one side, dances were held in your honour, and your word held undisputed sway in your part of the world. All things were possible.'[2] The same was true in most other parts of the country as the underground army appeared triumphant. For both the British army and IRA the period from July until December 1921 was a time of preparation for a possible resumption of war. The cessation of hostilities gave the SF counter state, especially the Dáil courts, an opportunity to function openly. This tended to reinforce the impression that the IRA had won. Initial euphoria was followed by great uncertainty. Would the truce last or would war resume? If so, would both sides be better prepared and better armed? Would discipline be maintained within the Waterford Brigade? What settlement would emerge from the Anglo-Irish negotiations? Would it be the cherished prize of a thirty-two county sovereign republic or dominion status? How would the loyalist community be affected by any settlement? Workers wondered if their employers, especially the farmers, would enforce pay reductions. Which side would the IRA support if there was industrial unrest? These were the questions before the people of Waterford during the summer and autumn of 1921.

Speculation about moves for peace was confirmed in the *Waterford News* on 8 July.[3] On that day General Macready, GOC British troops in Ireland, attended a conference with de Valera in the Mansion House. On 9 July Richard Mulcahy informed all IRA units that 'active operations by our troops will be suspended as from noon, Monday July 11th.'[4] The truce was preceded by one of the bloodiest weekends of the conflict as many IRA units, some hitherto quiescent, hastened to make their mark.[5] Believing that the IRA was near breaking point, the truce came as a relief to Michael Collins and his GHQ staff.[6] By contrast many of his commanders in the field thought they could have sustained and intensified the struggle in the months ahead.[7] For Paddy Paul

> The Truce took us entirely by surprise. We were not expecting anything of the kind and, for myself, I can say that I felt rather disappointed. Other areas and other units had earned glory in the fight but we had been late starters and had not had time up to then to do anything worth while.[8]

George Lennon was more prescient and feared that a relaxation of the struggle would spell the end and that the men would not resume hostilities if negotiations broke down.[9] The truce was welcomed enthusiastically by the population at large and there were widespread celebrations.[10] Phelan Bros, Drapers and Tailors, of George's Street, Waterford, took advantage of the occasion to advertise an 'historic sale … in commemoration of truce week'.[11]

In accordance with the terms of the truce, liaison officers were appointed in each brigade area to smooth out any difficulties that might arise with the authorities. Lennon was the designated IRA liaison officer for Waterford with Paul as his deputy.[12] Once the immediate celebrations were over the IRA began to prepare for a resumption of hostilities. Few IRA officers expected the truce to last. Liam Deasy, O/C Cork No. 3 Brigade, described it as 'a breathing space which might last three or four weeks' during which time the IRA would have time to reorganize their forces.[13] Similarly, Benny McCarthy, adjutant Waterford Brigade, believed that the negotiations would falter and that there was 'not much likelihood of peace'.[14] A strong emphasis was therefore placed on training and on procuring arms.[15] Before the truce the IRA faced an acute shortage of arms and ammunition. Arms were no longer easily seized from the RIC and the Crown forces had successfully located and seized significant arms dumps, particularly in Dublin.[16] Tom Barry estimated that there were only about 100 rifles available to his men in Cork No. 3 Brigade; a shortage of weapons rather than men limited his operations.[17] In June 1921 the combined Waterford Brigades had a roll of 232 officers and 2,044 men but only 56 rifles and 45 revolvers.[18] GHQ warned that there could be 'no question of vacation or half-time work on the part of anybody engaged' in the procurement of war materials.[19] Rifles, revolvers and machine-guns had to be imported. Collins and the GHQ contemplated a large-scale operation to transform the arms situation. They were determined that in the event of renewed hostilities, every Volunteer would have a gun and would not have to count his cartridges before an engagement. Brigade officers also had to contend with an influx of recruits after the truce. A six-week officers' training camp was organized by Paul as brigade training officer. About fifty men completed the course and returned to their companies and battalions to impart the knowledge gained.[20] The opportunity was also taken to further restructure the brigade. In July a new 7th battalion of about 300 men was formed from companies previously in the 1st Battalion. It was headquartered at Ballymacarberry under the command of Seán Morrissey.[21] A thorough reorganization of all intelligence activities was carried out under the direction of Florence O'Donoghue, divisional intelligence officer. In November he deemed the Waterford Brigade to be satisfactory.[22]

As the IRA paraded, drilled and generally acted as a victorious army, the RIC and the British army could only look on in frustration. 'Outside the city of Waterford and the immediate neighbourhood of police posts,' the CI wrote, 'the control of affairs has passed into the hands of the rebels.'[23] Month after month police reports were filled with references to drilling, recruiting, musketry training and other such activities, which in the eyes of the authorities, were being carried on without any reference to the spirit of the truce. In compliance with strict instructions, the RIC made no attempt to interfere with these IRA activities. This further undermined morale in the beleaguered force. More damaging still was the realization that the force would be disbanded. Largely confined to barracks during the truce, the RIC had plenty of time to worry about their future. Would older members be able to retire peacefully and would the younger ones have a future in a new police service? The feelings of unease were captured by the *Constabulary Gazette*: 'the force is unsettled and discontent rife for a variety of reasons, chief of which is the uncertainty of the future'.[24] Prison officers also faced an uncertain future, their predicament exacerbated by daily contact with republican prisoners. In August and in October tensions rose when prisoners, including those in Waterford Prison, demanded improved conditions and prisoner-of-war status. On 9 October prisoners in Waterford began to destroy the interior of the prison but stopped when ordered to do so by the IRA liaison officer. Morale was further damaged when forty-four prisoners, including some from Waterford, tunneled their way out of Kilkenny Prison on 22 November and no attempt was made to re-arrest them.

In common with his counterparts in other counties, CI O'Beirne attempted to judge the mood of the local populace throughout the summer and autumn. In July he remarked how the 'possibility of the renewal of the "war" is not taken seriously by any section of the public whose main anxiety appears to be the financial terms of any settlement'.[25] But by September O'Beirne detected

> On the whole, there are less hopes of peace than during the preceding two months. It is certain however that the government offer has sown seeds of serious dissension in the ranks of Sinn Féin and if the gunmen decide to fight on the issue of an independent republic, they will become unpleasantly aware of this cleavage.[26]

He regarded the position of loyalists as 'pretty hopeless no matter how the matter ends' and bleakly suggested that if war was resumed they would lose 'everything they possess, including probably their lives'.[27] The RIC also kept a watchful eye on the trade union movement, noting the extensive organizing activity of the ITGWU and perceptively warning of a probable clash between 'the union and Sinn Féin'.[28] In many parts of rural Ireland it was becoming clear that the aims of organized labour and the IRA were not aligned.[29] The CI did not allude to the fact that the urban-based Volunteers, especially those in Waterford city, had more in common with rural trade unionists than with rural Volunteers.[30]

As the police watched the IRA with a degree of fatalism, the British army seethed. While scrupulously observing the terms of the truce, behind the scenes the generals vented their frustration in no uncertain terms. In October Macready suggested that 'advantage has been taken of the truce to convert the IRA, which was three months ago little more than a disorganized rabble, into a well-disciplined, well-organized and well-armed force'.[31] However accurate this assessment, it was probably conditioned by the public arrogance of the IRA during the truce and by deep resentment at suggestions that the British army had been defeated. Like the IRA, the army used public occasions to remind people of its presence. On Memorial Day, 11 November 1921, led by their band, the Devonshire Regiment paraded through the streets of Waterford. They were accompanied by two local bands, a large contingent of local ex-servicemen and by the dependents of the men lost on the *Formby* and the *Coningbeg*. Despite inclement weather, a large crowd watched the ceremonies on the Mall and the two-minute silence was observed impeccably. They then listened to Captain Redmond speak about the sacrifices made by Waterford, city and county, during the First World War.[32] The next day he officially opened a new club hall for Waterford ex-servicemen on Mayor's Walk and again recalled shared sacrifice to the cheers of his loyal followers.[33]

The terms of the truce made no mention of the Dáil courts but the IRA interpreted them to mean that the courts and the republican police could function without interference from the authorities. Encouraged by Austin Stack, the IRA set up republican police units, and these units took over the day-to-day administration of law and order. In east Waterford William Keane was appointed O/C of the republican police, heretofore non-existent in the city.[34] Keane and his western counterpart, Patrick Ormonde, set up small police sections in every parish. Soon republican police, identifiable by armbands, were a common sight at sports meeting or fairs, while the RIC stayed in barracks. The demand for the services of the republican police was so great that some had to be made full-time. Most petty crimes were reported to them rather than to the RIC. For example, the *Waterford News* reported the recovery and return of stolen tweed valued at £10 in November.[35]

The truce allowed district courts, which heard more serious cases, to function in Waterford for the first time. Although provision had been made for them during the War of Independence, they rarely functioned anywhere and in Waterford not at all. On 25 October a public sitting of the Waterford district republican court was held in the council chamber of city hall. The adjudicating officers were Fr Kelleher, Dr Vincent White, the mayor, Councillor P.W. Kenny, chairman of the county council, and Luke Larkin, president of Waterford Workers' Council. Many of the claimants and defendants were legally represented and a large number of cases were heard.[36] Various newspaper reports suggest that the only Crown courts functioning were those dealing with compensation claims by members of the Crown forces or their dependents.

The other key task of the republican government – raising revenue – also continued at this time. The cost of maintaining the republican police, IRA training camps and men on full-time duty put an immense strain on the meagre resources of the Waterford Brigade. An arms levy, which had been collected in the west of the county, was now extended to the east and to the city with amounts of up to £150 being claimed from businesses and individuals.[37] On behalf of the Chamber of Commerce, Edwin Jacob wrote to Cathal Brugha, minister for defence and TD for Waterford, to ascertain if contributions were voluntary. The chief liaison officer confirmed that they were but a subsequent notice in the local press stated that the levy had been authorized, that all were expected to contribute and that the proceeds would be used to put 'the Brigade in a state of efficiency'.[38] To many people the distinction between a levy and a voluntary contribution collected by armed men was academic. The imposition of this levy contributed to growing ill-feeling towards the IRA and a lack of support for the republican side during the Civil War.

During the truce there was an immediate and understandable relaxation of IRA discipline. The ASU came down from the hills, fêted as heroes. Michael Shalloe recalled being 'allowed into the town and to dances and such like without much restraint.'[39] As weeks and months passed, however, IRA discipline continued to deteriorate everywhere. As Piaras Béaslaí, IRA adjutant-general, put it, 'the magic of the name "IRA" was abused daily. The man with a gun in his hand learned to be a law unto himself.'[40] In east Waterford there were numerous reports of houses being searched and having valuables stolen under the pretence of republican police investigating robberies.[41] Pax Whelan described one particular gang as 'worse than the Tans'.[42] Following a series of bank robberies Whelan carried out a full investigation, including parading suspects before the bank-managers.[43] The culprits, among them Michael Bishop, were identified and imprisoned in a cottage near Kilrossanty. A number were convicted and sentenced to be deported from Ireland.[44] However, they only went as far as Dublin, where they later joined the National army. Although this action put a stop, at least temporarily, to major armed crime, many IRA members continued to act as if they were above the law and in doing so alienated much of the local population. Disputes about the collection of levies and the wave of robberies reflected a breakdown in IRA discipline, which courts martial could stop but not reverse.

Waterford was central to plans by IRA GHQ to import a significant quantity of arms. This scheme continued during the truce period, even though if discovered they would breach the terms of the agreement and could precipitate a resumption of war. By June 1921 two attempts to smuggle large arms shipments into Ireland had failed. A plan to ship 500 Thompson submachine guns from

New York collapsed when the US Revenue discovered the weapons in the hold of a ship about to sail for Ireland.[45] Another plan to ship arms from Italy to West Cork came to nothing.[46] In late 1920 Collins sent Robert Briscoe to Germany to purchase arms, which were plentiful after the First World War.[47] Fluent in German and posing as a representative of a wool export business from Ballinasloe, he bought small quantities of arms that were transferred to a warehouse in Hamburg.[48] In May 1921 Briscoe returned to Ireland to prepare for the shipment of the arms and travelled to Waterford to finalize the details of the proposed landing at Helvick with Pax Whelan.[49] Before he left for Hamburg Briscoe was assured that an experienced mariner had been found to sail from Hamburg to Helvick. That sailor was Charlie McGuinness, one of the most colourful characters of the War of Independence.[50] McGuinness purchased a large deep-sea trawler, the *Anita*, and joined Briscoe in Hamburg in August. As they were about to sail, however, they were raided by the German police, the guns were seized and McGuinness was arrested. He was only fined though and the guns were returned to him.[51]

The discovery of the *Anita* and the subsequent court case caused uproar. Lloyd George raised the issue at a plenary session of the Anglo-Irish peace talks on 21 October and, after a stormy exchange of views, warned Collins and Griffith that the British government was willing to take the 'necessary action' to deal with this breach of the truce. Collins did not bow to the implied threat but agreed not to import arms into Ireland.[52] The Royal Navy was ordered to step up patrols, both on the coast of Ireland and outside the ports of Bremen and Hamburg.[53] Knowing that the *Anita* was being watched, Briscoe and McGuinness bought a small tug named *Frieda*. On 28 October it slipped out to sea with a German crew under the command of McGuinness with a cargo of 300 guns and 20,000 rounds of ammunition. Briscoe meanwhile sent a prearranged telegram that the arms were on their way to Liam Mellows, IRA director of purchases.[54]

It was estimated that it would take the *Frieda* about three days to cover the 800 miles from Hamburg to Helvick. Mellows sent a despatch to Pax Whelan and preparations to receive the cargo were made. A watch was instituted at Helvick on 30 October. Mellows himself travelled from Dublin to join the waiting Volunteers. The agreed signal was a single distress flare following which two fishing boats would put out to offload the arms. An all-night vigil followed but there was no signal. After a week of waiting and watching they concluded that the ship must have sunk with all hands and Mellows returned to Dublin.[55] No sooner had the *Frieda* left Hamburg than she ran into heavy weather. McGuinness was forced to take shelter in the harbour of Terschelling, one of the Friesian Islands, and did not resume his voyage until the morning of 2 November. In the meantime much of the coal had been consumed but he could not risk calling into a port to refuel. Due to fog off Helvick no signals were noticed and McGuinness made for Waterford harbour.[56] The escape of the *Frieda* had not gone unnoticed by the British and a flurry of activity followed. A telegram from GHQ in Dublin to the naval commander at Queenstown ordered destroyers to patrol the coasts from Youghal to Kilkee while the RIC at the ports in Cork, Kerry and Clare were ordered to be alert for any strange ship putting into harbour.[57] But the authorities were looking in the wrong place.

McGuinness sailed into Waterford on 10 November and with all his fuel spent he dropped anchor in the south channel behind an island just east of the city. Giving his crew, none of whom could speak English, strict instructions to remain out of sight, McGuinness rowed ashore and walked three miles into the city. According to his own account, he enquired at a parochial house for the address of Dr White. The parish priest refused to help him on the grounds that he did not support SF and McGuinness was forced to enquire from passers-by. After he eventually located White's house and convinced him that he was genuine, together they called on Larry McCarthy, the local ferryman. They then made their way down-river by boat. The sight of the *Frieda* and her cargo was all the proof that White needed and returning to Waterford he began to organize a small group to offload the guns. The next evening, again using the ferry, they went down the river and unloaded the guns. Although there were two British destroyers in the port, the operation was completed without detection.[58] The following morning White sent a message to Pax Whelan and that afternoon the first of a series of cars arrived to bring the guns and ammunition to the prearranged hiding place at Keatings of Kilrossanty, from where they were distributed to the Southern and Midland Divisions of the IRA.[59] Although McGuinness greatly exaggerated the amount of arms brought in, it was nonetheless substantial. In the five months between the truce and the Treaty, the IRA imported 51 machine-guns, 313 rifles, 637 revolvers and automatics and 80,000 rounds of ammunition.[60] This was far more than they had managed in the twelve months preceding the truce and most of it came in aboard the *Frieda*.

The truce period from July to December 1921 had seen a consolidation of SF control over much of the country. The open displays by the IRA, the public functioning of the Dáil courts and the administration of local authorities, all combined to present an image of victory for SF. At the same time, George Lennon's forebodings had been justified. There had been a major deterioration in IRA discipline both in Waterford and nationally. It was therefore clear to many observers that the Anglo-Irish war would not resume. Instead the thoughts of many people turned to what settlement would emerge from the on-going discussions in London. For workers and employers alike it was a tense time of stand-off as they waited for an almost certain dispute. For all parties the truce period was a time of uncertainty, which could only be resolved when a peace settlement was agreed.

7 'My constituents suggested ... ratification':[1] from Treaty to Civil War, December 1921–June 1922

On the morning of 7 December news that a treaty had been signed between Britain and Ireland was announced. Although the majority wanted peace and were prepared to accept compromises inherent in a treaty, the signatories were subject to a torrent of recrimination on their return from London.[2] The cabinet, the Dáil and finally the IRA split over the settlement. Seven months later, Civil War began despite efforts to avoid it.[3] In the interim the euphoria of seeing the British army depart gave way to a sense of despair as disorder prevailed in many areas. The issue of wage rates, particularly for agricultural labourers, re-emerged and occasioned serious strife. This chapter explores how reaction to the Treaty and Civil War affected Waterford.

Like the majority of national and local newspapers that supported the Treaty, the *Munster Express*, the *Dungarvan Observer* and the *Waterford Standard* were all strongly in favour: only Downey and his *Waterford News* opposed it. The *Waterford Standard*, organ of the local unionist community, was particularly supportive of the oath of allegiance and Ireland's continued membership of the British empire.[4] Both Catholic and Church of Ireland hierarchies and clergies were almost unanimously in favour. At a special meeting on 13 December, the Catholic bishops urged members of the Dáil to 'consider the best interests of the country and the wishes of the people'.[5] Bishop Hackett of Waterford and Lismore was a strong and vocal supporter of the settlement. He was, according to Pax Whelan, 'good before the Truce or as good as a bishop could be – after the Treaty he was pro-Treaty but not antagonistic.'[6] Robert Miller, his Church of Ireland counterpart, who had succeeded the retired Bishop O'Hara in 1919, likewise endorsed the Treaty, emphasizing the importance of the oath and the empire to his flock.[7] Among the diocese's secular Catholic clergy, Patrick Murray has identified sixteen pro-Treaty priests (including eight parish priests) and eight anti-Treaty curates.[8] Waterford Corporation too was supportive. At a special session on 3 January 1922 a motion was passed which recognized that 'the Treaty, although not ideal, offers a basis for freedom by giving us control of our vital national resources. We therefore strongly urge all local representatives to vote for the ratification of the present treaty.'[9] Waterford County Council, however, failed to reach agreement but concluded with a motion expressing faith in the elected representatives to reach the right conclusion.[10] It is estimated that 328 public bodies throughout the country passed motions in favour of the Treaty.[11]

On Wednesday 14 December the 124 SF members of the second Dáil assembled to debate the Treaty. The debate was adjourned for Christmas on 22 December and resumed on 3 January. The break allowed TDs to return to their constituencies and listen to the views of their constituents. Vincent White was the first of the five representatives of the Waterford-East Tipperary constituency to speak on 6 January. He was unequivocal in his support for the Treaty:

> when I went to my constituents in Waterford during Christmas, they suggested to me that it deserved ratification. We have in this Treaty not the shadows but the substance. We have complete control over our trade and commerce. We are entitled, if we so wish, to have a standing army ... and, finally, we have the evacuation of the British forces, bag and baggage, from Ireland.[12]

Immediately afterwards, Séamus Robinson, representing the east Tipperary part of the constituency, voiced his vehement opposition, concluding that there was a *prima facie* case of treason against Michael Collins and Arthur Griffith.[13] Éamon Dee from Dungarvan also spoke against the Treaty but with more reasoned and principled arguments.[14] The following day Cathal Brugha flatly rejected the Treaty.[15] Waterford's fifth TD, Frank Drohan, did not vote. Unable to reconcile his personal opposition to the Treaty with the overwhelmingly supportive stance of his constituents, he resigned his seat.[16] That evening the Treaty was approved by sixty-four votes to fifty-seven. Subsequent events, particularly the June election, showed that White had faithfully reflected the views of his constituents. Brugha, on the other hand, lived up to his reputation as a recalcitrant republican who refused to accept the oath of allegiance incorporated in the Treaty: in this, he represented the militant wing of the IRA, including the Waterford Brigade. At Westminster Captain Redmond waited until near the end of the debate before expressing his view on the Treaty. Speaking on 8 March 1922, he accused the then Liberal government that had caused the failure of the Home Rule Act of 1914 (his father's life's work) of political cowardice and a lack of generosity. In particular, he deplored partition. Conscious that he represented 'not only myself and my constituents, but also the great body of the people of the South of Ireland who are not represented in this house', he recommended the Treaty unreservedly.[17] This was Redmond's last contribution in the House of Commons.

Even before the Treaty was ratified by the Dáil the British government commenced a process of normalization and demilitarization.[18] Beginning on 9 December thousands of internees were released and arrived home to rapturous receptions.[19] One homecoming was not so happy, however. After a failed attack on the Ardmore RIC station, Declan Hurton and his brother had been arrested and sent to Ballykinlar internment camp. Following his release on 9 December Hurton travelled home by train. At Thurles station a hand-grenade was thrown at one of the carriages by a member of the RIC and seriously injured a number of passengers, including Hurton who died a week later. Local IRA members believed that Sergeant Thomas Enright was responsible and he was shot dead in Kilmallock on 14 December 1921.[20]

After the Treaty was approved by the Dáil, the British army began to evacuate more than 50,000 soldiers and their equipment.[21] All detachments were withdrawn to permanent barracks. Posts such as Dungarvan, Lismore, Kilmacthomas and Cloncoskeraine House were evacuated and troops concentrated in Fermoy, Clonmel or Waterford city. The Devonshires were one of the first units to leave Ireland. On 31 January an advance party left Waterford for the regimental depot in Devonport. A week later the main body left the Infantry Barracks and paraded behind their band to the Clyde Wharf. They were watched by a large crowd who cheered the departing troops. One local newspaper commented: 'Although we are pleased to see them go, it will be remembered that at all times 1st Devons have upheld the best traditions of the British army'.[22] The Devonshires were briefly replaced by a detachment of the York and Lancaster Regiment which handed the barracks over to the IRA on 6 March.[23] Although Cork and Dublin were the main posts for embarkation, Waterford was used quite extensively. Throughout February and March special trains brought British troops to Waterford North Station; from there they marched to waiting ships. A special canteen was set up on Clyde Wharf to feed the troops before they boarded. Small detachments often accompanied train-loads of baggage. One such baggage guard consisting of an officer and seven other ranks was attacked by about forty men at Waterford station on 9 March. Shots were fired and one soldier was slightly wounded before the party was disarmed and allowed to proceed.[24] Apart from that isolated incident, the departure of British soldiers through Waterford passed off peacefully. By April the last of the troops staging through Waterford had left and remaining units were concentrated in Dublin and Cork.

When the RIC was disbanded, members were concentrated in a few main urban centres before transfer to Gormanstown for the final discharge. RIC officers from Waterford, Tipperary and Kilkenny moved in convoys to Waterford city from where they were transported by naval vessels to Dublin. One group of about fifty RIC was ambushed by an IRA party under Paddy Paul at Dunkitt, three miles from Waterford city. The police surrendered without resistance and handed over their arms. They were stored in IRA arms dumps near Kilrossanty and were later used by the anti-Treaty Waterford Brigade to resist National army troops under Paul's command.[25] Details of the RIC convoy's movement had been given to Moses Roche, an officer in the

Kilmacthomas Company, by a friendly policeman.[26] By 11 March the RIC had left Waterford. The *Munster Express* reported how

> Large crowds witnessed the handing over of the various premises to the Provisional Government's representative. It is officially stated that 'until further notice, the headquarters of the 4th Battalion IRA and the Republican police forces will be at Lady Lane Barracks'.[27]

Following the departure of the RIC and the British army, maintenance of law and order rested in the hands of the republican police who patrolled the streets and investigated crime. Republican courts were held openly, attended by litigants of all classes. The IRA occupied the Castle Barracks in Dungarvan and the military barracks in Waterford. As soon as the British troops left, a maintenance party of eighty-two men, commanded by George Lennon, occupied the Infantry Barracks while a further thirty-two took over the Artillery Barracks.[28] The presence of the IRA in Waterford city was not universally welcomed. Some Volunteers later recalled the open hostility shown by crowds of Redmondite supporters, especially by families who had lost relatives during the First World War.[29]

As the country drifted towards civil war, rival factions within the IRA sought to position themselves to best advantage by occupying barracks and acquiring arms. Although the Waterford Brigade had declared itself anti-Treaty, there was a sizeable minority, especially members of the East Waterford and city units, who supported it. The latter billeted themselves in the Artillery Barracks. Both sides used the time to build up their strength. Some officers and men slipped away to Dublin to join the new National army. Quartered at Beggars' Bush and other barracks in Dublin, they could draw on the resources of the fledgling state for finance and equipment. The republican forces had no such option. They depended on local levies and were equipped with the arms used during the War of Independence and whatever had been smuggled in or captured since the truce. In May republicans staged a co-ordinated series of bank robberies across the country, targeting Bank of Ireland branches in particular.[30] The branch on Meagher Quay in Waterford city was robbed of £15,000 by unmasked IRA Volunteers in uniform.[31] At the same time, the anti-Treaty IRA set up training camps, one of which was at Lackendarra Lodge in the Comeragh Mountains: there, on 12 May 1922 local Volunteer, Seán Morrissey, was accidentally shot dead by a comrade.[32] His funeral to Knockboy graveyard was a display of military strength by the Waterford Brigade as hundreds of armed men in uniform escorted the cortège. It was the last public appearance in Waterford of a united IRA as thereafter the pro and anti-Treaty factions split. Paddy Paul left for Dublin and was commissioned into the National army. When he subsequently returned to Waterford to assess the situation he was promptly arrested by his former comrades. Confined in a cell in the guard-room of the Infantry Barracks, he went on hunger strike. After ten days he was transferred to the Infirmary from where he escaped dressed as a nurse and made his way back to Dublin.[33] When he next visited Waterford he did so as second-in-command of the National army force that attacked the city. His local knowledge proved a significant advantage to the government forces.

The deepening split in the ranks of the IRA in Waterford mirrored that within the organization at a national level. As the Provisional government of the Irish Free State (IFS) began to exercise its authority, the IRA translated vocal opposition into action. Representatives of all anti-Treaty units met in Dublin on 26 March and repudiated the authority of the Dáil. Delegates also vested control of the IRA in a sixteen-man elected executive that included Pax Whelan.[34] While this reflected his growing stature as a hard-line republican, it also meant that he spent much of the next three months in Dublin, leaving Lennon in command of the Waterford Brigade. Most, but not all, of the Waterford Brigade followed Whelan's leadership.[35] The IRA executive authorized the imposition of levies and other fund-raising activities and the seizure of barracks and other posts.[36] Robbery and commandeering in the name of the Republic became commonplace, eroding popular support for the anti-Treaty position. On the night of 13 April the executive and forces loyal to it occupied the Four Courts in Dublin, thereby posing a challenge to the authority of the IFS.[37]

Although there is no evidence of a systematic campaign against loyalists and Protestants in Waterford city and county, there were instances of opportunistic violence.[38] Ex-RIC members returning to their homes after demobilization were an obvious and easy target. When ex-Sergeant Patrick Golden, who had been in charge of Kilmanahan Barracks, returned to his home in Waterford in April, his house was surrounded by armed men and he was advised to leave the country; he did so the next day.[39] Timothy Gleeson, a former head constable from Tallow, and James Coogan, an ex-sergeant from the city, had similar experiences.[40] The latter claimed that 'all the disbanded RIC had left the city having received notices to quit the country'.[41] When James O'Donoghue, an RIC constable who had served in Tyrone, returned home to Cappoquin, he was peremptorily ordered out of the town at gunpoint by republicans. His brother, Vincent, an engineering officer with the Cork No. 1 Brigade who was strongly against the Treaty, was appalled. For him it was 'just one of the many acts of bullying and brutal tyranny indulged in at that time by petty local Republican "warriors" to show their arrogant authority and self-importance'.[42] In the case of other loyalists, the pressure applied was economic. Hugh Jones, a solicitor in Waterford city, who worked as the Crown solicitor for Wexford during the War of Independence, claimed that from February 1922 his business was boycotted and that it did not return to normal until 1925.[43] William Roe, a Methodist shopkeeper in Lismore, was forced to leave the county after repeated threatening letters warned him 'to clear out or we will riddle you with bullets when you least expect it'.[44] In all, about thirty loyalists in the city and county alleged that they had been intimidated.[45] When two city residents were ordered to leave at gunpoint the local IRA battalion condemned the action and warned the perpetrators of 'stern measures' should they be apprehended. At the same time the IRA supplied an armed guard for the home of the editor of the *Waterford Standard* when he was threatened.[46] In a letter to the *Church of Ireland Gazette*, Revd C. Stanley, rector of Kilmacthomas, claimed that interference with five tombstones in his parish was the work not of the IRA but of 'one or two hooligans ... either in a drunken state or through pure evilmindedness'. He also stated that 'I personally have suffered no inconvenience in any way from members of the IRA and have received nothing but respect from them, although they know well that I have no sympathy with their views'.[47] The violence may have been opportunistic rather than ideologically motivated, nevertheless it engendered fear among the minority community. In her study of Waterford, Tipperary and Limerick, Gemma Clark has shown that a threatening, sectarian atmosphere pervaded the small isolated Protestant communities in these counties.[48]

The state of anarchy within the county also facilitated another gun-running episode. In March 1922 Charlie McGuinness and Robert Briscoe, both of whom were anti-Treaty, again ran arms from Hamburg aboard a schooner called *Hannah*. On 3 April the guns were unloaded at Helvick into vehicles that had apparently come from the newly established Northern Ireland state.[49] It may be that these guns, with the connivance of Collins, were used to arm the IRA within Northern Ireland. McGuinness then sailed the *Hannah* to Wexford where he sold it.[50]

Almost as soon as the vote on the Treaty in the Dáil was complete, both sides took their cases to the people and spent much time at public meetings up and down the country arguing the merits of their respective views. Early in March, after de Valera announced that he would form a new republican party to contest the forthcoming general election, he began a speaking tour of Munster, delivering a series of speeches that were at best irresponsible and at worst incitement to civil war. He began his tour in Dungarvan on 16 March where, guarded by armed members of the Waterford Brigade, he claimed that the Treaty 'barred the way to independence with the blood of fellow Irishmen', for its acceptance would mean that freedom could only be won by civil war. Warning his audience that if they did not fight today they must fight tomorrow, he proclaimed: 'When you are in a good fighting position, then fight on'.[51] The next day he spoke in Carrick-on-Suir and told a large crowd that if the Treaty was accepted 'the fight for freedom would still go on; and the Irish people, instead of fighting foreign soldiers, would have to fight the Irish soldiers of an Irish Government set up by Irishmen ... it was over the bodies of the young men he saw around him that day that the fight for Irish freedom may be fought'.[52] Later that day in Thurles he infamously told a review of Volunteers that 'they would have to wade through Irish blood ... to get Irish freedom.'[53] Although de Valera had little, if any, influence on members of the IRA executive, his speeches were dangerous and irresponsible and, in the eyes of many, fixed the blame for the subsequent civil war on his shoulders.

Government ministers were not slow to respond to de Valera. On Sunday 26 March Michael Collins addressed a massive crowd, variously estimated at up to 12,000, on the Mall in Waterford city.[54] He was accompanied by Joe McGrath, minister for labour, Seán Milroy, TD, and Ernest Blythe, TD. Introduced by Dr White, who chaired the meeting, as 'the man who won the war', in an impassioned address Collins attacked de Valera's reckless speeches:

> Mr de Valera and his followers are proving themselves to be the greatest enemies that Ireland has ever had. He can perpetuate disunion, can give you the loss of all that you have won, can give you anarchy – a full measure of that anarchy of which his tactics have already given you an unpleasant sample. He cannot give you a republic. Mr de Valera is no more able to give you a republic now than he was last July when he accepted the Truce.[55]

The other speakers were equally assertive and all were received with cheers. Attempts to heckle and to shout 'Up de Valera' were few and were quickly stifled. Efforts had been made to prevent the meeting taking place. The railway signals had been cut at Ballyhale, delaying Collins's train by two hours and a platform erected on the Mall for the speakers had been set alight. However, the strong support for White, not to mention Redmond's influence, ensured a hearing for Collins. That was not the case in Dungarvan the following day. Collins's journey there was slow and circuitous as every road was blocked by felled trees; it took him three hours to make the thirty-mile trip. Speaking from the back of a lorry to a crowd of about 3,000, he got a good reception at first but when he began to defend the Treaty the crowd surged forward and pushed the lorry towards the harbour. Alarmed, Collins's bodyguard drew their revolvers and fired over the heads of the crowd which scattered.[56] A pattern had been established: pro-Treaty speakers could be assured of a hearing in the city but risked life and limb in the west of the county; the converse was true for anti-Treaty speakers. In the weeks that followed public meetings were usually accompanied by violence.

This changed suddenly following the announcement of the Collins–de Valera pact. On 19 May Arthur Griffith moved that the Dáil dissolve itself and an election be held on 16 June. The next day it was announced that Collins and de Valera had agreed that a joint panel of pro- and anti-Treaty candidates would contest the election and form a government.[57] Article 5 of the agreement allowed 'that each and every interest is free to go up and contest the election equally with the National Sinn Féin Party'.[58] The Dáil accepted this agreement and dissolved itself. Political violence immediately subsided and both sides urged support for the panel candidates. In Waterford-East Tipperary the pro-Treaty side nominated Vincent White and the anti-Treaty side nominated Cathal Brugha, Séamus Robinson and Éamon Dee: both sides agreed on Dan Breen as the fifth candidate. Immediately after the election was called, the press urged non-panel candidates to stand. Many did so despite intimidation by republicans. According to Michael Hopkinson, Breen 'persuaded' a farmer's candidate in the Tipperary part of the constituency to stand aside by having a group of armed men besiege the man's home for hours and wound him with a gunshot.[59] John ('Jack') Butler, a Labour candidate, received death threats but boldly declared that he was 'not afraid of Dan Breen or of his gun levelled at my temple'.[60] In all, five non-panel candidates stood: Nicholas Phelan and Jack Butler for Labour; Nicholas Fitzgerald and Daniel Byrne for the Farmers' Party; and John P. Mandeville as an Independent. The campaign opened quietly and on 5 June de Valera and Collins again appealed for support for panel candidates. Efforts were made to demonstrate unity. When de Valera visited Waterford on 12 June as part of his nationwide tour, White shared the platform and presided at the meeting. He declared: 'I come here tonight with my colleagues to ask you in the name of Ireland and as Irishmen to vote for the panel candidates. I only regret that we had not come together like this long ago'. Likewise, de Valera announced: 'We are here tonight irrespective of the views we have on the Treaty question to ask the electors of Waterford to vote for the panel candidates'. While de Valera accepted the right of non-panel candidates to stand, he did not 'think that they should do so at present' and appealed to them to stand aside.[61] The Labour and Farmers' candidates had no intention of doing so. There may have been an uneasy truce between the SF factions, but there was no such peace between the other groups. The fact that a countywide farm labourers' strike was in progress added to the tension and the violence.[62] The well-organized flying pickets of the ITGWU proved adept at harassing the political meetings of their opponents who responded in kind. The election was part of the greater struggle between workers and employers. Whichever side polled better in Waterford would claim a moral victory in the class war between farmers and labourers. The *Munster Express* forecast that Labour would be crushed between the rival SF parties.[63]

Polling day passed off peacefully even though there were reports of widespread personation. Counting of the ballots started on Monday 19 June.[64]

Vincent White topped the poll and was elected on the first count as was John Butler of Labour. The other successful candidates were Cathal Brugha, Daniel Byrne and Nicholas Phelan, the second Labour candidate. Non-panel candidates secured a small majority of the votes in Waterford. Pro-Treaty candidates secured 70 per cent of the vote, a clear endorsement of White's stance. For Labour it was an electoral triumph – 31 per cent of the votes against just 17 per cent for the Farmers' Party. If Labour were the winners, the Republicans were the losers. In an election widely seen as a referendum on the Treaty, nationwide they received only 130,000 votes compared to 239,000 for IFS candidates and 235,000 for non-panel candidates.

Conscious of their humiliating climb-down on wages in 1921, the WFA prepared for a renewed campaign in 1922. At its AGM in January the secretary bullishly claimed 'illegal Labour doctrines had been countered in the parishes of Rathgormac and Ballinameela. £100,000 had been collected for farmers' organisation in Waterford, now we must work to get all farmers into the organisation. The hour of action is at hand.'[65] The ITGWU was equally well prepared and just as confident of victory. With an extensive branch network throughout the country, the labour leadership was sure of its ability to mount a countrywide strike and to call out workers in other industries in support. Both sides spent the spring making bellicose speeches and it came as no surprise to anyone when the WFA announced that it would not participate in the annual conference to set wage rates. The ITGWU's response was immediate and it called a countywide strike effective from 22 May.[66]

Even before the strike started, the unity of the farmers had begun to crumble, especially in east Waterford. By the second day many farmers adjacent to the city had agreed to maintain the existing wage rates for another year. Where farmers would not agree, picketing, blacking of goods and boycotting by shop and factory workers quickly forced many of them to surrender. On 27 May the *Voice of Labour*, the organ of the ITGWU, declared: 'Waterford Will Win – First stages of farm fight are heartening, Dungarvan already settled'. A week later the paper was even more triumphalist: 'Waterford winning all the way. Farmers Flogged in Five-day Fight'.[67]

While the collapse of farmer resistance in the east was quick and ignominious, it was a different story on the estates along the Blackwater Valley. Led by Sir John Keane and the Duke of Devonshire, farmers there announced a reduction in the farm labourers' wage from 38s. to 30s. per week. Keane, the public persona of the large landowners, was especially targeted. On 7 June labourers occupied his estate and declared a 'soviet', milking his prize herd and distributing any money realized.[68] However, the so-called soviet did not last long because the local IRA unit announced that it was opposed to actions against private property. On 19 June fifty-seven labourers went back to work on the Dromana estate. Although other groups held out

for longer, the landowners triumphed. Emily Ussher gives a vivid description
of the siege of Cappagh House by labourers who were reinforced by trade
union activists from Waterford city. Despite shortages of food and being prevented from caring for their stock, the Usshers held out. Blockades were
broken, supplies secured and escorted to the farms, and boycotting was not
sustained.[69] Finally, on 5 August the strike collapsed on the Keane,
Devonshire, Villiers-Stuart, Musgrave and Ussher estates. The ITGWU
claimed victory on the farms in east Waterford but the large landowners in
the west showed that the union could be beaten.

The role of the IRA in the strike varied in different parts of the county.
In the east, many Volunteers from the city came from a trade union background. In advance of a strike meeting in Kilmacthomas, some of George
Lennon's comrades confronted the strikers and held them at bayonet point
before allowing them to proceed with the meeting on condition that it was
orderly.[70] Jack Edwards, trade union activist and a member of that IRA party,
put his position more succinctly: 'When it comes to firing I know where I am
going to fire'.[71] The IRA stance was different in west Waterford where many
members, especially those who joined during the truce, were sons of farmers
and hostile to the labourers. They believed the warning in the *Irish Farmer*:
'It is only wages today, it will be land tomorrow'.[72] According to Emmet
O'Connor, there was intermittent IRA interference with union pickets near
the Cork border. The labourers also had to contend with 'direct action' by a
so-called 'Farmers' Freedom Force'.[73]

By June 1922 Waterford city and county had degenerated into a state of
anarchy and uncertainty. Commandeering of goods and bank robberies by
republicans as well as opportunistic violence against loyalists left many
Waterford people feeling helpless with no recognized force of law and order
to turn to. The result of the general election had shown clearly that the
people had accepted the Treaty and the showing by non-pact candidates
demonstrated a desire for 'normal' politics. The killing of Field Marshal Sir
Henry Wilson in London on 22 June by members of the IRA precipitated a
crisis. Under intense pressure from the British government, Collins and his
colleagues issued the republican garrison of the Four Courts with an ultimatum – either evacuate the building or be attacked. The ultimatum was
rejected and the Civil War began.

8 'We strove ... to keep a few peaceful things going':[1] Civil War and social strife, July 1922–December 1923

At 4.15 a.m. on 28 June 1922 the Civil War began. Situated in the republican heartland and garrisoned by resolutely anti-Treaty forces, Waterford city and county inevitably became the scene of fighting. The city was attacked and captured by the IFS National army in July and Dungarvan likewise in August. As in the rest of the country, the capture of the main centres of population did not end the fighting. For another eight months, guerrilla warfare, death and disruption affected the country including Waterford, where the mountainous areas of the county became one of the last strongholds of republican resistance. Whether the republican forces had sufficient popular support to sustain a campaign of guerrilla warfare was a key issue. But Waterford was convulsed by more than civil war. The long simmering dispute between farmers and their labourers finally erupted into a prolonged and violent strike in 1923 as workers resisted demands for wage reductions.

At first sight the military situation did not appear to favour the National army. Nine of the sixteen IRA divisions opposed the Treaty. These included the 1st Southern, the 2nd Southern and the Dublin Brigade, the strongest and most experienced units in the country. In manpower, the anti-Treaty IRA outnumbered their opponents more than two to one and dominated Munster, Connacht, the three counties of Ulster and Dublin city. Yet, they quickly and irretrievably lost their advantage owing to a lack of unity and an absence of planning. As fighting continued in Dublin and republican units throughout the country concentrated on securing their own localities, only one attempt was made to assist the beleaguered republican forces in the capital. A column of 200 men from the Tipperary Brigades and a few Waterford Volunteers advanced as far as Blessington in County Wicklow on 1 July but dispersed when faced with the National army. Meanwhile, Liam Lynch, chief of staff of the republican forces, planned to establish a 'Munster Republic', a move which he believed would frustrate the creation of the IFS. The Munster Republic would be defended along the grandiosely named 'Limerick–Waterford Line', which followed the River Suir from Waterford to Cahir and from there via Tipperary town to Limerick. The republican forces did not have sufficient manpower, equipment, training or planning expertise to establish a cohesive defensive line. Instead they concentrated on garrisoning Waterford and Limerick and other towns along the line and waited for the inevitable attack.[2]

The Waterford garrison comprised between 200 and 300 men drawn mainly from the Waterford Brigade, commanded by Pax Whelan, with some Volunteers from Cork No. 1 Brigade. They were armed with rifles, revolvers and a few Thompson submachine guns. Indiscipline fatally undermined any prospects of successfully defending Waterford city. In July a column from the Cork No. 1 Brigade was billeted in Dungarvan as a reserve.[3] As part of the preparations to meet the government attack, the republican forces occupied and fortified a number of buildings along the quays: the Adelphi Hotel, the County Club, Reginald's Tower, the GPO, the Granville Hotel, the *Munster Express* offices and Breen's Hotel. The frontline was to be the river. No attempt was made to put outposts on Mount Misery because they could be easily isolated. The jail, the Infantry Barracks and the Artillery Barracks were also occupied as second line positions. All ships berthed on the North Wharf were ordered to cross to the south side of the river. Although wireless equipment was removed from the ships, there is no indication that it was utilized by republicans. Upriver, the bridges at Fiddown and Carrick-on-Suir were blown up. The drawbridge on the railway bridge was raised and the control equipment was dismantled to prevent it being lowered. Small patrols in commandeered vehicles monitored the roads east to Cheekpoint and west to Portlaw to detect any National army flanking movement. The drawbridge on Redmond Bridge, which had been raised each night and lowered during the day, was raised on Monday 17 July and the lifting controls removed.[4] Their preparations complete, the republicans waited for the inevitable attack. As they did so, Maurice McGrath, captain of the Rathgormac Company was accidentally shot and killed.[5]

On 14 July Collins ordered Commandant-General John T. Prout, a decorated US army veteran, who commanded about 800 National army troops in Kilkenny, to advance on Waterford.[6] On capturing the city, he was to move quickly to Carrick-on-Suir and Clonmel. Prout had detailed knowledge of the republican positions in Waterford from Paddy Paul, his second-in-command. Paul produced three different plans: to cross up-river at Fiddown and attack the republican left flank; to cross down-river and attack the right flank or to assemble a motorized column led by three or four Rolls Royce armoured cars to rush the bridge and capture it before it could be raised. The latter was not feasible as armoured cars were not available and the bridge had already been raised. An up-river crossing would leave the troops open to a flank attack by the strong republican force in Carrick-on-Suir under Dinny Lacey. Therefore, Prout and Paul agreed on a down-river crossing. To fix the defenders' attention, the main body of troops would be positioned in Sallypark and Ferrybank on the north bank of the Suir and on the commanding heights of Mount Misery as if preparing for a direct assault across the river. Having fought in the First World War, both Prout and Paul decided to rely heavily on their single 18lb field gun, knowing the effect that artillery fire would have on the anti-Treaty IRA who had never previously experienced it.[7]

Prout's forces left Kilkenny before noon on Tuesday 18 July. Although they met no resistance, their advance was hindered by road blocks. Just after 6 p.m. scouting parties approached the city. The first of these appeared on Mount Misery at 6.45 p.m. and drew sustained fire from the republican positions along the quays. The troops withdrew behind the crest of the hill without loss. At the same time, as another patrol led by Commandant Heaslip and Captain Edward O'Brien, a native of Waterford, began descending the lower slopes towards the railway freight yard, they too came under fire. Volunteer Michael Costelloe was wounded and died two days later. Having reached Sallypark and Ferrybank the National army troops lined the roads and railway lines and exchanged fire with the republican strongholds along the quays. Firing continued until nightfall and as darkness fell silence descended on the city. That night Whelan dispatched a message to Liam Lynch appealing for ammunition and for an attack to be launched by Lacey's Tipperary Brigade.[8]

Wednesday 19 July began with desultory sniping. The 18lb field gun was brought across the golf links and manoeuvred into a position from where it could command the city with direct fire. Paul took charge of laying the gun and at 10.40 a.m. he fired at the jail. Throughout the day a steady fire was maintained on the jail and both barracks while troops on opposite sides of the river exchanged fire. Two civilians, Joseph Dwan and William Long, were killed. In response to the shelling, Whelan evacuated both barracks and transferred his headquarters to the jail. As was their practice, the republicans set both buildings alight, although this did not deter a large mob from entering and looting the premises. Just before midnight, the fire at the Infantry Barracks reached the magazine which exploded, killing one looter and severely injuring many others. The looting was halted temporarily but soon resumed; by morning the two barracks were empty, gutted shells.

The next day the National army prepared to cross the River Suir. At Gyles Quay, about three miles downriver, they found a few small rowing boats which were used after midnight to ferry 100 men, led by Captains Mackey and O'Brien, across to the southern shore. Avoiding the road and the occasional republican patrol, they moved along the river bank and within a few hours were in position near the city. The republican position had been decisively turned. At about 1.45 a.m. Mackey led his men into the rear of the County Club while O'Brien led a party of twenty through the back door of the Adelphi Hotel. A surprised sentry was captured and within minutes the garrisons of the hotel and the County Club were captured without a shot being fired. The adjoining Imperial Hotel was unoccupied. All buildings on the east side of the Mall were now in IFS hands. Reginald's Tower was the next target; it too was unoccupied, the garrison having retreated to the GPO leaving a quantity of arms and explosives behind. Alerted by this activity, the republican forces in the GPO opened up intense small arms fire and, for a time, the National army advance was halted.[9]

Most of the fighting on 20 July centred on the GPO. Soldiers led by Captain O'Brien advanced to within twenty yards of the building but no further. To break the stalemate, in the afternoon the 18lb field gun was moved from Mount Misery to the North Wharf, directly opposite the post office, and the National army fired six shells, devastating the interior of the GPO. The republicans withdrew to the Granville Hotel but one of their men, John 'Bonny' Doyle, was shot in the head by a sniper and subsequently died in hospital on 5 August.[10] Having taken the GPO, the National army resumed their advance along the quays. Republican resistance briefly centred on the Granville Hotel but an attack on the rear of the building trapped the defenders and at about 6 p.m. Jeremiah Cronin and his eighteen-strong garrison were forced to surrender. The other positions along the quays were evacuated by the anti-Treaty IRA, some of whom made their way to the jail while others left the city. Darkness put an end to the military engagement but shops and other premises along the quay were looted and stripped of anything moveable before Free State soldiers managed to enforce a curfew.[11] Over thirty separate claims for compensation arising from damage or looting during the siege were subsequently lodged with the IFS government.[12]

By Friday 21 July the only centre of republican resistance left was the jail manned by about twenty Volunteers under the command of Patrick Power. When small arms fire failed to dislodge the garrison, the 18lb field gun was once again deployed and shelled the jail from Sallypark. One of the gun crew was wounded by a sniper from Bilberry. Covering fire was provided by a Lancia armoured car but Sergeant James Howlett, who was using a Lewis gun to suppress the fire from Bilberry, was shot in the head and died instantly. After five shells hit the gate house in quick succession the republicans were forced to evacuate: they successfully ran the gauntlet across Ballybricken to Chapel Lane and from there joined up with others who were leaving the city. National army troops reached the jail within twenty minutes but not before looting of the prison had begun. That evening the drawbridge of Redmond Bridge was lowered by hand, the event being marked by a volley from the watching troops. The fighting in Waterford was effectively over. A few snipers remained but were of nuisance value only.[13]

In his despatch on 18 July Whelan correctly contended that the key to a successful defence of Waterford was a flank attack on the Free State forces by the Tipperary No. 3 Brigade. On Wednesday Dinny Lacey assembled his men in Carrick-on-Suir to launch the attack. He divided his men into three columns of 50 with a reserve of 100 men under Dan Breen. One column was to establish a blocking position at Mullinavat to prevent the arrival of National army reinforcements from Kilkenny while the other columns attacked the troops on Mount Misery from the rear. Breen's force was held in reserve to exploit any success. Using commandeered transport, the force reached Kilmacow around noon. The column sent to Mullinavat met a National army ration party travelling to Kilkenny and opened fire. The engagement lasted two hours but there were no casualties to either side. On hearing the sound of firing, Lacey assumed that he had lost the key element of surprise and retreated to Carrick-on-Suir, destroying bridges and blocking roads en route. By nightfall the republican force was back at its base having accomplished nothing.[14] Meanwhile, Prout and Paul were unaware of any threat. Whelan had also appealed to Cork comrades for assistance. Liam Deasy, O/C 1st Southern Division, ordered the column under Pa Murray to advance eastwards from Dungarvan but it did not reach Waterford city in time.[15] Whereas Whelan blamed the Cork men, claiming that 'the first column from Cork came up as we were just evacuating, but they didn't want to fight', for their part, the Cork contingent complained about a lack of cooperation from their Waterford comrades.[16] Waterford city fell far more readily than might have been expected. As Hopkinson put it, 'even by the standards of the Civil War, the fall of Waterford demonstrated an extreme unwillingness on the part of the republicans to fight and a complete failure of co-operation between the various anti-Treaty forces.'[17] To the citizens of Waterford who, oblivious of danger, had gathered at street corners and every vantage point to watch the fighting, it seemed that a vast amount of ammunition had been expended. 'More ammunition was fired than in the whole of the Battle of the Somme' one local veteran is supposed to have remarked sardonically. Yet, there were only three military fatalities: Costelloe and Howlett of the National army, and Doyle on the republican side. About ten members of the National army and an unknown number of republicans were wounded. There were at least six civilian deaths, including a 10-year-old girl who was shot as she ran to get bread during a lull in the fighting.[18] Many more were wounded, especially by the explosion in the Infantry Barracks. One girl, Mary Hearne, aged just 15, had a leg blown off in that explosion while Martin Flynn, a 14-year-old boy, was very badly burned in the same incident. On Saturday 22 July captured republicans were taken to Kilkenny. For his leadership and bravery throughout the siege, Captain Edward O'Brien was promoted to lieutenant-commandant.[19]

The end of republican resistance in Waterford city, coupled with the fall of Limerick to Free State forces on 20 July, meant that both ends of the much vaunted 'Waterford-Limerick line' were in government hands. While the National army forces in Limerick advanced quickly southwards towards

Bruree and the most sustained fighting of the whole conflict, Prout was content to occupy Waterford city, despite orders from Collins to move promptly on Carrick-on-Suir. Instead he initiated a recruiting campaign and was gratified to inform Dublin that he was securing a good supply of recruits, many of them veterans of the First World War. A shipment of 500 rifles arrived on board the *Helga* to arm the new recruits.[20] On leaving the city, the anti-Treaty IRA retreated only as far as Butlerstown Castle, three miles away. There they set up headquarters and also occupied Whitfield House and Mount Congreve.[21] Neither side engaged in aggressive patrolling. It was not until 29 July that Prout began to advance towards Carrick-on-Suir. He overestimated republican strength to the west of the city, reporting 220 in Portlaw alone, for which reason he advanced along the north bank of the river. After some stiff fighting, Carrick-on-Suir fell on 4 August and Clonmel on 9 August.[22] Prout could now turn his attention to Dungarvan, which after the fall of Cork on 10 August, was one of the last towns still in republican hands.

The indiscipline and carelessness that had cost the republican forces dearly in Waterford city continued to undermine their effectiveness. The advancing National army met with no resistance. One of the defenders of Butlerstown Castle, Sonny Cullinane, later recalled how the garrison was captured without firing a shot because the men had gained access to the wine cellars.[23] Demoralized, the republican forces made no effort to defend Kilmacthomas but continued their retreat to Dungarvan. By now some were also becoming increasingly aware that people at large wanted peace. Many simply dropped out and went home.[24] In the words of one Volunteer, 'when I reached Dungarvan I decided to take no further part in the fighting so I went home'.[25] The retreat was not without loss. On 14 August John Dobbyn was killed by the accidental discharge of a comrade's rifle.[26]

As the National army continued its progress towards Dungarvan, Pax Whelan rallied his men for a last stand. At a brigade council meeting on 30 July it was evident that his command was disintegrating as individuals and even whole companies had gone over to the Free State.[27] The most that could be done was to delay the National army advance before reverting to guerrilla warfare. On 4 August a party of men under Mick Mansfield, brigade engineer, blew up the middle arch of the road bridge at Ballyvoile and one of the nine arches of the magnificent railway viaduct there, which later collapsed.[28] At this stage there was an expectation that a line of defence would be established along the steep ravine of the River Dalligan. However, late on 8 August word reached republicans in Dungarvan that the National army contingents had landed by ship in Cork. The men of the Cork brigades immediately left for home on a commandeered train.[29] In their wake they blew up the railway bridge at Cappoquin and attempted to demolish the road bridge but only succeeded in cratering it. With less than 100 men now remaining in Dungarvan, and knowing that meaningful resistance was impossible, Whelan had his men set fire to the castle barracks that night. The next day the coastguard station at Ballinacourty was set ablaze. Whelan formed his men into three ASUs, each comprising about twenty men armed with rifles and Lewis guns. The ASU under Thomas Keating's command was to operate in the east of the county from a base near Kilrossanty, another under Paddy Curran was in the west while the third, under Jack O'Meara, was based in the Nire Valley in north Waterford. Whelan and his brigade staff were to go underground near Dungarvan to control operations.[30] Once again the IRA was an underground army but now they could no longer count on the support of the people. They were also fighting former comrades who knew the safe houses and the mountainside shelters. In reverting to low-intensity warfare Whelan was implementing the change in strategy adopted by the anti-Treaty IRA. On 14 August the republican *Poblacht na hÉireann War News* announced a 'resumed war of independence'.[31] A week later the republican GHQ issued instructions to all brigades to establish ASUs.[32]

On 22 August a National army column led by Paul finally entered Dungarvan to a warm welcome from the local people and members of the UDC.[33] Even in the republican heartland of west Waterford the people wanted peace and law and order. All towns in County Waterford were now in the hands of government forces. The conventional phase of the Civil War was over but a more deadly phase had begun. On the night of 15 August word reached the troops billeted in Ballybricken Jail that the unoccupied police barracks in nearby Shortcourse was on fire. A patrol under the command of O'Brien was dispatched to investigate the scene. Rushing ahead of the patrol, he broke open the barracks door but was fired on and fatally wounded. His attackers escaped into the gathering crowd.[34] At O'Brien's funeral Bishop Hackett strongly condemned the attack and all armed resistance to the new government.[35] The attack bore all the marks of a carefully planned, targeted ambush. Four days later an incident occurred in Kilkenny Jail which in republican eyes was linked to O'Brien's death. On 19 August Jack Edwards, a republican captured in Waterford, was shot dead by a sentry.[36] According to his brother Frank, 'It was known to be a reprisal for the shooting of a Free State officer, a Captain O'Brien, in Waterford'.[37] Two other republican prisoners from Waterford died in custody in disputed circumstances. Patrick Mangan of Lismore, a prisoner in Cork Jail, took part in a protest on 24 September and was killed when the guards opened fire.[38] John Walsh of Kilmacthomas was captured in March 1923 and taken to Kilkenny Jail where he was interrogated, badly beaten and shot. He died of his wounds on 14 March.[39] Andrew Power of Ballygunner was another republican who died in custody. He served on the Western Front with the Irish Guards and spent a period as a prisoner of war. Following his demobilization in 1919 he returned home and joined the local IRA battalion. In August 1922 he was arrested at his father's house and detained in Ballybricken Jail before being transferred to Kilkenny. Power contracted diphtheria and died in Kilkenny Jail on 28 January 1923.[40]

During the period September to December 1922 the Waterford Brigade initiated and sustained a guerrilla campaign in the county and city at a more intense level than during the War of Independence. Thomas Keating's ASU was first into action. On 26 August, while a detachment under Mossy Roche sniped at the National army troops in Tramore Coastguard Station, Keating and the main body attacked the garrison at Whitfield Court. The estate steward described the events in a letter to Lady Susan Dawney who was with her husband, Major Dawney, in India:

> They were shooting at one another all day and it was a terrible battle. Then in a bizarre turn of events, They stopped for a cup of tea and both sides greatly admired your Ladyship's antirrhinums![41]

There were no casualties. The ASU and Roche's detachment withdrew to the safety of Kilrossanty, or so they thought. On the morning of 2 September ten members of the ASU were surprised and captured while in camp.[42] Their failure to take the rudimentary step of posting sentries exposed an unforgiveable overconfidence and failure to grasp that the situation had changed. In the words of Mick Mansfield: 'Things were very different now to what they were in 1920–1921. No place was safe for us now as the people were divided in their allegiance to the republic or Free State. It was impossible to know who was friendly or who was not'.[43] A month later Keating's ASU was dealt another devastating blow when a section was captured in a farmhouse near Kilmacthomas. The captures virtually eliminated the ASU as a fighting force.[44] As Jack O'Meara's ASU was operating in conjunction with forces under the command of Dan Breen, mainly in south Tipperary, armed resistance in Waterford centred on Paddy Curran's unit in the west of the county and on the few activists in the city. Throughout September Curran's ASU concentrated on sniping attacks on National army garrisons in Dungarvan, Lismore and Cappoquin and on the armed post at Youghal Bridge. There were no reported casualties to either side during these attacks. Occasionally the army would respond by sending strong patrols into areas perceived as 'republican strongholds'. On 29 September one such patrol was ambushed near Ballinamult and three soldiers were wounded.[45] During September there were a number of National army fatalities. On 6 September two soldiers died when their vehicle crashed near Kilmeaden.[46] On 27 September Sergeant-Major Thomas Murray was accidentally shot while preparing for sentry duty in Lismore Castle.[47] A few days later, Volunteer Myles Broughton was killed in the same way also in Lismore Castle.[48] Civilian fatalities were inevitable. During one sniping attack in Waterford city on 4 September Mrs Katie Walsh was fatally wounded while sitting by a window in her house.[49]

During October there was an increase in violence in Waterford. Military posts in Waterford and Dungarvan came under sniper attack almost nightly. Although the attacks rarely resulted in casualties, they did create an atmosphere of siege for the embattled National army. One soldier was seriously wounded guarding the GPO in Waterford on 10 October when fired on from Ferrybank. Army intelligence suspected that a group led by Patrick Sinnott and Thomas Partridge were responsible for most of the sniping attacks in the city but, despite repeated searches, the National army failed to capture them.[50] Occasionally, individual soldiers walking in the streets were held up and relieved of their arms. On 14 October Sergeant Stan Furlong was walking in Sallypark when he was held up by three masked men. He drew his revolver and in the ensuing gun-battle he was seriously wounded; his attackers escaped.[51] Apart from sniping at the garrison in Dungarvan, Paddy Curran's ASU fired at any military traffic travelling between Dungarvan and Waterford or Fermoy. The troops in Dungarvan responded by sending strong patrols into the mountains to search for the column. On 22 October two members of such a patrol were killed, Patrick Foley and Laurence Phelan.[52] Corporal James Dunne was accidentally shot by a comrade in their billet at Dungarvan. It was a tragic end to a varied military career. Dunne had served in the First World War with the Connaught Rangers and had participated in the mutiny in India in protest against British policy in Ireland for which he had been sentenced to a long term of imprisonment. Released following the Treaty, he joined the National army as soldiering was the only occupation he knew.[53] For many people the republican forces seemed to have made much of Waterford, outside of the major towns, ungovernable. But on 20 October, in an indication of growing government confidence, thirty-eight members of the new unarmed Garda Síochána, under the command of Superintendent Brennan, occupied the former RIC barracks in Lady Lane.[54]

The conflict continued in much the same vein during November with sniping at garrison posts and ambushes on roads. Paddy Paul recognized that the Dungarvan area was the centre of republican resistance and therefore reinforced his troops there. They had an early success when they captured Pax Whelan and his brother Seán (the brigade intelligence officer).[55] From documents in Pax Whelan's possession, the IFS forces appear to have traced republican bank accounts and confiscated £1,800 – a serious blow to the anti-Treaty side. As a member of the IRA executive, Whelan was a prized capture and he was transferred to Mountjoy Prison in Dublin. Just days before his arrest, Seán Whelan sent a gloomy assessment to IRA headquarters, report-

ing that in Waterford the republican side lacked the popular support necessary to sustain a guerrilla campaign and that people were giving information
to the government forces. Although individuals and groups could maintain the
struggle for a period, the republican movement in Waterford clearly lacked
the popular support to sustain a guerrilla campaign over the longer term.[56] On
13 November troops from Dungarvan surrounded Ballymacarberry. Members
of Jack O'Meara's ASU, who were staying in the village, managed to shoot
their way out and escape into the mountains. Two National army soldiers
were wounded.[57] The next day Paul brought further reinforcements to
Dungarvan and inspected the troops. When he set out to return to Waterford
on 15 November his convoy was ambushed and one soldier was wounded.
After a brisk exchange of fire lasting about thirty minutes, the ambushing
party dispersed as reinforcements arrived.[58] The same week saw further
tragedy in Waterford city. On the 13th three men entered Boyce's pawnshop
on Michael Street to purchase four sets of binoculars. When they produced a
slip of paper instead of money Charles Boyce, son of the proprietor, tried to
take back the binoculars. One of the men shot Boyce dead. All three then ran
off, dropping the slip of paper which was marked: 'Receipt – F.H. Adj. 4th
(City) Battalion'. It was believed that F.H. referred to Frank Heylin, one of
the leading republicans in the city. The National army raided his home and
arrested him but since they could find no evidence, they had to release him
a week later.[59] The month ended with a resurgence of activity near
Kilmacthomas which saw four members of the National army wounded in
three ambushes. Intelligence sources blamed Thomas Keating and his newly
re-formed ASU.[60]

There were a number of republican attacks on the railway during
December. The government forces scored a success when they arrested Tom
Partridge and Pat Sinnott – both of whom ranked high on the wanted list –
following an attack on a military lorry.[61] On 10 December a large party of
armed and masked men disarmed the military guard at Waterford North
Station and set fire to the goods depot. The blaze could be seen from all over
the city and contemporary estimates put the damage at between £50,000 and
£100,000 – an enormous sum. The lack of co-operation by the local fire
brigade was noted by the intelligence office for Waterford.[62] A week later
Keating's column stopped a train near Kilmeaden and burned it. Other
attacks on trains and railway stations followed and the service between
Durrow and Waterford city could only operate with a military escort.[63] The
line was forced to close for a period.[64] The destruction of the railways in
Waterford was part of a wider republican campaign against the country's rail
network.[65] The civilian death toll increased in December. John O'Shea was
shot by a sentry at the jail when he failed to halt. Pierse Murphy, an ex-soldier, was shot dead on Doyle Street on New Year's Eve by a man dressed in

military uniform. On the same night another civilian, Thomas Cullen, was mortally wounded while walking near the Artillery Barracks. At both inquests military witnesses claimed that they had been fired on and were returning fire but this was disputed by other witnesses.[66] The six-month period from July to December 1922 was marked by twenty-five deaths in Waterford city and county: ten National army, four IRA and at least eleven civilians. By comparison, the equivalent period in 1920 had seen seven people killed – three RIC, one British army, one IRA and two civilians. Added to this, the destruction of rail and road infrastructure and the resultant disruption to normal life made the prospect for the New Year bleak. There appeared to be no end in sight to the internecine struggle and the cycle of killings.

This widespread guerrilla warfare and the government's apparent inability to counter it necessitated drastic action. On 30 September 1922 a draconian public safety bill was approved by the Dáil which established military courts with the power to impose the death penalty for a broad range of offences, including possession of arms.[67] No appeal could be made against the decision of a military court. An amnesty for the possession of arms drew little response. At first there was widespread scepticism about whether the powers would be used but a month later these were dispelled when on 17 November four men were executed in Dublin for possessing revolvers. A week later Erskine Childers was executed for possession of a small pistol, given to him by Michael Collins. When in reprisal, republicans shot and killed Seán Hales, a TD who had voted for the public safety bill, on 8 December the government executed Liam Mellows, Dick Barrett, Rory O'Connor and Joe McKelvey, four prominent republicans who had been in custody since July. Death penalties had to be confirmed by the National army Command O/C. Prout, O/C Waterford Command, first exercised his new powers when John Phelan and John Murphy were executed in Kilkenny Military Barracks on 29 December 1922. A practice also began whereby executions were stayed on condition that no further incidents occurred in a particular area. The condemned men were effectively being held hostage for the behaviour of their republican comrades.[68]

Michael Fitzgerald and Paddy O'Reilly, both natives of Youghal and active members of Cork No. 1 Brigade, were captured near Clashmore and lodged in Waterford Jail on 4 December 1922.[69] They were sentenced to death in early January. Peter Cuddihy of Waterford city was also sentenced to death but was reprieved.[70] Prout confirmed the sentences but no date was set for the executions. Anti-Treaty supporters campaigned for a reprieve and during the first week in January over 2,000 signatures were collected in Youghal and the surrounding district.[71] Meanwhile other avenues were also explored. According to Pax Whelan, prominent land owners such as Mrs Holroyd-Smith of Ballinatray House were asked to intercede with the government and did so but to no avail.[72] While all of this was going on, Fitzgerald and O'Reilly endured the uncertainty of not knowing if or when they would face a firing squad.

In the city, sniping at the GPO, the jail and the military barracks continued on a nightly basis in January 1923. Five soldiers escorting Labour Exchange officials as they collected money from the Bank of Ireland in O'Connell Street were attacked on 5 January. Private Christopher Sweeney died instantly and two others were seriously wounded. The attackers escaped but without the cash.[73] Three days later the body John Ivory of Faithlegg, a member of the pre-Treaty IRA but who had taken no part in the Civil War, was found in a ditch near Crooke church. He had been shot twice at close range, once in the head and once in the neck.[74] No motive for the killing was established. In west Waterford the daily round of sniping at military posts and attempted ambushes continued but with little success. Searches by the National army in the Dungarvan area led to a large number of arrests of known republican sympathizers or activists; they were subsequently interned.[75]

It is not known if the continuing violence influenced Prout who decided to let the executions of Fitzgerald and O'Reilly proceed. At 4 a.m. on 25 January they were informed that they would be executed at 8 a.m. in the Infantry Barracks. They were allowed attend mass and receive the sacraments. In their final poignant letters to their families Fitzgerald and O'Reilly were resigned to die, forgave their enemies and said goodbye to their loved ones.[76] Their last request, that they die together, was granted and refusing blindfolds they were shot.[77] The bodies of Fitzgerald and O'Reilly were buried within the barracks but in October 1924 they were re-interred in Youghal. Republicans believed that the British government had intervened to prevent any reprieve of Fitzgerald who had been the triggerman for a landmine attack on a party of the Hampshire Regiment in Youghal in May 1921 that killed members of the regimental band, including three band boys.[78] There is no evidence to support this. The IFS government did not need external pressure in its steely determination to break the republican struggle and to preserve the democratic institutions of the fledgling state. To this end, Patrick Hogan, minister for agriculture, advocated the application of extensive executions for a limited time 'but within that time they ought to be going with machine-like regularity'.[79] His cabinet colleague, Kevin O'Higgins, agreed and called for executions in every county.[80] A total of thirty-four prisoners were executed in January 1923.

Between February and May 1923 the republican military effort throughout the country disintegrated. Many factors contributed to the collapse, especially the ongoing executions. As an officer of the 1st Southern Division put it: 'If we intensify war it will mean losing some of our best men who will be executed'.[81] A Kerry officer told Ernie O'Malley: 'It was no good carrying out an operation for our prisoners inside in gaol would have been taken out and shot'.[82] Many of these prisoners had come to recognize the futility of the armed struggle. On 6 February prisoners in Limerick issued an appeal to their comrades still fighting: 'A continuation of the present struggle is waste of blood and has developed into a war of extermination. We think it has gone far enough and ought to stop now'.[83] In a further propaganda coup the government issued a similar statement from Liam Deasy, O/C 1st Southern Division, who had been captured on 18 January and sentenced to death. His execution was suspended on condition that he would urge republicans to end their armed struggle. Deasy's letter was widely publicized and, coupled with a shrewdly timed offer of amnesty to anyone willing to surrender, dealt a further blow to republican morale. The *Cork Examiner* reported that prisoners in Clonmel and Waterford had issued statements supporting Deasy's appeal.[84] In an effort to bolster the spirit of his men, Lynch released a statement on 9 February claiming that the IRA was 'in a stronger military position than at any period in its history. The war will go on until the independence of one country is recognised by our enemies, foreign and domestic. Victory is within our grasp'.[85] To some, the statement embodied Lynch's undoubted integrity and courage and his indomitable spirit which was keeping the republican effort alive. But for many others it reflected his failure to face the reality that the war was lost.

The National army also improved its counterinsurgency efforts and reorganized its command structure in Waterford. Prout's performance as O/C Waterford Command was much disparaged. Among his critics was William T. Cosgrave, president of the executive council of the IFS. As TD for Kilkenny he received letters from prominent citizens following the capture of Callan and Thomastown by a republican column in December. They blamed the indiscipline of Prout's troops for this.[86] Mulcahy regarded Prout as too weak to enforce proper discipline and from 13 January 1923 responsibility for west Waterford was transferred to the Cork Command.[87] The 40th Battalion in Fermoy and the 42nd Battalion in Youghal were reinforced and began aggressive patrols in the republican heartland of the Knockmealdown Mountains. With the 14th Battalion in Waterford and the 64th Battalion in Clonmel, there were now approximately 2,300 troops actively searching for the small republican ASUs. National army intelligence estimated the strength of the republican forces in Waterford city and county at 155 men.[88] The National army also set up a network of posts throughout the county. The 40th Battalion had seven posts in County Waterford. Each was strongly fortified and garrisoned by an officer and at least thirty men. These posts were too strong to be successfully attacked by the IRA. While there are many reports in the operational files of posts being sniped at, there were few recorded casualties. Desultory sniping at a fortified post might create an illusion of republican military activity but it was no substitute for real offensive action and held out no prospect of ultimate victory.

In early 1923 in Waterford, as in other parts of the country, the republican forces suffered setback after setback. Bereft of money and support they were increasingly reliant on robbery to fund their activities. Friday was pension payment day and on 9 February three members of the IRA approached the busy sub-post office in Poleberry in Waterford city. As they entered the building they were confronted by soldiers inside waiting for them. They ran onto the street but were fired on by more troops stationed outside. Clearly, the raid had been expected. Thomas Walsh, a 23-year-old boot-maker from Mayor's Walk, and 18-year-old Michael Moloney lay dead on the pavement. Nicholas O'Neill was wounded but escaped.[89] The death of two of their members was a huge blow to the IRA in the city as was the realization that the troops, forewarned, had been lying in wait for them.

The Waterford–Dungarvan railway line continued to be a favourite target for republicans. On 2 February a breakdown train left Waterford to remove the wreckage caused by a derailment near Durrow Station. Just as the work was completed the train was seized by a group of armed men who sent the unoccupied train speeding towards the broken Ballyvoile viaduct.[90] It toppled into the ravine some 200 feet below. Later that month republicans started a campaign of burning the houses of prominent government supporters.[91] The first to be burnt on 19 February was the mansion of Sir John Keane who had been appointed to the IFS Senate.[92] The same night the homes of Caroline Fairholme and Arthur Hunt were also burnt.[93] Fairholme was convinced that her well-known loyalism during the War of Independence was the reason why she was singled out.[94] Three nights later the country house of the Poer O'Shea family at Gardenmorris was destroyed.[95] These attacks further alienated the people from the republicans. Terence Dooley contends that a significant number of the 300 'big houses' burned during the period 1920–3 were destroyed by local agitators whose primary concern was to expel local landlords and redistribute their lands.[96] There is no evidence of an agrarian motivation in the Waterford burnings. Between February and April 1923 seven big houses were burned in Waterford compared to twenty-nine in Tipperary, nineteen in Cork, eleven in Wexford and five in Kilkenny.[97] The month was also noteworthy for the continuing success of the sweeps organized by the National army. Dozens of men were rounded up and sent to internment camps.

During March the killing continued. On the 4th troops from Clonmel discovered a body in a field near Clerihan. Riddled with bullets and labelled 'convicted spy', it was identified as that of Sergeant Thomas McGrath of the National army. He had been stationed in Waterford and attached to the Intelligence Department.[98] In west Waterford Paddy Curran's ASU tried to sustain military activity. On the night of 6 March troops stopped a car at Grange. The five occupants opened fire and tried to escape in the darkness. Two did so but Tom Mooney, Bill Lennon and Richard Morrison were captured. Lennon, who had been active in the West Waterford Brigade before the truce, had joined the National army when Dungarvan fell to the government forces. In October, however, he deserted and re-joined his comrades on the republican side. He was now in double jeopardy. Not only could he be court-martialled and sentenced to death for being captured bearing arms but he could face the same fate as a deserter. A number of deserters had been captured near Dublin and executed in January. Aware of this, his companions carried out a daring operation and rescued him from hospital.[99] On the morning of 12 March part of Paddy Curran's column started to demolish Killongford Bridge. Their activities were reported to the garrison in Dungarvan and troops were immediately dispatched. While fifteen men under the command of Lieutenant Brown approached along the main road, other troops led by Commandant Walsh attempted to surround the column from the Two Mile House direction. A confused fire-fight that lasted two hours ended with the withdrawal of the republicans.[100] In the city the only incident of note was an unsuccessful attempt to disarm a National army officer.[101] Many west Waterford men operated with the Cork No. 2 Brigade. One of them was 19-year-old Thomas Greehy of Lismore who was killed by the explosion of a mine at Kilwatermoy near Tallow on 10 March. It is not clear whether this was the premature explosion of a mine that he was preparing or a booby trap laid by Free State forces.[102]

Liam Lynch convened a meeting of the IRA executive in the Nire Valley from 23 to 26 March to review the national situation. Most of the leading republicans were present. De Valera also attended; he was allowed to speak but was not given any voting rights.[103] Mick Mansfield, O/C Waterford Brigade since the arrest of Whelan, reported on the state of his brigade.[104] He told the meeting that even though his numbers were small and lacked arms and ammunition, he would continue the struggle as long as the IRA executive wished him to do so.[105] There were similar reports from other brigade commandants. A motion proposed by Tom Barry: 'That in the opinion of the executive further armed resistance and operations against the Free State Government will not further the cause of Independence of the country' was defeated by six votes to five. Knowing the risk of having the entire republican leadership assembled in one place and warned by scouts of National army patrols in the area, they dispersed and returned to their own areas.

Fully aware that the Knockmealdown and Comeragh Mountains was one of the last areas where the republican commanders could meet, the National army began to sweep the area aggressively. The garrisons in the ring of surrounding posts – Waterford city, Carrick-on-Suir, Clonmel, Clogheen, Cahir, Mitchelstown, Fermoy, Lismore, Cappoquin, Dungarvan and Kilmacthomas – were all reinforced. Strong patrols, at times numbering up to 100 men, covered the area daily. Bridges over the Blackwater and the Suir were guarded around the clock. When the weather permitted, aircraft from Fermoy supported the troops on the ground and restricted the movement of republicans. To further hinder movement, all boats on both rivers were impounded.[106] Fishermen protested about loss to their livelihood but in vain. The pressure soon paid dividends. After the March executive meeting, Lynch had spent a few days near Callan, County Kilkenny, before returning to the Knockmealdown Mountains to attend another meeting. As he and his companions made their way across the mountains on 10 April, they were spotted by a National army patrol which opened fire. Lynch was fatally wounded and died that evening in Clonmel.[107] His death was a major blow to the republican cause since it was his resolute spirit and belief in final victory that had sustained the military campaign. Other republican losses followed. On 14 April Austin Stack was captured near Ballinamult 'alone and unarmed, lying in a ditch and looking haggard and care-worn with some days' growth of beard, without collar or overcoat'.[108] Over the next few days other prominent republicans such as Todd Andrews were captured in the neighbourhood.[109]

In Waterford Keating embodied the flame of resistance much as Lynch had done on a national level. The day after Lynch was killed Keating and Paddy Landers of Modeligo were spotted near Coolnasmear by an army patrol which opened fire. Keating was severely wounded and thrown into the back of a lorry. He was brought first to Cappoquin and kept there for a few hours before being brought to Dungarvan Hospital. Surgery failed to save him and he died on 12 April. Many believed that prompt medical attention could have saved his life.[110] Militarily, the republican effort was on its last legs and it was only a matter of time before surrender. Meeting in late April, the surviving members of the IRA executive elected Frank Aiken as chief of staff, ordered a suspension of offensive operations and authorized de Valera to enter peace negotiations with the government. A National army military summary in May was devastatingly accurate: 'Reports point to the fact that in almost every command their organization is absolutely broken or else hampered in such a way as to render it almost impossible for them to carry out any major operation.'[111] While de Valera sought vainly for a fig-leaf, relentless harrying of the remaining republican activists continued. On Sunday 6 May Paddy Paul had a notable success near Waterford city. Acting on intelligence received, he surprised a group of nine republicans and apprehended them. Those arrested included the remaining activists in the city such as John O'Connor, O/C City Battalion, and Michael Hunt, 'probably the most active local irregular'.[112] This effectively ended the Civil War in Waterford. On 24 May Aiken published a ceasefire order and ordered the dumping of arms. On the same day de Valera issued his stirring call to 'the soldiers of the legion of the rearguard' advising that:

> Further sacrifice on your part would be now in vain and continuance
> of the struggle in arms unwise in the national interest. Military victory
> must be allowed to rest for the moment with those who have destroyed
> the republic.[113]

The ceasefire came too late for Thomas Mackey, a young republican from
Tallow, who was shot while trying to evade a patrol on 24 May. He was the
last Waterford fatality of the struggle.[114]

During 1923 Ireland was torn by social strife and class conflict as well as
Civil War. In excess of 1.2 million work days were lost that year to strikes
and lock-outs as workers and employers clashed over pay rates. By 1921 the
post-war boom that had sustained the wartime demand for labour had given
way to recession. Retrenchment and cutbacks were the order of the day as
employers sought to reduce their costs.[115] In response, the trade unions vowed
to defend their hard-won gains and rallied to the slogan 'Not a penny off the
pay, not a minute on the day'. However, employers could now count on government backing as law and order was re-established throughout the country.
The government demonstrated a new-found confidence in its dealings with
the threat of industrial unrest. Since February 1922 it had temporized in
negotiations with the powerful Post Office Workers' Union. A commission of
enquiry into the cost of living for postal workers bought time. When it finally
reported in September, the cabinet promptly rejected its findings and
announced pay cuts of 11 per cent. A three-week national postal strike failed
to move the government from its stance and the union was forced to accept
the lower wage rates.[116] The scene was set and such a scenario was to be
repeated many times both locally and nationally in 1923.

In Waterford city and county during 1923 there were thirteen strikes
involving more than 3,000 workers.[117] Those organized by gas workers and
farm labourers were distinctive for the length of the stoppage and the bitterness of the struggle. The strike involving the city gas workers began on
Friday 26 January 1923 as an inter-union dispute between the dockers' union
and the ITGWU over the unloading of coal.[118] The inter-union row was soon
entangled in a discussion on the future of the company, with management
insisting on a reduction of labouring staff from seventy to forty with the latter
having to work a 12-hour day for the same wages as their existing 8-hour day.
An all-out strike followed and the workers occupied the gasworks, declaring
a 'soviet' and hoisting the red flag. Pat Keating, leader of the strikers, personally raised the flag and called for sympathetic strike action by other workers at the AGM of the local ITGWU branch. His call was greeted with
cheering and applause but that was the extent of the support he received as
the national leadership of the ITGWU moved to distance itself from such
radical actions. As the occupation of the gasworks continued the men tried to

maintain supply to the city and to collect monies owed for the gas. At 8.00 p.m. on Saturday 10 March the army moved in, evicted the men and removed the flag. The soviet was over but the strike continued. The gas supply was now shut down completely. Various attempts to mediate failed as management sought a wage reduction in addition to the thirty redundancies and the extended working day. It was not until August that a conference under the chairmanship of Vincent White, the mayor, negotiated an end to the dispute. The men, broken by debt and hunger, came back on management terms after seven long months. Keating was offered his job back but refused it in favour of a friend. This emphatic defeat for the workers marked a further step in the retreat of socialism.

Equally long and bitter was the strike by the farm labourers in east Waterford. Buoyed up by their partial victory in the west of the county in 1922, and confident of government backing, the WFA prepared for conflict. At its AGM in February 1923 the secretary stated that the WFA was in a good and financially sound position with a membership of 289. Sir John Keane was again elected chairman.[119] The ITGWU was not idle either. Conscious of the trend of wage reductions, it prepared for battle and was mandated by its members to seek a county-wide renewal of the 1922 wage rates when that agreement expired on 14 May 1923. On that day both sides met at the Granville Hotel. Keane tabled the farmers' final offer: 30s. per week for a six-day week (a reduction of 8s.) and the abolition of all bonuses. He admitted: 'It is not a generous wage but it is as much as the industry can stand'. Unsurprisingly, the workers rejected the offer. A strike began on 19 May.[120] Both sides expected a tough battle but it was doubtful they realized just how long and bitter the dispute would be.

As soon as the strike was declared, well prepared picketing plans were implemented as 1,500 labourers in the east of the county struck. As had been previously agreed, labourers in the west stayed in their jobs. An appeal from the ITGWU to other workers for solidarity met an immediate and gratifying response. Dockers, railwaymen, carters, creamery workers, shop assistants and factory workers all refused to handle the farmers' produce. On the very first day of the dispute the strikers scored a notable victory. A consignment of butter arrived at the city docks to be loaded on the Fishguard boat. The dockers refused to handle it and other labourers were called in to load it. They did so under the protection of a strong military presence which kept a hostile crowd at bay with fixed bayonets. When the butter was finally loaded the ship's crew refused to sail the vessel while the blacked cargo was in the hold. In exasperation and conscious of his timetable, the ship's captain ordered the butter to be unloaded and steamed away leaving it on the quayside. The cross-channel shipping companies – the Clyde Shipping Company and the Great Western Shipping Company – subsequently announced that they would not accept such consignments for the foreseeable future. It was first blood to the strikers.[121]

In countering the solidarity of the workers the farmers were able to rely on government support in the shape of the National army. From the beginning, the workers used pickets to block the roads to prevent movement of goods to and from farms. The farmers appealed to the local military to keep the roads open and within days were provided with military escorts to move their goods. This led to a significant escalation of the dispute. On 29 May the *Munster Express* reported:

> A convoy of carts went into Hall's stores, Hannover St., (Waterford) to obtain grain. Almost every second cart was guarded by a soldier with a rifle. At Hall's, the storemen walked out and have since been locked out. Farmers acted as their own porters. Guards kept the large crowd in check. On returning, the convoy was ambushed at the Sweep by rifle and revolver fire from a distance. Some sacks were holed. The military returned fire and gave chase: the officer in command being slightly wounded.[122]

Alarmed by this, Paul appealed for reinforcements. On 1 June 250 troops arrived by special train, members of the Special Infantry Corps raised specifically to suppress whatever the government deemed to be 'common criminality' and under the command of Colonel Patrick Dalton, a native of Waterford.[123] More arrived the following week until the 6th and 11th Battalions of the Corps, each with a strength of over 300, were deployed in small detachments from the city to Dungarvan. These troops proved decisive in breaking the strike. Their reports paint a picture of very active patrols, enforcement of a curfew and arrests.[124] The approach taken by the soldiers can be gauged from an undated wireless message sent by Dalton to the O/C 11th Battalion: 'Clean up this area at once. Use your own discretion re. action to be taken. Use no half measures. Make an example of the place.'[125]

The striking labourers responded in kind. Acts of arson, intimidation and physical assault were commonplace. Goods were seized, where possible, and destroyed. Cattle and other livestock were stolen and sometimes killed. Occasional sniping attacks on military escorts added to the sense of tension and siege. Although union officials routinely condemned the violence, groups of picketers continued to take the law into their own hands. Any attempt to move farm produce to the factories and mills was met by mass picketing. Two nights of rioting on Ballybricken followed an attempt to move pigs to Denny's bacon factory.[126] When baton-charging gardaí failed to disperse the picketers, troops with fixed bayonets were used. A curfew was introduced and anybody caught without a pass was liable to arrest. The ordinary courts were dispensed with and courts-martial used to hand out summary convictions. Ballybricken Jail could not cope and a temporary prison camp was established in the grounds of the courthouse. Nine labourers were arrested in Fenor when a search of a cottage by the troops uncovered a shotgun. The men were tried, convicted and detained in the temporary prison. A report from Paul in October revealed that over an eight-month period 371 men had been arrested and detained, 173 for agrarian offences.[127]

The WFA did not rely on government efforts alone to break the strike. They chartered a ship, *The Lady Belle*, to bring supplies for strikebound farmers into Dungarvan. The dockers refused to unload the ship but traders and farmers did the task themselves. A general strike in Dungarvan in support of the dockers was short-lived.[128] More and more farmers and traders were joining together to ensure that essential supplies got through and key services were maintained. Other farmers favoured direct action. Unity among the farmers was maintained ruthlessly. According to the WFA, there was 'no wavering and none would be allowed'.[129] Union sources claimed that farmers who had reached local agreement with their labourers were intimidated into repudiating the agreements after their property was damaged by reprisals. When James Baird, a local union organizer, declared that the farmers did not own the land but that it belonged to all the descendants of the dispossessed Irish, he unleashed a torrent of condemnation of 'Bolshevism' from every pulpit.[130] The *Munster Express* reported that 'many farmers, who had at the beginning of the dispute signed out, have now abjured these agreements'.[131] The labourers themselves were often attacked and beaten by groups of masked men. According to Emmet O'Connor:

> A group of vigilantes, styling themselves the 'White Guards' initiated a systematic campaign of terror against labourers and branch secretaries. During the second week of September union activists had their cottages raided and burned by masked and armed men. Throughout the month, car-loads of vigilantes toured the countrywide, waylaying strikers and pistol whipping them.[132]

In the autumn the violence and bitterness of the strike showed no signs of abating. More and more workers in farming-based factories and services were laid off. In November Keane assured his members that even if the dispute was to continue into 1924 they could draw financial support from an all-Ireland strike fund.[133] On the other hand, the labour leaders spoke of a fight to the finish and a resort to occupation of factories. Several attempts at mediation, including one in October by the minister for agriculture on behalf of the ITGWU, were rejected by the farmers. The WFA now saw an opportunity to smash the union and to return to the pre-1917 relationship between farmer and labourer. They declared that they would not deal with the ITGWU but that each farmer would talk directly to his own labourers. Behind the rhetoric, the strike leaders were becoming desperate as they considered their options: direct action would be crushed by the military and a general strike would not have the support of their union. The strike was now costing the ITGWU over £1,500 per week, an outlay it could ill afford. William O'Brien, president of the ITGWU, travelled to Waterford and met the strike committee. He told them that the union could not fund the strike and that strike pay would cease immediately.[134] The announcement that even the meagre strike pay was to be stopped was a bombshell. Facing starvation the workers had no option but to end the strike on 8 December 1923. Local leaders tried to put a brave face on it and issued a statement: 'In order to save the organisation locally, it was decided that all should return to work forthwith and await a favourable opportunity to recover lost ground.'[135] But there was no question of every man returning to work. Individuals were taken back as and when the farmer decided and on the pay and conditions dictated by the farmer. The most militant did not get their jobs back and either migrated elsewhere or emigrated to Britain or America. Organizationally, the ITGWU collapsed and all but disappeared. It would be many years before there would even be an attempt to restart a local branch network outside of Waterford city. The WFA had won a decisive victory.[136]

It had been a terrible period for Waterford city and county. Death and destruction had scarred both people and infrastructure. Workers and republicans alike had been defeated. These losses had left both groups disillusioned and with uncertain futures as 1923 drew to a close. National army intelligence reports from Waterford for May and June contained dire warnings of republicans and strikers combining their efforts: 'The irregular element in Waterford is ingratiating itself with labour and has succeeded in working up the labour organisations against the Government.'[137] The general weekly summary struck an alarmist note in June 1923:

> The policy of the strikers lends itself particularly to the Irregulars, who, having for the most part, dumped their arms, and being of the labouring community themselves, are only too willing to carry out any operations which may suggest themselves. As a result of the Irregular support, the labourers in general have come to adopt an attitude of opposition to the Government, but on the other hand, the Farmers' organisation is now wholeheartedly in support of the Government and Army.[138]

Despite such warnings there was no evidence of any structured involvement by the republicans in the farm labourers' strike or in other labour disputes. The IRA fought their military struggle mostly in the west of the county; the workers fought their battles mostly in the city and in east Waterford. The dream of militant socialist republicanism remained just that – a dream. Neither the end of the Civil War nor the end of the farm labourers' strike was greeted with any enthusiasm in Waterford. Rather, the dominant emotions were weariness and relief with a widespread desire to look forward to the future. But what were the challenges and opportunities confronting Waterford and the IFS in 1923? After a decade of political, social and military conflict, how would the people of Waterford respond to the challenges of healing the wounds of war and building a new state?

9 'Ireland shall get her freedom and you still break stone':[1] Waterford in 1923

On 18 June 1924, eleven years after the opening of Redmond Bridge, another bridge opened in Waterford, or more accurately, reopened. On that day the Cork to Rosslare express travelled over the rebuilt Ballyvoile viaduct, the first train to do so in two years. In contrast to the opening of Redmond Bridge, this was a low-key event. There was no fanfare, speeches or public ceremonial. But, in its own way, the reopening of Ballyvoile viaduct had huge significance as it marked the completion of the rebuilding of the infrastructure in Waterford city and county and thus the elimination of the physical scars of the revolution. The emotional and political scars would take far longer to heal. On the same day Captain Redmond spoke in the Dáil on a motion concerning the Boundary Commission. Although he made no reference to the Ballyvoile viaduct or to the reopening of the line, he was no doubt conscious of his father's role eleven years before when Ireland's future was firmly focused on securing a home rule parliament. After a decade of revolution that had convulsed the country, the political future of the twenty-six county IFS dominion was now firmly in the hands of Redmond and his colleagues in a parliament that had far greater powers than had ever been envisaged under home rule. But this came at the high price of a fractured society, a limited largely agrarian economy and the physical destruction of war. All presented significant challenges for the Irish people. For some it was the challenge arising from victory, of building the new state; for others it was the crushing aftermath of defeat; for all it necessitated coming to terms with new realities. For the people of Waterford – republicans, government supporters, workers, and southern unionists – the events of 1923 defined political life in the county for a generation.

Under the IFS constitution the government was obliged to call an election before the end of the year. Cosgrave and his colleagues, anxious to capitalize on their victory in the Civil War, favoured an early contest and a general election was set for 27 August 1923. The number of Dáil seats was increased from 128 to 153 and the constituencies revised. Waterford city and county formed one four-seat constituency. In many ways this was the first relatively normal election since 1910 with every constituency contested by a variety of parties and candidates. The government contested the election under the banner of their newly formed party, Cumann na nGaedheal. Though confident of victory, the campaign was lacklustre and uninspiring. The new party did not have sufficient time to create a branch network throughout the country.[2] There was not a single functioning branch of Cumann na nGaedheal in

Waterford. Instead the government relied on a combination of pro-Treaty SF
branches and individual activists. Cumann na nGaedheal nominated Dr
Vincent White and Michael Brennock from Dungarvan. A week before
polling, the *Munster Express* doubted the prospects of the government candidates because under the panel arrangement at the previous election 'a number
of farmers and labourers gave their second preferences to the pro-Treaty candidates and the Unionist vote, perhaps one thousand-strong, was cast solidly
on the pro-Treaty side. Other candidates now appeal to this element.'[3]

The foremost candidate appealing to pro-Treaty voters and supporters of
Cumann na nGaedheal candidates was Captain William Redmond, who re-
entered the electoral scene after an absence of two years. He knew that he had
a solid electoral base in his heartland of Ballybricken and that he could rely
on the support of former UIL stalwarts and on the large number of ex-servicemen, approximately 2,000, in the constituency. Judging by contemporary
newspaper accounts, his campaign was the best organized and the most
enthusiastically supported. At well-attended public meetings from Lismore to
Waterford city, he reminded his audience of his father's long service to the
country, of the Parnellite tradition that he embodied, and of the need for representation not riven by factionalism. Redmond's campaign culminated in an
eve-of-poll meeting on the Mall, one of the largest ever held in the city.
Emphasizing his political pedigree, Redmond stated that he belonged to no
party but stood on his own feet, and would represent all his constituents
impartially.[4] The meeting ended with a parade to Ballybricken stopping at the
ex-servicemen's club on Mayor's Walk for further speeches.

For republicans, both nationally and locally, it was a very difficult election
campaign. The ceasefire order did not bring a cessation or even a reduction of
activity by the security forces as relentless sweeps and searches for the few
activists still at large continued. There was no immediate decrease in the size
of the National army and the Garda Síochána expanded its presence into every
village. There was little overt opposition to the new police force and its presence was generally welcomed. Some IRA men remained on the run.[5] Some
attempted to return home but many were arrested and interned.[6] More than
10,000 potential republican election workers or candidates were in prison. In
addition, the SF party was without funds and its remaining branch network
was under constant harassment by Gardaí and the National army as meetings
were broken up and canvassers were arrested.[7] SF's abstentionist policy and the
widespread destruction caused by the Civil War did little to win popular support. To counter these difficulties republicans relied on the emotive appeal of
a thirty-two county state and the sacrifice of those who had died for it. In the
Waterford constituency, SF put forward a formidable candidate – Cathal
Brugha's widow, Caitlín. She campaigned strongly throughout the constituency,
portraying herself as a reluctant candidate but one determined to guard the

republican spirit of her dead husband. On 9 August de Valera, who was in hiding, issued a ringing endorsement: 'In selecting Caitlín as her special champion, Waterford made a choice for which she will be honoured forever.'[8]

For the workers and farmers the election campaign was greatly complicated and highly charged by the strike actions. Although the gas workers strike ended four days before the election, the farm labourers' strike, which continued until December, was at its peak. Nationally and locally Labour entered the electoral fray in a confident mood. 'It is certain', the *Voice of Labour* proclaimed in an eve of poll headline, 'that the Labour Party in the new Dáil will be considerably stronger.'[9] One of the outgoing Waterford deputies, Nicholas Phelan, had been expelled from the party for failing to attend the Dáil and his place on the ticket was taken by James Baird. Both he and John Butler, the other sitting deputy, were union officials who were prominently involved in the farm labourers' strike. The Farmers' Party also viewed the election as a dimension of the strike. The *Munster Express* deemed the party 'particularly well organized, very active and financially strong.'[10] It nominated Nicholas Wall and Garret Flavin.

The election campaign between supporters and opponents of the Treaty was marked by violence, intemperate speeches and the disruption of meetings. When Richard Mulcahy, minister for defence and a native of the city, attempted to address a meeting on the Mall on 14 August, the Gardaí had to separate the fighting groups, baton-charge protesters and arrest many before Mulcahy could be heard. Republicans claimed that at their meeting the police wantonly baton-charged their supporters. SF used every occasion to remind the electorate about those who died during the Civil War. On 11 August a large procession was organized to mark the first anniversary of the deaths of John 'Bonny' Doyle and Jack Edwards. In her graveside oration in Ballygunner, Caitlín Brugha reminded those present of why the two men had died and urged that the republican struggle must go on.[11]

The parallel electoral battle between the workers and the farmers was equally bitter and violent. The Waterford correspondent of the *Times* noted that Waterford was unlike any other constituency because of the class struggle that underpinned the election. He reported a typical Labour speech in Tramore where the speaker, after reminding his audience that they had neither clothes, capital nor comforts, drew a box of matches from his pocket and said 'but we have these'. This was, the correspondent believed, 'an incendiary remark with a vengeance'.[12] He also reported a comment by Baird to the effect that no Irish farmer 'great or small had any right or title to the land he held other than acts of the English Parliament', which the correspondent suggested 'could only be construed in one way by landless men!'[13] In response, the farmers' candidates repeatedly denounced 'Bolshevism, land-grabbing and foreign doctrines', while claiming to be the true friends of the honest worker.[14] In marked contrast to the campaigns of other candidates, Redmond's was free of violence and the press commented on the orderliness and peaceful nature of his meetings – a far cry from his two campaigns in 1918.[15]

Polling took place on Monday 27 August. The turnout of over 70 per cent was similar to the rest of the country. The *Munster Express* reported that from 'the time the polling booths opened at nine o'clock there was a great rush of voters, so much so that long queues of people patiently waited their turn to record their votes.'[16] Harassment of republicans continued on polling day with arrests at polling stations and detention until the following day. After close of polling the ballot boxes were collected by military personnel and brought to the city on Tuesday. Counting started on Wednesday morning.

The election was a triumph for the republicans. Despite all the obstacles, Caitlín Brugha headed the poll and was elected on the first count.[17] This success showed clearly that, despite a crushing defeat in the Civil War, there was still a strong republican sentiment in the constituency. Conversely, the election was a disaster for Cumann na nGaedheal which failed to win a seat in the Waterford constituency. Although the government could derive some comfort from the fact that three-quarters of the electorate supported pro-Treaty candidates, the result was an electoral humiliation. The return of Captain Redmond was no surprise and there can be little doubt that had he stood in the 1922 election he would also have won a seat. With the exception of the Redmond factor, the pattern of voting in Waterford mirrored the national trend. Cumann na nGaedheal received 39 per cent of the national vote but this was its electoral high point. Thereafter, its share of the vote declined until it lost power to Fianna Fáil in 1932.[18] The farmers' vote declined marginally but Nicholas Wall retained a seat for the Farmers' Party. After the farmers won their industrial war with the farm labourers, they disappeared as an electoral force and transferred their votes to one of the other parties. Labour's share of the vote collapsed dramatically; it had almost halved since 1922. Although it had performed a responsible and constructive role as the opposition in the Dáil in 1922–3, this was of little import to working-class voters trying to cope with wage reductions or locked in bitter strikes. Indeed, the strikes convinced many voters who had supported Labour as the party of peace in 1922 to switch allegiance to Cumann na nGaedheal or Captain Redmond.[19] Baird, the more militant of the two Labour candidates, won more first preferences but John Butler attracted more transfers and won the last seat. The election result set the electoral pattern in the Waterford constituency for decades. Republican candidates (whether as SF or later as Fianna Fáil) were assured of at least one Dáil seat and often two; they also dominated local politics in the county. The city and east Waterford returned to the Redmond fold and returned a Redmond to the Dáil until the death of Captain Redmond's widow in 1952.[20] In 1933 Cumann na nGaedheal absorbed the Redmondite organization and only then did it become a real electoral force in Waterford.

For the Labour Party the events of 1923 proved traumatic. The defeat of the workers in the gasworks in August and the collapse of the farm labourers' strikes in December had a devastating impact on the individuals involved, on their families and on the wider labour movement. Those fortunate enough to be re-employed were compelled to work longer hours for less pay and were burdened with debts incurred trying to feed their families during the lengthy disputes.[21] Many had no option but to emigrate to England or the US and did not return. Workers who had not been involved in labour disputes also experienced pay reductions. Wages in agriculture-related industries followed those of the farm labourers and shrank by as much as 10s. a week, a reduction of 25 per cent. The building trades followed suit as did the county council. Local authority labourers were a benchmark for unskilled labour in the country. Acutely aware of this, on 27 November 1923 the minister for local government directed local authorities to reduce labourers' wages in line with the pay scales in their districts. Waterford County Council duly cut the weekly pay of its 400 road labourers from 45s. to 36s.[22] Thereafter, wages for all workers remained static or declined slightly. The hard-won gains of the war years and the post-war boom had been lost.[23] The defeat of the ITGWU in the farm labourers' dispute marked the end of the union in rural Waterford. Branch after branch closed. In 1924 the Dungarvan branch was the only one still in existence outside Waterford city; in 1926 it too folded.[24] Without the income from the members' dues, the union could not support its full-time officials and a cycle of decline in trade unionism in Waterford set in. The Waterford city branch continued to organize labourers, transport employees and other general workers but by 1925 annual remittances to head office had fallen to £417, less than half the 1922 figure.[25] This decline was not reversed until the industrialization drive of the 1930s. Notably, the revival was without the syndicalist and class-driven ideology of the revolutionary decade. There were no further instances of red flags flying over seized buildings or the declaration of soviets.[26] The ITGWU branch network was the lifeblood of the Labour Party in Waterford and contributed significantly to the party's success in 1922.[27] Its collapse in 1923–4 was a disaster for the party and resulted in decades spent in the political doldrums. The Labour Party lost its sole Waterford seat in 1927 and did not regain it until 1948.

The unionist community in Waterford and in the IFS generally suffered major population loss in the period between the censuses of 1911 and 1926. In the twenty-six counties, the non-Catholic population declined by 33% compared to a decline of just over 2% for Catholics.[28] The respective decline in Waterford was 40%.[29] Allowing for the withdrawal of British army personnel and First World War deaths, it is estimated that nationally about 20%

of the non-Catholic population left the IFS for economic or voluntary reasons.[30] In Waterford this figure was 28%.[31] These rates are similar to those
for the surrounding counties of Wexford, Kilkenny, Tipperary and Cork.[32] A
sense of apprehension about the transition to national independence in 1922
and the anarchy that characterized that change contributed to this exodus as
did the emerging Gaelic, Catholic and nationalist ethos of the new state. The
sentiment of C.P. Crane, a Tipperary resident magistrate, would have been
echoed by many: 'I had been brought up under the union jack and had no
desire to live under any other emblem.'[33] Reflecting on the departure of some
her landed neighbours, Emily Ussher believed that 'every empty house has
left the country less able to pay its way and stands desolate in its own little
puddle of unemployment'.[34]

Those who remained in Waterford adapted quickly to the changed circumstances despite Goff-Davis's observation that 'Protestants continued to be
the upper class but they no longer had political power. They remained the
same but everything around them changed.'[35] She did, however, remark that
many thought of themselves as Irish.[36] In stark contrast to other counties, all
of the big houses destroyed in Waterford during the Civil War were rebuilt.
Some Protestants embraced the opportunities presented by the new state and
followed the exhortations of the editor of the *Waterford Standard*, at the time
of the Treaty: 'There is much that we can contribute to the building up of
the new Ireland. We will give it in full measure.'[37] Several of the landed aristocracy and gentry participated in the running of the nascent state. Led by
Sir John Keane's active role in the Senate, this group included the Strangman
and Jacob families, Captain William Goff-Davis and Beverley Ussher. All
played a leading role in developing the state and its institutions at a national
and local level.

For the 12,000 interned republicans neither the ceasefire nor the general
election hastened their release. The government insisted that releases would
only follow a signed promise not to take up arms again. Few republicans
signed and there was only a trickle of releases. In desperation, prisoners
turned to one of the traditional weapons of republican prison protest – the
hunger strike. A protest in Mountjoy against prison conditions began on 13
October and spread rapidly to other prisons and internment camps. By the
end of the month it was claimed that 8,000 prisoners were refusing food.[38]
Outside the prisons their supporters tried to rally support. In Dungarvan and
Waterford city posters appeared listing those from the area on hunger strike.[39]
From the beginning, however, the hunger strike had no clearly defined purpose and rapidly disintegrated when the resolve of the weak was broken. After
three weeks some protestors took food and were soon followed by hundreds
of others.[40] On 23 November the hunger strike was called off but not before
Denis Barry and Andy O'Sullivan of Cork died.[41] By holding firm the gov-

ernment had won a notable victory. Internees began to sign the declaration and a steady stream of releases followed. Moses Roche was one of the last to be released in April 1924.[42] Thereafter, only those convicted on specific charges were detained.

Some republicans continued to be the subject of intensive police enquiries. On 6 February 1924 three men from Passage East were arrested and charged in connection with the killing of John Ivory in January 1923.[43] A week later three others, who were still interned, were also charged with the same offence.[44] The only evidence presented in court was that they were known republicans and had been seen near the scene on the night of the murder. On 12 April their trial collapsed due to lack of evidence and they were released to a jubilant crowd of supporters gathered outside the city courthouse.[45] Thomas Tobin, a recently released prisoner, and Dermot O'Mahony, who was still an internee, were charged in January 1924 with the killing of Cissie Ryan, during the attack on Lieutenant Spain. The state's case against both men was much stronger in this instance and included eye-witness identification by Spain and a fellow soldier, Corporal Mulcahy. The trial eventually opened in the Central Criminal Court in Dublin on 2 July. The accused pleaded not guilty. The case against O'Mahony was dismissed but Tobin was found guilty and sentenced to penal servitude.[46] He was released the following year. Thus, whether in prison, on the run or in exile, 1923 marked a low point for Waterford republicans. Tired and disillusioned, it must have seemed that the effort of the previous ten years had been in vain. Unable to find work and with their opponents seemingly entrenched in power, many of them emigrated.[47] Among them was Michael Shalloe who recalled: 'We decided that there nothing for us but to quit our native land'.[48] Some returned in the 1930s when a Fianna Fáil government created a more congenial atmosphere but many never came back.

The economic policy of the IFS was best summed up by Patrick Hogan, minister for agriculture, who stated that 'national development is practically synonymous with agricultural development'.[49] The government had the power to formulate a new economic direction but instead espoused a conservative policy of low taxation and free trade based on Ireland's comparative advantage in pastoral agriculture. There would be no 'New deal', 'Great leap forward' or five-year plans. Instead Ireland would continue its traditional role as a supplier of butter, bacon and beef to the British market. But even here there were obstacles to overcome. As James Meenan commented, 'the windfall of a near-monopoly of the British market' during the war was an opportunity to establish the reputation of Irish produce. This was not taken and 'when the war was over and supplies from Denmark and overseas were again available, the British consumer had only too clear a memory of bad eggs and worse butter from Ireland'.[50] With an economy heavily dependent on agriculture and agri-

cultural products, Waterford city and county was a microcosm of the country
as a whole. When agriculture enjoyed a modest upturn in the aftermath of the
Civil War the Waterford dairy industry benefitted from the establishment of
new co-operatives. The new Dungarvan Co-operative Creamery, unusually for
the time, manufactured milk powder and cheese as well as butter.[51] Unlike the
farmers, agricultural labourers did not benefit. Their numbers declined amid
deteriorating wages and conditions. The bacon–curing factories of the city also
enjoyed a degree of prosperity as they regained market-share in Britain but the
reduced wages of the workers meant that this was not shared equally. In
Waterford, as in the rest of the country, the response to Hogan's slogan of
'one more cow, one more sow and one more acre under the plough' was dis-
appointing and did not provide any basis for sustained economic development.
Furthermore, the focus on agriculture in the IFS made it difficult to stimu-
late the small domestic manufacturing sector since most available government
funds were used to provide credit for agriculture and related industries. As a
result no new factories opened in Waterford in the post-revolutionary years.[52]
In this Waterford differed little from the rest of the country. Despite traditional SF rhetoric very few protective tariffs were introduced which might
have allowed local industries to develop.[53] In 1923 it was hoped that the creation of a ministry of fisheries would herald a period of investment in the fishing industry. Such hopes proved illusory as external market difficulties and a
lack of investment ensured that there was little development of the industry in
Waterford or in other coastal counties.[54] That other staple of the Irish economy, the building trade, had an even briefer revival. The need to repair the
city and county's infrastructure in the wake of the Civil War resulted in a
small but significant injection of capital. Road and rail bridges had to be
repaired and burnt buildings reconstructed. The rebuilding of the infantry barracks in the city gave some employment but this was completed in January
1924. During the general election in 1923, W.T. Cosgrave promised a major
programme of public housing but the results were very modest. Three
schemes, totalling just forty-six houses, were built in Waterford city in 1923
at a cost of £30,276.[55] Thereafter, investment in public housing ceased until
the 1930s despite an acute housing shortage. The *Waterford News* made the
remarkable observation that between the 1891 and 1911 censuses the number
of houses decreased by fifty-eight to 4,791, notwithstanding an increase in the
city's population of 1,261 persons over the same period.[56]

   The absence of a programme of investment and development meant that
poverty and unemployment were not tackled with the inevitable consequence
that emigration, which had virtually ceased during the First World War and
the immediate post-war years due to the economic boom, resumed in 1923.
The first meeting of Waterford Corporation in 1924 noted the growing
number of unemployed in the city and the distress and poverty evident in

many areas.[57] The demobilization of the National army after the Civil War added to the number of people out of work. The 1926 census, the first since 1911, showed that the population of County Waterford fell by 6.4 per cent between 1911 and 1926, slightly above the national figure of 5.5 per cent but very similar to the figures for surrounding counties. While the population of the main urban centres – Waterford city and Dungarvan – dropped only marginally, the population of rural Waterford fell by 10 per cent.[58] Most of this decline occurred between 1923 and 1926 with the recession in agriculture and the drop in the need for farm labourers. With no growth in industry in the urban centres to absorb the surplus labour, as in previous generations, the emigrant ship remained the only resort.

Cultural life in Waterford might have been expected to have changed profoundly as a result of the revolution and the policies of the IFS government in respect of the Irish language. There is no evidence of any such cultural shift. The voluntary enthusiasm for Irish as an expression of nationality that had infused the Gaelic League suffered in the disillusion of the post-Civil War years. Nationally, the number of branches fell from 819 in 1922 to just 139 in 1924; in Waterford only one branch affiliated to the League in 1924.[59] Butler described the apathy and disillusion that permeated the Gaelic League in Waterford and the struggle to keep that single branch alive.[60] The story was similar across the country.[61] Although Irish was proclaimed as the national language in the IFS constitution, this was largely aspirational. Both nationally and in Waterford the number of Irish speakers continued to decline. In Waterford county the proportion of Irish speakers declined by almost one-third from 38 per cent in 1911 to 26 per cent in 1926.[62] The 1926 report of the Gaeltacht Commission classified most of the county as either 'Fíor-Gaeltacht' (where Irish was the normal everyday language of all generations) or 'Breac-Gaeltacht' (where English was the everyday language but with a significant number of Irish speakers in the population). However, these boundaries were 'benevolently inflated' and when the Gaeltacht boundaries were revised in 1956 only the tiny enclave of Ring and Old Parish was classified as a Gaeltacht.[63] The failure of the new state to promote the language imaginatively could not be blamed on the normal excuses – partition, the British government and the Civil War. What could have been a noble venture became instead a sorry tale of dismal failure.[64]

While there is broad agreement that the changes wrought in Ireland during the period 1912–23 were revolutionary, equally there is a consensus that these changes affected different parts of the country to varying extents. Every county was different. Several key questions need to be explored in the context of the Irish Revolution and how it affected Waterford. What level of support was there in Waterford for the revolution and how does this support compare with the neighbouring counties of Wexford, Kilkenny, Tipperary and Cork? What changed during the revolution? Who benefitted from this change? How did the Waterford of 1912 differ from that of 1923? Support for the revolution and the attendant levels of violence have been analysed by a number of commentators.[65] Within that comparative context a clear pattern emerged. Support for SF in Waterford county, as expressed in electoral support and financial contributions, was on a par with its neighbouring counties. Waterford city was different. More than half of the electorate opted to support Captain Redmond; this made Waterford unique in southern Ireland. SF failed to win the political battle there and this undoubtedly affected the level of revolutionary violence in east Waterford. Revolutionary violence, measured in terms of its victims meaning those killed by bullets or bombs, when normalized for population shows a clear trend: Waterford was twice as violent as Wexford or Kilkenny but only half as violent as Tipperary and about one third as violent as Cork.[66] When comparing east and west Waterford one finds that in the latter there was a strong, active IRA presence, whereas people in the east played little part in revolutionary activity. In the city and its hinterland there was a much greater focus on labour and the struggle for a socialist future.

The most marked change to have occurred between 1912 and 1923 was at a political level. In 1912 the IPP had a virtual monopoly of power in Ireland at both parliamentary and local levels. Within six years that monopoly had been broken by SF. In turn its monopoly of power collapsed amid the bitter divisions of the Civil War. From the ruins of that conflict a new political élite emerged as the victors formed Cumann na nGaedheal: conservative, reactionary and dedicated to upholding the Anglo-Irish Treaty.[67] The losers ultimately formed Fianna Fáil – conservative, socially more progressive than its opponents and dedicated to dismantling the same treaty. For many years and through many elections arguments over the Treaty replaced normal political debate. Waterford county became a Fianna Fáil stronghold while Cumann na nGaedheal prospered in the city after it absorbed Captain Redmond and his supporters. Though some IPP stalwarts such as Redmond or the Esmonde family in Wexford played a part in the politics of the new state, power had passed irrevocably from their hands. Members of that other pillar of the old establishment, the landed gentry, continued to live in their mansions surrounded by the demesne lands. As a member of the IFS Senate, Sir John Keane took an active part and spoke strongly in favour of free speech and freedom of assembly but opposed the Shannon hydroelectric scheme as a step towards nationalization. Keane represented his class well and remained a senator until 1943, being nominated successively by Cosgrave and de Valera.[68] In business the dominance of the merchant class in the city, most of whom were members of the Church of Ireland or Quaker communities, continued. The farmers emerged from the decade, their lands and property intact, and continued to provide the same produce for the same markets. After 1923 Labour, both nationally and in Waterford, was marginalized for almost two decades.[69] The defeat of the workers in their various disputes was reflected in the collapse of the trade union and Labour Party organizations in Waterford. Both workers and republicans had seen their hopes dashed. The workers had lost all the gains made during the First World War and the immediate-post war boom. Unemployment was increasing again and once more the emigrant ship beckoned. For republicans the euphoria that greeted the truce had given way to the disappointment of the Treaty and the bitterness of Civil War defeat.

Families of all classes and creeds mourned the loss of fathers, sons and brothers killed between 1912 and 1923, the majority of them in the service of the British army on overseas campaigns. Old comrades associations in Waterford remained strong and vibrant, especially in the city, for many years afterwards. Those who died during the War of Independence or on the republican side during the Civil War were commemorated annually and roadside memorials were erected to their memory. Only the National army soldiers who gave their lives for the new state were forgotten.

A decade of revolution had occasioned much bloodshed and change in Waterford; nonetheless many aspects of life remained the same. The economic structure of the city and county had not changed to any great extent between 1912 and 1923. Farmers and their interests still dominated while the urban poor eked out their existence. Several of the landed aristocracy and gentry such as Sir John Keane participated in the political and economic life of the IFS. Although a Redmond still represented Waterford politically, Captain William was a minority voice, whereas his father, John, had been leader of a powerful national political party. But Captain Redmond sat in a parliament in Dublin which had significant powers and the freedom to progress eventually to an independent republic. By any standards the Irish revolution was a conservative one. The ruling political class had changed and a new state had emerged, one that was a compromise between the home rule aspirations of the IPP and the thirty-two county republic of SF. The revolution had both winners and losers and the failure to make social progress marked out the losers. In his Lenten pastoral of 1924 Dr Hackett, Catholic bishop of Waterford and Lismore, suggested that

> Everyone who loves Ireland must rejoice at the happy change which has taken place during the past months. By degrees conditions have become normal. The observance of the Divine Law has become more evident, social order has been again established. Thank God the outlook is not gloomy. The hope that our country has a happy and prosperous future, that our children may once more merit the esteem and respect of nations seems well founded.[70]

In the bishop's eyes the restoration of the social order was a victory but for others it was a defeat. In August 1923 Liam Curham, vice-president of Waterford Workers' Council, told an election rally:

> They were told that the day that the Free State Treaty was signed that they had obtained the greatest Magna Carta the world had ever seen. Well now they, the workers, had no work and they could lie out in the fields or stand on the quay and look up at the flag on Reginald's Tower and say 'Now we are Free'. Free to go home and starve with their wives and children.[71]

While at least there was now the possibility of political, economic and social progress for all the people of Waterford, his members were still breaking stones.

Notes

CHAPTER ONE *'The coming prosperity': Waterford in 1912*

1 Taken from a speech by John Redmond on 10 Feb. 1913.
2 *Waterford News (WN)*, 12 Feb. 1913; *Munster Express (ME)*, 12 Feb. 1913; *Irish Independent (II)*, 11 Feb. 1913.
3 *WN*, 12 Feb. 1913; *ME*, 12 Feb. 1913.
4 W.E. Vaughan & A.J. Fitzpatrick (eds), *Irish historical statistics: population, 1821–1971* (Dublin, 1978), p. 10.
5 Ibid., pp 310–11; David Fitzpatrick, 'Emigration, 1871–1921' in W.E. Vaughan (ed.), *A new history of Ireland; vi, Ireland under the Union, II, 1870–1921* (Oxford, 1996), pp 612–14.
6 Vaughan & Fitzpatrick, *Population*, pp 34–5.
7 Ibid., p. 35.   8 Ibid., p. 67.
9 Ibid., p. 66.
10 Bernard Canning, *Bishops of Ireland, 1870–1987* (Donegal, 1987), p. 303; Patrick Power, *A compendious history of the United Dioceses of Waterford and Lismore* (Cork, 1937), p. 40.
11 John M. Hearne, *Waterford Central Technical Institute, 1906–2006: a history* (Waterford, 2006), pp 6–7.
12 *Irish Catholic Directory 1912*, pp 247–51.
13 *ME*, 6 Feb. 1913.   14 Power, *Compendious history*, p. 41.
15 Canning, *Bishops*, p. 68.
16 Diary entry May 1902 (Waterford City Library (WCL), Robert Dobbyn diaries).
17 Henry Stewart O'Hara, 'Address to synod of Waterford and Lismore, 27 June 1913', *Church of Ireland Gazette*, 2 July 1913.
18 *Church of Ireland Gazette*, 16 Jan. 1914.
19 R.B. McDowell, *The Church of Ireland, 1869–1969* (London, 1975), p. 73.
20 Henry D. Gribbon, 'Economic and social history 1850–1921' in Vaughan (ed.), *A new history, vi*, pp 260–356; Liam Kennedy, 'Traders in the Irish rural economy, 1880–1914', *Economic History Review*, 32:2 (May 1979), 201–10.
21 Peter Solar, 'The agricultural trade of the port of Waterford 1809–1909' in William Nolan and Thomas P. Power (eds), *Waterford: history and society: interdisciplinary essays on the history of an Irish county* (Dublin, 1992), pp 495–518.
22 Andy Bielenberg, *Ireland and the industrial revolution: the impact of the industrial revolution on Irish industry, 1801–1922* (London, 2009), pp 55, 75, 81.
23 Proinnsias Breathnach, 'The development of the dairy industry in County Waterford' in Nolan & Power (eds), *Waterford*, pp 707–11.
24 Sylvester Ó Muirí, 'The commercial development of fishing in Waterford' in Criostóir Mac Cárthaigh and Dónal MacPolin (eds), *Traditional boats of Ireland: history, folklore and construction* (Cork, 2008), pp 365–7.
25 County Inspector (CI) Waterford, Apr. 1913 (TNA, CO 904/89).
26 Rosamond Jacob diaries (NLI, Jacob papers, MS 32,582); Emily Ussher, 'True story of a revolution', n.d. (TCD, Ussher papers, MS 9,269), Anita Goff-Davis, *Walled gardens* (London, 1991), pp 14–20.
27 Thomas Fewer, *Waterford people: a biographical dictionary* (Waterford, 1998), pp 60–1.
28 Census of Ireland 1911, County of Waterford [Cd 6050], vol. vi, pp 72–6.
29 Local Government Board of Ireland, *Report on the sanitary circumstances and administration of Waterford County Borough, 1910–11*, pp 407–33.

30 Francis Devine (ed.), *A capital in conflict: Dublin city and the 1913 lockout* (Dublin, 2013), pp 145–6.
31 Seán O'Faoláin, *Bird alone* (Oxford, 1985), pp 297–8.
32 Census of Ireland 1911, Agricultural statistics of Ireland with detailed report for the year 1910, HC 1911 [C.5964]; Province of Munster [Cd 6050], vol. vi; Province of Leinster [Cd 6050], vol. xi.
33 E. Rumpf and A.C. Hepburn, *Nationalism and socialism in twentieth-century Ireland* (Liverpool, 1977), p. 54.
34 Census of Ireland, 1911, Province of Munster county and city of Waterford [Cd. 6050], vol. v, pp 84–6.
35 Murray Fraser, *John Bull's other homes: state housing and British policy in Ireland, 1883–1922* (Liverpool, 1996), pp 41–5.
36 Emmet O'Connor, *A labour history of Waterford* (Waterford, 1989), p. 134.
37 Fewer, *Waterford people*, p. 79.
38 *Constabulary list and directory for half year commencing 1 July 1912* (Dublin, 1912), pp 10, 48–9, 73, 120–1; Brendan Byrne, 'Law, order and the RIC in Waterford 1920–21: a chronology', *Decies*, 55 (1999), 117–26.
39 For example, CI Waterford, Mar. 1912 (TNA, CO 904/92).
40 E. Whyte (ed.), *Irish military guide with which the Dublin and the Curragh (official) military directories of Ireland are incorporated, including the navy, the militia and the Royal Irish Constabulary* (Dublin, 1912).
41 A.S. Aldridge, 'Youngest to die', *Decies*, 55 (1999), 185–6.
42 Born John James Shee in 1860, he changed his name to O'Shee in 1900. See Patrick Maume, 'John James O'Shee', in *DIB*.
43 Dermot Meleady, *Redmond: the Parnellite* (Cork, 2008), p. 195.
44 Brian M. Walker, *Parliamentary election results in Ireland, 1801–1922* (Dublin, 1978), pp 378–9.
45 Ibid., p. 378.   46 *II*, 10 Jan. 1913.
47 *ME*, 15 Feb. 1913.
48 Fraser, *John Bull's other homes*, pp 151–2; Minutes, 1 Dec. 1914 (Waterford City Archives (WCA), Waterford Corporation minute book).
49 Matthew Potter, *The municipal revolution in Ireland: a handbook of urban government in Ireland since 1800* (Dublin, 2009), p. 164.
50 *WN*, 5 Jan. 1912; O'Connor, *Waterford*, pp 126–7.
51 Potter, *Municipal revolution*, p. 163; Daniel Dowling, *Housing in Waterford* (Waterford, 1988), pp 22–6.
52 Brian McNally and Maurice McHugh, *Comhairle Chondae Phortláirge, 1899–1999: comóradh an chéid* (Waterford, 2000), pp 1–12.
53 O'Connor, *Waterford*, pp 117–18.
54 Emmet O'Connor, *A labour history of Ireland, 1824–1960* (Dublin, 1992), pp 68–9.
55 *ME*, 16, 23 Oct. 1908; *WN*, 16, 23 Oct. 1908.
56 Conor McCabe, 'The context and course of the Irish railway disputes in 1911', *Saothar*, 30 (2005), 21–32.
57 O'Connor, *Waterford*, pp 124–8.
58 Irene Fahy, 'Councillor Mary Strangman and the health of the city', *Decies*, 56 (2000), 189–205.
59 Leeanne Lane, 'Rosamond Jacob: Nationalism and Suffrage' in Louise Ryan and Margaret Ward (eds), *Irish women and the vote* (Dublin, 2007), pp 171–87.
60 *II*, 11 Feb. 1913.   61 *WS*, 24 Feb. 1912.
62 *ME*, 12 Feb. 1937.
63 Minute book of the United Irish League National Directory (NLI, MS 708), pp 1900–5.

64 Ibid., 1910.
65 Ibid.; Michael Wheatley, *Nationalism and the Irish party: provincial Ireland, 1910–1916* (Oxford, 2005), pp 22–43.
66 *WN*, Jan., Feb. 1913; *ME*, Jan., Feb. 1913.
67 León Ó Broin, *Revolutionary underground: the story of the Irish Republican Brotherhood, 1858–1924* (Dublin, 1976), pp 60–96.
68 Correspondence with Dr Matthew Kelly, Oxford University.
69 Ibid.
70 Matthew Kelly, *The Fenian ideal and Irish nationalism, 1882–1916* (Woodbridge, 2006), pp 142–4; Owen McGee, *The IRB* (Dublin, 2005), pp 280–309.
71 RIC Crime Branch Special Report 1905, 1909 (TNA, CO 904/117, 118).
72 Ó Broin, *Revolutionary underground*, pp 140–51; Diarmuid Lynch, *The IRB and the 1916 Rising* (Cork, 1957), pp 28–38.
73 Liam Walsh (BMH WS 1,005, pp 1–3).
74 Seán Matthews (BMH WS 1,022, pp 1–4).
75 Patrick C. O'Mahony (BMH WS 118, pp 1–4). O'Mahony was originally from Kerry.
76 Damian Lawlor, *Na Fianna Éireann and the Irish revolution 1909 to 1923* (Offaly, n.d.), pp 7–31.
77 Patrick Hearne (BMH WS 1,742, pp 1–3); James Nolan (BMH WS 1,369, pp 2–3); Jacob diaries 1914 (NLI, Jacob papers, MS 32,582).
78 CI Waterford, Feb. 1914 (TNA, CO 904/92).
79 David Cullinane, *Céad Sinn Féin* (Waterford, 2005), p. 33.
80 Portláirge '84 *Comóradh an Chéid* (Dublin, 1984), p. 2.
81 Matthew Butler, *The Gaelic League in Waterford* (Waterford, 1944), pp 22–4; Jacob diaries 1912, 1913, 1914 (NLI, Jacob papers, MS 32,582).
82 Census of Ireland 1911 Munster, Cd 663, HC 1912; Brian Ó Cuiv, 'Irish language and literature, 1845–1921' in Vaughan (ed.), *A new history, vi*, pp 431–2.
83 Michael Bance, *Smokey Joe: the life and times of a provincial newspaper editor* (Dublin, 1994), p. 44.
84 Fewer, *Waterford people*, p. 44.

CHAPTER TWO *'We have fought and we have won': Waterford and home rule, 1912–14*

1 Speech by John Redmond to his Waterford supporters on 25 Jan. 1914, *ME*, 31 Jan. 1914.
2 *II*, 12 Apr. 1912.
3 O'Connor, *Waterford*, p. 128; idem, *Ireland*, pp 87–8.
4 CI Waterford, Nov. 1913 (TNA, CO 904/91); ibid., June 1914 (TNA, CO 904/93).
5 *II*, 15 Apr. 1912; Denis Gwynn, *The life of John Redmond* (London, 1932), p. 202; Dermot Meleady, *John Redmond: the national leader* (Dublin, 2014), p. 215.
6 *ME*, 27 Mar. 1912.
7 Gwynn, *Redmond*, p. 202; Daniel M. Jackson, *Popular opposition to Irish home rule in Edwardian Britain* (Liverpool, 2009), pp 146–7.
8 F.S.L. Lyons, 'The developing crisis 1907–1914' in Vaughan (ed.), *A new history, vi*, pp 129–31; Alvin Jackson, *Home rule: an Irish history, 1800–2000* (Oxford, 2003), pp 109–11.
9 Alan Ward, *The Irish constitutional tradition: responsible government and modern Ireland, 1782–1992* (Dublin, 1992), p. 65.
10 F.S.L. Lyons, 'The watershed, 1903–7' in Vaughan (ed.), *A new history, vi*, pp 121–2.
11 *II*, 1 Apr. 1912.   12 Jackson, *Home rule*, pp 110–11.
13 *ME*, 20 Apr. 1912.   14 *WN*, 12 Apr. 1912.

15 *II*, 12 Apr. 1912.
16 Jackson, *Home rule*, pp 106–41; Paul Bew, *Ireland: the politics of enmity, 1789–2006* (Oxford, 2007), pp 367–71; idem, *John Redmond* (Dundalk, 1996), pp 35–7; Cornelius O'Leary and Patrick Maume, *Controversial issues in Anglo-Irish relations, 1910–1921* (Dublin, 2004), pp 9–45.
17 *ME*, 3 May 1912.   18 *WN*, 3 May 1912.
19 *WS*, 24 Apr. 1912.
20 Andrew Scholes, *The Church of Ireland and the third home rule bill* (Dublin, 2010), pp 32–6.
21 *WS*, 24 Apr. 1912; *Church of Ireland Gazette*, 24 Apr. 1912; R.B. McDowell, *Crisis and decline: the fate of the southern Unionists* (Dublin, 1997), p. 46.
22 *WS*, 5 June 1912.   23 *Church of Ireland Gazette*, 5 July 1912.
24 *WS*, 5 June 1912.   25 CI Waterford, June 1912 (TNA, CO 904/86).
26 *WS*, 15 June 1912.   27 *WN*, 14 June 1912.
28 *WS*, 17 June 1912.   29 Ibid., 5 Oct. 1912.
30 PRONI, Ulster Covenant online, www.proni.gov.uk, accessed 10 Feb. 2013.
31 *Church of Ireland Gazette*, 3 July 1914.
32 Rosemary Cullen Owens, *Smashing times: a history of the Irish women's suffrage movement* (Dublin, 1984), pp 48–52.
33 *WN*, 12 Apr. 1912.   34 *WS*, 10 Apr. 1912.
35 *Evening Herald*, 19 July 1912; Owens, *Smashing times*, pp 57–8.
36 *WN*, 2 Aug. 1912.   37 CI Waterford, Jan. 1914 (TNA, CO 904/92).
38 *ME*, 20 Sept. 1913; *WN*, 20 Sept. 1913; *ME*, 12 Nov. 1913.
39 Thomas P. Dooley, *Irishmen or English soldiers?: the times and world of a southern Catholic Irish man (1876–1916) enlisting in the British army during the First World War* (Liverpool, 1995), p. 99.
40 *ME*, 20 Sept. 1913.   41 *WS*, 17 Sept. 1913.
42 Ibid., 27 Sept. 1913; *ME*, 4 Oct. 1913.
43 *WN*, 19 Sept. 1913.   44 *WS*, 12 Nov. 1913.
45 *WN*, 24 Oct. 1913.   46 Ibid.
47 *WS*, 3 Jan. 1914.   48 CI Waterford, Nov. 1913 (TNA, CO 904/91).
49 *ME*, 30 Aug. 1913; *WN*, 18 Oct. 1913.
50 Gwynn, *Redmond*, p. 249.   51 *ME*, 31 Jan. 1914.
52 Ibid.
53 Ibid.; CI Waterford, Jan. 1914 (TNA, CO 904/92).
54 *Freeman's Journal (FJ)*, 26 Jan. 1914; *II*, 26 Jan. 1914; *Cork Examiner (CE)*, 26 Jan. 1914.
55 *II*, 26 Jan. 1914   56 *Irish Times (IT)*, 27 Jan. 1914.
57 *WS*, 14 Feb. 1914.
58 Jacob diaries 1914 (NLI, Jacob papers, MS 32,582).
59 *Hansard (Commons)*, 24 Feb. 1914, vol. 58, cols. 1691–727.
60 Minutes, 1 Mar. 1914 (WCA, Waterford Corporation minute book).
61 Ussher, 'True story of a revolution', p. 2.
62 Ibid., p. 3.   63 CI Waterford, Mar. 1914 (TNA, CO 904/92).
64 *II*, 28, 29, 30 May 1914.   65 *ME*, 17 May 1914; *WN*, 17 May 1914.
66 CI Waterford, May 1914 (TNA, CO 904/93); *ME*, 17 May 1914.
67 *ME*, 29 May 1914; *WN*, 29 May 1914; CI Waterford, May 1914 (TNA, CO 904/93).
68 *ME*, 30 May 1914.   69 *An Claidheamh Solais*, 1 Nov. 1913.
70 F.X. Martin, *The Irish Volunteers, 1913–1915: recollections and documents* (Dublin, 1963), pp 69–83.
71 Ronan Fanning, 'Richard Mulcahy', *DIB*; Maryann Gialanella Valiulis, *Portrait of a revolutionary: General Richard Mulcahy and the founding of the Irish Free State* (Dublin, 1992), p. 7.
72 Patrick C. O'Mahony (BMH WS 118, p. 4).

73 Marnie Hay, *Bulmer Hobson and the nationalist movement in twentieth-century Ireland* (Manchester, 2009), pp 127–9; Bulmer Hobson, *Ireland: yesterday and tomorrow* (Tralee, 1968), pp 50–1.

74 Aodagán O'Rahilly, *Winding the clock: O'Rahilly and the 1916 Rising* (Dublin, 1991), pp 98–100; Breandán Mac Giolla Choille (ed.), *Intelligence notes, 1913–1916* (Dublin, 1966), pp 104–9.

75 *ME*, 31 Jan. 1914.   76 Ibid., 14 Mar. 1914.

77 CI Waterford, Apr. 1914 (TNA, CO 904/93).

78 CI Waterford, May 1914 (ibid.).   79 Ibid.

80 *ME*, 26 July 1914.   81 Ibid., 11 July 1914.

82 Ibid., 18 July 1914; *WN*, 18 July 1914.

83 Minutes, 10 June 1914 (WCoA, Waterford County Council minute book).

84 CI Waterford, June 1914 (TNA, CO 904/93).

85 Lil Conlon, *Cumann na mBan and the women of Ireland* (Kilkenny, 1969), pp 7–16; Cal McCarthy, *Cumann na mBan and the Irish Revolution* (Cork, 2007), pp 9–21.

86 *WN*, 23 Jan. 1914; Jacob diaries 1914 (NLI, Jacob papers, MS 32,582); Leeann Lane, *Rosamond Jacob: third person singular* (Dublin, 2010), pp 69–71.

87 McCarthy, *Cumann na mBan*, p. 27; Conlon, *Cumann na mBan*, p. 8.

88 Jacob diaries 1914 (NLI, Jacob papers, MS 32,582).

89 Martin, *Irish Volunteers*, pp 43–7.

90 P.A. Murphy to Redmond, 22 June 1914 (NLI, John Redmond papers, MS 15,257/3).

91 RIC IG, Oct. 1914 (TNA, CO 904/95).

92 CI Waterford, Apr. 1914 (TNA, CO 904/93).

93 Jackson, *Home rule*, pp 135–8; Bew, *Ireland*, pp 370–1; O'Leary & Maume, *Controversial issues*, pp 42–4.

94 Brigade states for Waterford, 28 July 1914 (NLI, Maurice Moore papers, MS 10,551/2).

95 Timothy Bowman, *Carson's army: the Ulster Volunteer Force, 1912–22* (Manchester, 2007), pp 101–3.

96 CI Waterford, July 1914 (TNA, CO 904/94).

97 Mac Giolla Choille (ed.), *Intelligence notes*, pp 120–31; Gerry White and Brendan O'Shea, *'Baptised in blood': the formation of the Cork Brigade of the Irish Volunteers, 1913–1916* (Cork, 2005), pp 39–50.

98 CI Waterford, Aug. 1914 (TNA, CO 904/93).

99 *WS*, 1 Aug. 1914; *WN*, 1 Aug. 1914.

100 Seán Matthews (BMH WS 1,022, pp 3–5).

101 *ME*, 1 Aug. 1914; *WN*, 1 Aug. 1914.

102 *WN*, 30 July 1914.

103 Address to diocesan synod of Waterford and Lismore, 23 June 1914, *Church of Ireland Gazette*, 27 June 1914.

104 Ronan Fanning, *Fatal path: British government and Irish revolution, 1910–1922* (London, 2013), pp 125–8; Gwynn, *Redmond*, pp 335–43; Meleady, *Redmond: the national leader*, pp 281–4.

CHAPTER THREE *'Waterford has done its duty magnificently': war, rebellion and Waterford, 1914–16*

1 Address by John Redmond to a public meeting in Waterford, *ME*, 4 Dec. 1915.

2 Max Hastings, *Catastrophe: Europe goes to war 1914* (London, 2013), pp 59–62.

3 Catriona Pennell, *A kingdom united: popular responses to the outbreak of the First World War in Britain and Ireland* (Oxford, 2012), pp 164–71.

4 Patrick Callan, 'Recruiting for the British army in Ireland during the First World War', *Irish Sword*, 17 (1987–8), 42–56.

5 Ibid., 44
6 David Johnson, *The interwar economy in Ireland* (Dundalk, 1989), pp 3–4.
7 Wheatley, *Nationalism*, pp 192–5, 216–18; Patrick Maume, *The long gestation: Irish nationalist life, 1891–1918* (Dublin, 1999), p. 200.
8 *WS*, 5 Aug. 1914.   9 Dooley, *Irishmen or English soldiers*, pp 104–20.
10 *WS*, *ME*, 7 Aug. 1914.   11 *WS*, 21 Aug. 1914; *ME*, 21 Aug. 1914.
12 *WS*, 27 Feb. 1915.   13 Ibid., 8 Aug. 1914
14 Gwynn, *Redmond*, p. 356.
15 Maume, *Long gestation*, pp 147–51; Jackson, *Home rule*, pp 143–4 gives a more nuanced analysis of Redmond's position and support for the war effort.
16 Jackson, *Home rule*, pp 147–9.
17 Pennell, *A kingdom united*, pp 165–89; Joseph P. Finnan, *John Redmond and Irish unity, 1912–1918* (New York, 2004), pp 78–83; Wheatley, *Nationalism*, pp 196–203.
18 Meleady, *Redmond: the national leader*, pp 298–9.
19 *ME*, 8 Aug. 1914.   20 *WN*, 16 Sept. 1914.
21 *WS*, 8, 15 Aug. 1914.
22 Gordon to Moore, 4 Aug. 1914 (NLI, Moore papers, MS 10,551/2).
23 *WS*, 23 Dec. 1914.   24 CI Waterford, Aug. 1914 (TNA, CO 904/94).
25 Eoin P. Ó Caoimh, 'Redmond's change of policy, Aug.–Sept. 1914' in Martin (ed.), *Irish Volunteers*, p. 151.
26 Maume, *Long gestation*, pp 147–51; Pennell, *A kingdom united*, pp 194–7.
27 Minutes, 6 Oct. 1914 (WCA, Waterford Corporation minute book).
28 Christopher M. Kennedy, *Genesis of the rising, 1912–1916: a transformation of nationalist opinion* (New York, 2009), pp 94–5; David Fitzpatrick, *Politics and Irish life, 1913–21: provincial experiences of war and revolution* (Dublin, 1977), p. 112.
29 Gwynn, *Redmond*, pp 391–2.   30 Jackson, *Home rule*, pp 144–5.
31 Martin (ed.), *Irish Volunteers*, p. 152.
32 *ME*, 3 Oct. 1914.   33 Mac Giolla Choille (ed.), *Intelligence notes*, p. 110.
34 Hobson, *Ireland*, pp 58, 70.
35 Table showing the original strength of the Irish National Volunteers and indicating approximately how the various battalions divided as result of meetings held from 24 September, date of secession, up to and including 31 Oct. 1914 (NLI, Redmond papers, MS 15,258).
36 Thomas Cleary (BMH WS 972, p. 5); Michael Mansfield (BMH WS 1,188, p. 1).
37 *ME*, 10 Oct. 1914.   38 *FJ*, 12 Oct. 1914.
39 Ibid., 6 Feb. 1915. Lonergan was charged with causing grievously bodily harm but was acquitted.
40 *ME*, 15 Nov. 1914.   41 *WS*, 21 Nov. 1914.
42 CI Waterford, Sept. 1914 (TNA, CO 904/94).
43 Ibid., Sept. 1915 (TNA, CO 904/98).
44 Thomas Dooley, 'Politics, brass bands and marketing: army recruiting in Waterford city, 1914–1915', *Irish Sword*, 18 (1991), 205–19.
45 Catriona Pennell, 'More than a curious footnote: Irish voluntary participation in the First World War and British popular memory' in John Horne and Edward Madigan (eds), *Towards commemoration: Ireland in war and revolution, 1912–1923* (Dublin, 2013), p. 39.
46 *ME*, 13 Feb. 1915; *WN*, 26 Feb., 30 Apr. 1915.
47 Dooley, *Irishmen or English soldiers*, pp 103–7.
48 Ibid., pp 106, 146.
49 Dooley, 'Politics, brass bands and marketing', 216.
50 *ME*, 27 Mar. 1915.   51 Gwynn, *Redmond's last years*, p. 187.
52 *ME*, 27 Mar. 1915.

53 Day memorial, Christ Church cathedral, Waterford.
54 *WS*, 27 Mar. 1915.   55 Patrick Paul (BMH WS 877, p. 2).
56 CI Waterford, Mar., Apr., May and June 1915 (TNA, CO 904/96-7).
57 *ME*, 17, 24 July 1915.   58 *WS*, 4 Dec. 1915.
59 Dooley, 'Politics, brass bands and marketing', 205.
60 CI Waterford, Jan. 1915 (TNA, CO 904/95).
61 *ME*, 29 Mar. 1915; WS, 11 Dec. 1915.
62 *WS*, 17 July 1915.
63 James McConnel, 'Recruiting sergeants for John Bull?: Irish Nationalist MPs and enlist-
     ment during the early months of the Great War', *War in History*, 14:4 (2007), 424.
64 CI Waterford, July 1915 (TNA, CO 904/97).
65 Tom Burnell, *The Waterford war dead: a history of the casualties of the Great War* (Dublin,
     2010), pp 50, 275.
66 Ibid., p. 47.   67 *WN*, 5 Sept. 1914.
68 Burnell, *War dead*, p. 99.   69 *WN*, 11 Dec. 1914.
70 Eileen Reilly, 'Women and voluntary war work' in Adrian Gregory and Senia Pašeta (eds),
     Ireland and the Great War: 'a war to unite us all'? (Manchester, 2002), pp 49–72; Pennell,
     A kingdom united, pp 72–6, 168–71.
71 *WS*, 2 Sept. 1914.
72 Stannus Geoghegan, *The campaigns and history of the Royal Irish Regiment. Volume II from
     1900 to 1922* (London, 1927), pp 25–8.
73 *WS*, 20, 24 Mar. 1915; *ME*, 27 Mar. 1915.
74 *WN*, 17 Sept. 1915.
75 Ibid., 3 Mar. 1915; Patrick McCarthy, 'The life and death of Timothy Quinlisk: the
     Waterford connections to Roger Casement's Irish brigade', *Decies*, 68 (2012), 45–61.
76 Eibhear Walshe, *Cissies abattoir* (Cork, 2009), pp 20–1; John Smith, 'The Oldcastle pris-
     oner of war camp', *Ríocht na Midhe*, 21 (2010), 212–50.
77 Repatriation of Andrea Volmer, 1915 (NAI, CSORP, 1915/19,396).
78 *WS*, 19 Jan. 1914.   79 Ibid., 14 Aug. 1914; *WN*, 14 Aug. 1914.
80 O'Brien to Moore, 30 Apr. 1915 (NLI, Moore papers, MS 9,714).
81 R.A. Kelly and W.J. Smith to Moore, 7 June 1915 (NLI, Moore papers, MS 10,551/2).
82 Padraic Colum and Maurice Joy (eds), *The Irish rebellion of 1916* (New York, 1916), p. 184.
83 *FJ*, 13 Jan. 1915.   84 *ME*, 3 Apr. 1915.
85 Maume, *Long gestation*, p. 160.   86 *ME, WS*, 25 Aug. 1915.
87 CI Waterford, Nov. 1915 (TNA, CO 904/98).
88 *WN, ME*, 29 May 1915.
89 *WS*, 29 May 1915; CI Waterford, June 1915 (TNA, CO 904/100).
90 Fitzpatrick, *Politics*, p. 112; Kennedy, *Genesis*, p. 198; Michael Laffan, *The resurrection of
     Ireland: the Sinn Féin party, 1916–1923* (Cambridge, 1999), pp 8–9.
91 Stephen Gwynn, *John Redmond's last years* (London, 1919), p. 193.
92 Bew, *Ireland*, p. 372.   93 Wheatley, *Nationalism*, p. 206.
94 F.S.L. Lyons, 'The Rising and after' in Vaughan (ed.), *A new history*, vi, p. 207.
95 CI Waterford, Apr. 1915 (TNA, CO 904/96).
96 *WS*, 15 May, 1915.
97 CI Waterford, Mar. 1915 (TNA, CO 904/96); *ME*, 26 June 1915.
98 *WN*, 21, 28 May 1915.   99 CI Waterford, Oct. 1915 (TNA, CO 904/98).
100 O'Connor, *Waterford*, p. 135.
101 George D. Kelleher, *Gunpowder to guided missiles: Ireland's war industries* (Cork, 1993), pp
     179–80, 187.
102 Minutes, Mar. 1915 (WCA, Waterford Corporation minute book).

103 Des Cowman, *Perceptions and promotions: the role of Waterford Chamber of Commerce, 1787–1987* (Waterford, 1988), p. 52.
104 *ME*, 8 Aug. 1914.
105 D. French, *British economic and strategic planning, 1905–1915* (London, 1982), p. 99.
106 Dooley, *Irishmen or English soldiers*, p. 112.
107 *ME*, 6 Feb. 1915.   108 Dooley, *Irishmen or English soldiers*, p. 113.
109 O'Connor, *Waterford*, p. 135.
110 Thomas Dunne, 'A history of Waterford labour' [unpublished manuscript] (WCL).
111 'General rate of weekly wages in 1915 of permanent male Irish agricultural labourers not living in free houses or receiving allowances of any kind' (NLI, Joseph Brennan papers, MS 26,195).
112 Fitzpatrick, *Politics*, p. 242; RIC IG, Mar. 1916 (TNA, CO 904/99).
113 Patrick C. O'Mahony (BMH WS 118, p. 2); Seán Matthews (BMH WS 1,022, p. 4).
114 J.J. O'Connell, 'History of the Irish Volunteers' (NLI, Bulmer Hobson papers, MS 13,168).
115 CI Waterford, Apr. 1915 (TNA, CO 904/96).
116 Ibid., Dec. 1915 (TNA, CO 904/98).
117 *ME*, 24 Mar. 1916; CI Waterford, Mar. 1916 (TNA, CO 904/99).
118 *ME*, 7 Aug. 1915.   119 Ibid., 21 Aug. 1915.
120 Manchester martyrs meeting in Waterford, Nov. 1915 (NAI, CSORP, 1915/20038).
121 O'Connell, 'Volunteers' (NLI, Hobson papers, MS 13,168).
122 Seán Matthews (BMH WS 1,022, p. 5).
123 Maeve Cavanagh-McDowell (BMH WS 258, p. 7).
124 Marie Perolz (BMH WS 246, p. 3).
125 Seán Matthews (BMH WS 1,022, p. 5).
126 Ibid., p. 5; Patrick C. O'Mahony (BMH WS 118, p. 6).
127 F.X. Martin, 'Eoin MacNeill on the Easter Rising', *IHS*, 12:47 (1961), 268, note 54.
128 William Walsh (BMH WS 1,005, pp 5–6).
129 Maeve Cavanagh-McDowell (BMH WS 258, p. 10).
130 Seán Matthews (BMH WS 1,022, p. 6).
131 Maeve Cavanagh-McDowell (BMH WS 258, pp 10–11); Jim Maher, '1916 in Kilkenny' in John Bradley and Michael O'Dwyer (eds), *Kilkenny through the centuries* (Kilkenny, 2009), pp 477–83.
132 Patrick C. O'Mahony (BMH WS 118, pp 6–7); Terence O'Reilly, *Rebel heart: George Lennon flying column commander* (Cork, 2009), p. 28.
133 Patrick C. O'Mahony (BMH WS 118, p. 7).
134 William Walsh (BMH WS 1,005, p. 6).
135 Nioclás Ó Gríobhtháin, 'Domhnall Ó Buachalla agus óglaigh na Rinne', *An Linn Bhuí*, 5 (2001), 185–93.
136 Records of the Great Southern & Western Railway Company, June 1916 (Irish Railway Record Society Archives, file no. 2659 Sinn Féin Rebellion).
137 Valiulis, *Mulcahy*, pp 13–20.
138 Geoghegan, *Royal Irish Regiment*, pp 102–4.
139 *1916 Rebellion handbook* (Belfast, 1998), pp 49–51.
140 Jim Herlihy, *The Dublin Metropolitan Police: a short history and genealogical guide* (Dublin, 2001), p. 177.
141 C.V. Buckley to Smith, 17 May 1916 (NLI, Moore papers, MS 10,551/2).
142 Smith to Moore, 30 Nov. 1916 (ibid.).
143 H.F.N. Jourdain, *History of the Connaught Rangers* (3 vols, London, 1926) ii, 485; CI Waterford, May 1916 (TNA, CO 904/101).

144 Charles Townshend, *Easter 1916: the Irish rebellion* (London, 2005), pp 301–10; Fearghal McGarry, *The Rising: Ireland: Easter 1916* (Oxford, 2010), pp 177–86.
145 *II*, 10 May 1916.
146 Dermot Keogh, 'The Catholic Church, the Holy See and the 1916 Rising' in Gabriel Doherty and Dermot Keogh (eds), *1916: the long revolution* (Cork, 2007), pp 250–308.
147 *ME*, 20 May 1916.
148 Minutes, 12 May 1916 (WCoA, Waterford County Council minute book).
149 Ibid., 5 May 1916.   150 *Church of Ireland Gazette*, 1 July 1916.
151 Minutes, 24 May 1916 (WCoA, Waterford County Council minute book).
152 Ibid., 17 June 1916.
153 CI Waterford, May 1916 (TNA, CO 904/100).
154 Inspector-General RIC, 'Public attitude and opinion in Ireland as to the recent outbreak' (TNA, CAB 37/147/38).
155 *WS*, 4 Dec. 1915.   156 Deaglán Ó Reagáin (BMH WS 1,233, p. 1).
157 CI Waterford, Dec. 1916 (TNA, CO 904/101).

CHAPTER FOUR *'An oasis in the political desert of Ireland': the resistable rise of Sinn Féin, 1916–18*

1 *ME*, 3 Jan. 1919.   2 Laffan, *Resurrection*, pp 77–168.
3 Burnell, *War dead*, pp 111, 229.   4 Ibid., p. 33.
5 Terence Denman, *A lonely grave: the life and death of William Redmond* (Dublin, 1995), pp 117–26.
6 *WN*, 22 June 1917.
7 Richard McElwee, *The last voyages of the Waterford steamers* (Waterford, 1992), pp 102–18.
8 Ibid., pp 132–6.   9 Burnell, *War dead*, p. 116.
10 CI Waterford, Mar. 1918 (TNA, CO 904/105).
11 Ibid., Jan. 1917 (TNA, CO 904/102).
12 Ibid., Feb. 1917 (ibid.)   13 Ibid., Oct. 1916 (TNA, CO 904/101).
14 Callan, 'Recruiting for the British army', 42–56.
15 CI Waterford, Sept., Oct. 1918 (TNA, CO 904/107); Callan, 'Recruiting for the British army', 45.
16 CI Waterford, Aug. 1918 (TNA, CO 904/106).
17 *WN*, 23 June 1916.   18 Ibid., 1, 22 Dec. 1916.
19 Ibid., 24 Nov. 1916.
20 CI Waterford, Sept. 1916 (TNA, CO 904/101), Oct. 1917 (TNA, CO 904/104).
21 CI Waterford, May 1916 (TNA, CO 904/100).
22 *WN*, 29 June 1916; *ME*, 29 June 1916.
23 CI Waterford, June 1916 (TNA, CO 904/100).
24 *WN*, 29 June 1916.   25 *ME*, 29 June 1916.
26 *WN*, 27 July 1916.
27 Caoimhe Nic Dháibhéid, 'The Irish National Aid Association and the radicalization of public opinion in Ireland', *Historical Journal*, 55:3 (Sept. 2012), 705–29.
28 William Walsh (BMH WS 1,005, p. 6).
29 CI Waterford, July 1916 (TNA, CO 904/101).
30 Laffan, *Resurrection*, pp 62–4; Eda Sagarra, *Kevin O'Shiel: Tyrone nationalist and Irish state-builder* (Dublin, 2013), pp 81–6.
31 *II*, 11 Sept. 1916.   32 Brigid Hourican, 'George Murnaghan', *DIB*.
33 CI Waterford, Feb. 1917 (TNA, CO 904/102).
34 'Maurice Quinlan, Waterford' (NAI, CSORP, 1916/5626, 1916/18630).
35 *WN*, 1 June 1917.   36 Ibid.; Vincent White (BMH WS 1,764, pp 1–2).

37 *ME*, 12 Oct. 1916; *WN*, 12 Oct. 1916; *FJ*, 10 Oct. 1916; *II*, 9, 10 Oct. 1916.
38 Ibid.   39 Ussher, 'True story of a revolution', p. 23.
40 'Meeting addressed by Mr John Redmond' (NAI, CSORP, 1916/5644).
41 Michael Laffan, 'The unification of Sinn Féin in 1917', *IHS*, 17 (1971), 353–79.
42 CI Waterford, May 1917 (TNA, CO 904/103).
43 *WN*, 11 May 1917; Jerome aan de Wiel, *The Catholic Church in Ireland, 1914–1918: war and politics* (Dublin, 2003), p. 174.
44 Laffan, *Resurrection*, p. 61.   45 Ibid., pp 106–10.
46 *WN*, 13 July 1917.   47 CI Waterford, Dec. 1917 (TNA, CO 904/104).
48 CI Waterford, Apr.–Nov. 1917 (TNA, CO 904/102–104).
49 CI Waterford, Sept. 1917 (TNA, CO 904/104).
50 Patrick C. O'Mahony (BMH WS 745, pp 1–2).
51 Laffan, *Resurrection*, pp 118–21.
52 Margaret Ward, *Unmanageable revolutionaries: women and Irish nationalism* (London, 1989), pp 125–6; Lane, *Jacob*, pp 127–30.
53 *WN*, 13 July 1917.   54 Butler, *Gaelic League in Waterford*, pp 56–7.
55 CI Waterford, Nov. 1917 (TNA, CO 904/104).
56 Waterford meeting proclaimed, Nov. 1917 (NAI, CSORP, 1917/27,553).
57 *ME*, 24 Oct. 1917; *WN*, 12 Oct. 1917.
58 Gwynn, *Redmond*, pp 592–6.
59 *ME*, 8 Mar. 1918; *WN*, 8 Mar. 1918; *WS*, 8 Mar. 1918.
60 Meleady, *Redmond: the national leader*, p. 456.
61 *II*, 15 Mar. 1918.   62 *ME*, 15 Mar. 1918; *WN*, 15 Mar. 1918.
63 Nicholas Whittle (BMH WS 1,105, pp 8–22); Vincent White (BMH WS 1,764, pp 2–11); Jeremiah Cronin (BMH WS 1,020, pp 1–3).
64 *WN*, 19 Dec. 1924.
65 Minute book of the Metropolitan Branch UIL, 19 Mar. 1918 (NLI, MS 16,185).
66 *ME*, 15 Mar. 1918; *WN*, 15 Mar. 1918.
67 *FJ*, 15 Mar. 1918.   68 Ibid.
69 CI Waterford, Mar. 1918 (TNA, CO 904/105); *WN*, 22 Mar. 1918.
70 CI Waterford, Mar. 1918 (TNA, CO 904/105).
71 *II*, 18 Mar. 1918.
72 *FJ*, 20 Mar. 1918; A.C. Hepburn, *Catholic Belfast and Nationalist Ireland in the era of Joe Devlin, 1871–1934* (Oxford, 2008), p. 193.
73 *II*, 23 Mar. 1918; *IT*, 23 Mar. 1918.
74 *ME*, 29 Mar. 1918; *WN*, 29 Mar. 1918.
75 *ME*, 29 Mar. 1918.   76 *II*, 25 Mar. 1918.
77 *FJ*, 25 Mar. 1918.   78 *II*, 25 Mar. 1918.
79 Hayden Talbot, *Michael Collins' own story told to Hayden Talbot* (Dublin, 2012), p. 43.
80 CI Waterford, Mar. 1918 (TNA, CO 904/105).
81 *II*, 25 Mar. 1918.   82 Ibid.
83 Laffan, *Resurrection*, pp 122–8.
84 Dillon to Asquith, 30 June 1918, cited in Laffan, *Resurrection*, p. 128.
85 Alan Ward, 'Lloyd George and the 1918 conscription crisis', *Historical Journal*, 17 (1974), 107–29.
86 *Hansard (Commons)* 10 Apr. 1918, vol. 104, col. 1569.
87 Cavan by-election poster 1918 (NLI, Prints and Drawings, Ephemera collection, MS 507741).
88 F.S.L. Lyons, *John Dillon: a biography* (London, 1968), pp 433–7.
89 Aan de Wiel, *Catholic Church*, pp 220–4.

90 O'Connor, *Waterford*, p. 142; O'Connor, *Ireland*, p. 91.

91 *ME*, 4 May 1918.

92 Ibid., CI Waterford Aug. 1918 (TNA, CO 904/105).

93 Laffan, *Resurrection*, pp 153–5.   94 Ibid., p. 154.

95 David Fitzpatrick, *Harry Boland's Irish revolution* (Cork, 2003), p. 104.

96 Uinseann Mac Eoin, *Survivors* (Dublin, 1980), p. 138.

97 Laffan, *Resurrection*, pp 156–61.

98 RIC IG, Nov. 1918 (TNA, CO 904/107).

99 *Dungarvan Observer* (*DO*), 4 Dec. 1918; *WN*, 4 Dec. 1918.

100 *DO*, 11 Dec. 1918.   101 *FJ*, 13 Dec. 1918.

102 Walker, *Parliamentary election results*, p. 9.

103 *WN*, 22 Nov. 1918.   104 *WN*, 23 Nov. 1918.

105 Vincent White (BMH WS 1,764, p. 11).

106 *ME*, 22 Nov. 1918.

107 CI Waterford, Nov. 1918 (TNA, CO 904/106).

108 Walker, *Parliamentary election results*, p. 9.

109 *WS*, 3 Jan. 1919; *ME*, 3 Jan. 1919.

110 *WS*, 17 Jan. 1919.   111 O'Connor, *Ireland*, pp 97–8.

112 Bob Kenny, 'The spatial dimensions of trade union organisation in Ireland– a case study' (MA, NUI Maynooth, 1985).

113 O'Connor, *Waterford*, pp 137–47.

114 Emmet O'Connor, *Syndicalism in Ireland* (Cork, 1988), pp 36–8; Anonymous, *Fifty years of Liberty Hall* (Dublin, 1959), pp 75–6.

115 Michael Laffan, 'In the shadow of the national question' in Paul Daly, Ronan O'Brien and Paul Rouse (eds), *Making the difference? The Irish Labour Party, 1912–2012* (Cork, 2012), p. 36.

116 *ME*, 23 Nov. 1919; Conor Kostick, *Revolution in Ireland: popular militancy, 1917–1923* (Cork, 2009), p. 121.

117 *ME*, 9 Aug. 1919; *WN*, 9 Aug. 1919.

118 Dunne, 'A history of Waterford labour'.

119 O'Connor, *Waterford*, p. 154.   120 Laffan, 'In the shadow', pp 36–9.

121 O'Connor, *Waterford*, p. 156.

CHAPTER FIVE *'Waterford has not done much'?: the War of Independence, 1919–21*

1 Declan Slattery (BMW WS 1,245, p. 2); Patrick Ormond (BMH WS 1,283, p. 7); James Mansfield (BMH WS 1,229, p. 3).

2 Denis Madden (BMH WS 1,103, p. 11); James Power (BMH WS 1,024, pp 2–3); Seán Matthews (BMH WS 1,022 p.10).

3 *Constabulary List and Directory*, no. 159 (Dublin, 1921); Byrne, 'Law, order and the RIC in Waterford', 117–26.

4 Jeremiah Cronin (BMH WS 1,020, p. 3).

5 *WN*, 21 Mar. 1919.

6 Edmund Downey, 'Report on the death of Michael Walsh and transcript of the inquest', unpublished account in the author's possession.

7 Laffan, *Resurrection*, pp 319–20; Arthur Mitchell, *Revolutionary government in Ireland* (Dublin, 1995), pp 57–65.

8 Mitchell, *Revolutionary government*, p. 59.

9 Patrick C. O'Mahony (BMH WS 745, p. 7).

10 Of this sum £11,600 was raised in England.
11 Dáil loan net amounts received, 1920 (NAI, DÉ/27).
12 David Fitzpatrick, 'The geography of Irish nationalism, 1910–1921', *Past & Present*, 78 (1978), 113–44.
13 *WN*, 21 Mar. 1919; *WS*, 21 Mar. 1919.
14 *WS*, 29 Apr. 1919; CI Waterford, May 1919 (TNA, CO 904/109).
15 Hepburn, *Catholic Belfast*, pp 202–3, 212.
16 *WN*, 23 Jan. 1921; *ME*, 23 Jan. 1921; *WS*, 23 Jan. 1921.
17 *ME*, 24 Jan. 1920; *WS*, 24 Jan., 7 Feb. 1920.
18 *ME*, 24 Jan. 1920.   19 O'Connor, *Waterford*, pp 143–58.
20 Brian McNally and Maurice McHugh, *Comhairle Chontae Phortláirge, 1899–1999* (Waterford, 1999), p. 19.
21 Laffan, *Resurrection*, pp 338–9.
22 Walker, *Parliamentary election results*, p. 103; Laffan, *Resurrection*, p. 339.
23 Copies of an tÓglach club system (TNA, CO 904/24/4).
24 *ME*, *WN*, 28 Feb. 1920.
25 Minutes, 3 July 1920 (WCoA, Waterford County Council minute book).
26 Minutes of Finance Committee, Nov. 1920 (ibid.).
27 Minutes, May 1921 (WCA, Waterford Corporation minute book).
28 Ibid., Mar. 1921 (WCA); Laffan, *Resurrection*, pp 330–1.
29 Charles Townshend, *The British campaign in Ireland, 1919–1921* (Oxford, 1975), pp 40–6, 59–67.
30 James Mansfield (BMH WS 1,229, pp 4–5); Tommy Mooney, *Cry of the curlew* (Dungarvan, 2012), pp 122–5.
31 CI Waterford, Jan. 1920 (TNA, CO 904/112).
32 Townshend, *British campaign*, pp 27–8; idem, *The Republic: the fight for Irish independence* (London, 2013), pp 115–16.
33 Thomas Brennan (BMH WS 1,229, pp 7–8); Patrick Paul (BMH WS 877, pp 8–9).
34 Mooney, *Curlew*, pp 137–8, 149–50; O'Reilly, *George Lennon*, pp 46–7; James Mansfield (BMH WS 1,229, pp 7–9); Seán and Síle Murphy, *The Comeraghs, gunfire and Civil War* (Waterford, 2003) pp 30–1.
35 Denis G. Marnane, 'The War of Independence in Tipperary town and district, part 3, the socio-economic background of the Tipperary Town volunteers', *Tipperary Historical Journal* (2013), 132; Joost Augusteijn, 'Why was Tipperary so active in the War of Independence?', *Tipperary Historical Journal* (2006), 210.
36 Murphy & Murphy, *Comeraghs*, pp 39, 176–7; Mooney, *Curlew*, pp 149–50; Michael Mansfield (BMH WS 1,188, pp 10–11).
37 War diary of The Buffs, 1920 (National Army Museum, London).
38 Office of the commander in chief and War Office: distribution of the army, June 1920 (TNA, WO 73/115).
39 Roger E. Robinson and Walter P. Aggett, *The bloody eleventh: history of the Devonshire Regiment* (3 vols, Devon, 1988), iii, 8; CI Waterford, Aug. 1920 (TNA, CO 904/112).
40 Byrne, 'Law, order and the RIC in Waterford', 120.
41 John D. Brewer, *The Royal Irish Constabulary: an oral history* (Belfast, 1990), pp 72–3.
42 CI Waterford to Divisional Inspector for Munster, 23 Aug. 1920 (NLI, Piaras Béaslaí papers, MS 33,913).
43 CI Waterford, Oct. 1920 (TNA, CO 904/113).
44 Mary Kotsonouris, *Retreat from revolution: the Dáil courts, 1920–24* (Dublin, 1994), p. 23.
45 *WN*, 27 Aug. 1920.
46 Mitchell, *Revolutionary government*, pp 136–8; Trevor Anderson, 'The Dáil Courts in Limerick', *North Munster Antiquarian Journal*, 49 (2008), 111–24.

47 Michael Curran (BMH WS 1,230, pp 8, 11); *WN*, 17 Sept. 1920.
48 Kotsonouris, *Retreat*, pp 47–50.
49 *WN*, 15 Apr. 1921; *WS*, 15 Apr. 1921; 'Non-attendance of jurors at Waterford Assizes', Mar. 1921 (NAI, CSORP, CR 1921/18472, 18478).
50 *WN*, 4 Mar. 1921.   51 Mitchell, *Revolutionary government*, pp 147–52.
52 Patrick Ormond (BMH WS 1,283, p. 15).
53 Tom Kelleher (BMH WS 758, p. 5).
54 'Lt. Col. Frederick Charles Yeo MBE MM, Summary of Service' (Devonshire Regimental Museum), Devon.
55 Denis Madden (BMH WS 1,103, p. 11); Michael Desmond (BMH WS 1,188, p 2).
56 Denis Madden (BMH WS 1,103, p. 13).
57 Michael Desmond (BMH WS 1,388, p. 8); George Kiely (BMH WS 1,182, p. 4).
58 Pat McCarthy, 'The RAF and Ireland, 1919–1922', *Irish Sword*, 17 (1989), 174–88; Douglas Muir, 'Aerial mail, 1919–22', *Irish Sword*, 27:110 (2010), 385–414.
59 Séamus O'Mahony (BMH WS 730, p. 5); Karl Hayes, *A history of the RAF and USNAS in Ireland, 1913–22* (Dublin, 1988), p. 71.
60 *WN*, 19 Nov. 1920; McCarthy, 'RAF', 71.
61 Michael Hopkinson, *The Irish War of Independence* (Dublin, 2002), pp 70–4.
62 Michael Shalloe (BMH WS 1,241, pp 4–5).
63 George Kiely (BMH WS 1,241, p. 6).
64 Mooney, *Curlew*, p. 159; Murphy & Murphy, *Comeraghs*, pp 45–6.
65 Richard Abbott, *Police casualties in Ireland, 1919–1922* (Cork, 2000), pp 119, 151–2; *CE*, 31 Dec. 1920; Seán Riordan (BMH WS 1,355, p. 5); Michael Mansfield (BMH WS 1,188, pp 15–16).
66 Michael V. O'Donoghue (BMH WS 1,742, pp 106–9).
67 Abbott, *Casualties*, p. 163; *DO*, 11 Dec. 1920; Mooney, *Curlew*, pp 196–7.
68 *CE*, 13 Dec. 1920; Summary of police reports, Dec. 1920 (TNA, CO 904/143).
69 *CE*, 29 Jan. 1921; *WN*, 3 Feb. 1921; Melanie O'Sullivan & Kevin McCarthy, *Cappoquin: a walk through history* (Cappoquin, 1999), p. 299.
70 Mooney, *Curlew*, p. 258; *WN*, 14 Apr. 1921; *CE*, 15 Apr. 1921.
71 Military court of enquiry, 22 June 1921 (TNA, WO 35/160); *CE*, 21 June 1921.
72 Townshend, *Republic*, pp 183–8; Hopkinson, *War of Independence*, pp 72–4.
73 General order, IRA GHQ, 4 Oct. 1920 (UCDAD, O'Malley papers, P17b/127).
74 Ibid.   75 O'Reilly, *George Lennon*, pp 62–7.
76 Jack O'Mara (BMH WS 1,305, p. 4).
77 Moses Roche (BMH WS 1,129, pp 8–9); Declan Slattery (BMH WS 1,245, p. 6); Ussher, 'True story of a revolution', pp 50–1.
78 Mooney, *Curlew*, pp 175–85; O'Reilly, *George Lennon*, pp 68–73; Murphy & Murphy, *Comeraghs*, pp 48–55; CI Waterford, Nov. 1920 (TNA, CO 904/113); Michael Mansfield (BMH WS 1,188, pp 13–15); Andrew Kirwan (BMH WS 1,179, pp 5–7); Éamonn Power (BMH WS 1,130, pp 11–12).
79 IG report Oct. 1920 (TNA, CO 904/113).
80 Charles Townshend, 'The Irish Republican Army and the development of guerrilla warfare 1916–21', *English Historical Review*, 94 (1979), 318–45.
81 Mac Eoin, *Survivors*, p. 3; O'Connor, *Waterford*, pp 159–60.
82 Kostick, *Popular militancy*, pp 131–4; O'Connor, *Ireland*, pp 107–8.
83 *Daily Herald*, 24 and 28 Apr. 1920.   84 *ME*, 1 May 1920.
85 'State of Waterford city report in the *Morning Post*' (NAI, CSORP, 1920/10,736, 11,062).
86 Charles Townshend, 'The Irish Railway strike of 1920', *IHS*, 21:83 (1979), 265–82; Kostick, *Popular militancy*, pp 140–6.
87 *WN*, 18 June 1920.   88 Ibid., 26 Nov. 1920.

89 Townshend, 'Railway strike', 271.   90 *ME*, 4 Sept. 1920.
91 O'Connor, *Waterford*, p. 145.
92 Emmet O'Connor, 'Agrarian unrest and the Labour movement in County Waterford, 1917–1923', *Saothar*, 6 (1980), 42–3.
93 Ibid., 43.
94 Mooney, *Curlew*, pp 161–2; Patrick Paul (BMH WS 877, pp 10–11); Michael Power (BMH WS 1,180, pp 3–6); CI Waterford, Sept. 1920 (TNA, CO 904/113); *ME*, 20 Sept. 1920; *WN*, 20 Sept. 1920.
95 National Graves Association, *The last post* (Dublin, 1986) p. 107; Michael Power (BMH WS 1,180, pp 6–7).
96 Patrick Paul (BMH WS 877, pp 12–15); Liam Walsh (BMH WS 1,005, pp 12–13).
97 Henry O'Keeffe (BMH WS 1,315, pp 4–5).
98 Patrick Paul (BMH WS 877, pp 17–20).
99 Denis Madden (BMH WS 1,103, p. 13).
100 Mooney, *Curlew*, pp 208–9; Murphy & Murphy, *Comeraghs*, pp 57–65; Sinn Féin, *Pickardstown ambush memorial booklet* (Waterford, 2010), pp 6–19; Patrick Paul (BMH WS 877, pp 17–25); Nicholas Whittle (BMH WS 1,105, pp 64–95); Thomas Brennan (BMH WS 1,020, pp 9–16); *ME*, 14 Jan. 1921; *WN*, 14 Jan. 1921; CI Waterford, Jan. 1921 (TNA, CO 904/114); William Sheehan, *British voices from the Irish War of Independence, 1918–1921* (Cork, 2005), pp 216, 244.
101 *WN*, 14 Jan. 1921.   102 Ibid.
103 *ME*, 14 Jan. 1921.   104 Ibid.
105 Patrick Paul (BMH WS 877, pp 24–5); Vincent White (BMH WS 1,764, p. 25).
106 Nicholas Whittle (BMH WS 1,105, pp 96–107).
107 Townshend, *Republic*, pp 217–18, 226–9.
108 Waterford Prison registers, Jan.–June 1921 (WCL).
109 P. Henchion, 'The graveyard inscriptions of County Cork – X', *Journal of the Cork Historical and Archaeological Society*, 79 (1974), 56; Letters of E. Mansfield from Ballykinlar (copies in author's possession).
110 *FJ*, 29 June 1921; *CE*, 27, 29 June 1921; Pat McCarthy, 'From Waterford to Ballykinlar – internment during the War of Independence', *Decies*, 70 (2014), 103–16.
111 Report from P. Whelan (O/C Waterford No. 2 Brigade) to chief of staff, 7 July 1921 (UCDAD, Richard Mulcahy papers, P/7A/19).
112 Report from 1st Division to GHQ enquiring into Tramore ambush including a list of participants and their statements, 7 July 1921 (UCDAD, Mulcahy papers, P/7A/22); Hopkinson, *War of Independence*, p. 122.
113 Patrick Paul (BMH WS 877, pp 27–9).
114 Jeremiah Cronin (BMH WS 1,020, pp 8–10).
115 Patrick Paul (BMH WS 877, pp 28–9).
116 Memo from Waterford No. 1 Brigade to chief of staff, 25 May 1921 (UCDAD, Mulcahy papers, P/7A/19); Thomas Brennan (BMH WS 1,104, p. 20).
117 Chief of staff to Waterford No. 1 Brigade and O/C 1st Division, 28 May 1921 (UCDAD, Mulcahy papers, P/7A/19).
118 Ibid.
119 Pax Whelan (UCDAD, O'Malley notebooks, P17b/95/78).
120 Whittle, *Waterford remembers*, pp 24–5; IRA casualties (IMA, Michael Collins papers, A/602); Thomas Cleary (BMH WS 972, pp 40–1); Patrick Paul (BMH WS 877, pp 34–5).
121 Report by Paul to GHQ, May 1921 (UCDAD, Mulcahy papers, P/7A/22).
122 Murphy & Murphy, *Comeraghs*, pp 68–75; O'Reilly, *George Lennon*, pp 105–11; Michael Curran (BMH WS 1,230, pp 10–12).

123 Michael Mansfield (BMH WS 1,182, pp 18–19); Deaglán Ó Reagáin (BMH WS 1,283, pp 6–8).
124 Murphy & Murphy, *Comeraghs*, pp 74–6; Mooney, *Curlew*, pp 230–4.
125 The action at the Burgery was a defining moment for the West Waterford Brigade and is well covered in the BMH and other sources. See Murphy & Murphy, *Comeraghs*, pp 79–98; O'Reilly, *George Lennon*, pp 111–35; George Lennon, 'Trauma in time' (unpublished memoir, Waterford County Library); 'The Burgery ambush, Dungarvan', *WN*, 5 Sept. 1924 (the author may be George Plunkett); Edmund Keohan, *History of Dungarvan* (Waterford, 1924), pp 31–41; CI Waterford, Mar. 1921 (TNA, CO 904/144); Michael Mansfield (BMH WS 1,182, pp 22–5); James Mansfield (BMH WS 1,129, pp 17–20); Jack O'Mara (BMH WS 1,305, pp 4–7).
126 Edmund Power (BMH WS 1,130, p. 20).
127 Military court of enquiry, 21 Mar. 1921 (TNA, WO 35/151A).
128 Abbott, *Casualties*, p. 205; Military court of enquiry, 6 Mar. 1921 (TNA, WO 35/149A); James Brennock (BMH WS 1,113, pp 13–14); Brewer, *Oral history*, p. 72.
129 CI Waterford, Mar. 1921 (TNA, CO 904/114).
130 Townshend, *British campaign*, p. 149.
131 Florence O'Donoghue, *No other law* (Dublin, 1986), p. 154.
132 James Mansfield (BMH WS 1,129, p. 20).
133 CI Waterford, Apr. 1921 (TNA, CO 904/115).   134 Ibid.
135 Mooney, *Curlew*, p. 258; RIC IG report Apr. 1921 (TNA, CO 904/115).
136 Denis Madden (BMH WS 1,103, p. 13).
137 Brigade intelligence reports, July 1921 (NLI, Florence O'Donoghue papers, MS 31,215).
138 Regimental war diary, 1st Battalion, The Buffs, 1920–1 (NAM).
139 Thomas Brennan (BMH WS 1,104, p. 22).
140 *CE*, 13 Sept. 1921; Military court of enquiry, 19 Sept. 1921 (TNA, WO 35/151B).
141 Denis Madden (BMH WS 1,103, p. 13).
142 Patrick Ryan (BMH WS 1,314, p. 6).
143 Military court of enquiry, 13 May 1921 (TNA, WO 35/158); James Mansfield (BMH WS 1,129, p. 22); Mooney, *Curlew*, pp 274–5.
144 CI Waterford, May 1921 (TNA, CO 904/115).
145 McCarthy, 'The Irish Rebellion in the 6th Divisional area', *Irish Sword* 27 (2010), 107–8; William Kautt, *Ground truths: British army operations in the Irish War of Independence* (Dublin, 2013), p. 158.
146 William Sheehan, *A hard local war: the British army and the guerrilla war in Cork, 1919–1921* (Stroud, 2011), pp 137–40; Townshend, *British campaign*, pp 176–7.
147 Michael Cummins (BMH WS 1,282, pp 10–12); Mooney, *Curlew*, pp 292–3; O'Reilly, *George Lennon*, pp 149–52; CI Waterford, June 1921 (TNA, CO 904/115).
148 Military court of enquiry, 7 June 1921 (TNA, WO 35/148).
149 Murphy & Murphy, *Comeraghs*, p. 109; Seán Tobin (BMH WS 757, p. 13); Mooney, *Curlew*, p. 313; C.R.B. Knight, *Historical records of The Buffs* (London, 1951), p. 3; Pax Whelan, Report for July 1921 (UCDAD, Mulcahy papers, P7/A/23).
150 Patrick Paul (BMH WS 877, p. 36).
151 Report on Waterford No. 1 Brigade divisional commandant to chief of staff, 10 June 1921 (UCDAD, Mulcahy papers, P/7A/19).
152 Lennon, 'Trauma in time'; Patrick Paul (BMH WS 877, p. 40).
153 Abbott, *Casualties*, pp 225–6; Michael Hallinan, 'The capture and execution of D.I. Potter' in Hallinan (ed.), *Tipperary county: people and places* (Dublin, 1993), pp 157–60; CI Tipperary, May 1921 (TNA, CO 904/115).

154 Abbott, *Casualties*, p. 254; *CE*, 10 June 1921; Séamus Babington (BMH WS 1,595, pp 137–40).

155 Abbott, *Casualties*, p. 254; *CE*, 4 July 1921; Report on action at Tallow, 8 July 1921 (UCDAD, Mulcahy papers, P/7A/18).

156 I am grateful to Dr Daithí Ó Corráin for clarification of this point.

157 Patrick Paul (BMH WS 877, pp 60–1).

158 Rosamond Jacob diaries, 28 Aug. 1918 (NLI, Jacob papers, MS 32,582).

159 Ernie O'Malley, *On another man's wound* (Dublin, 1936), p. 129.

160 Lena Keating, 'The Keatings of Comeragh – their part in the War of Independence, 1918–1922' (unpublished family memoir, copy in author's possession).

161 Augusteijn, 'Why was Tipperary so active?', 207–26; McCarthy, 'The Irish Rebellion in the 6th Divisional area', 64.

162 Gribbon, 'Economic and social history', p. 346.

CHAPTER SIX *'I cannot shake off a dread premonition': truce and gun-running, July–December 1921*

1 Lennon, 'Trauma in time'.

2 Frank O'Connor, *An only child* (London, 1961), p. 209.

3 Townshend, *British campaign*, pp 196–9; Hopkinson, *War of Independence*, pp 192–7; *WN*, 8 July 1921.

4 Circular to all officers commanding units, 9 July 1921 (UCDAD, Mulcahy papers, P7/A/21).

5 Townshend, *British campaign*, p. 198.

6 Ibid., p. 193.   7 Hopkinson, *War of Independence*, pp 195–7.

8 Patrick Paul (BMH WS 877, p. 40).

9 Lennon, 'Trauma in time'.

10 *DO*, 15 July 1921; *ME*, 15 July 1921; *WN*, 15 July 1921.

11 *DO*, 15 July 1921.   12 O'Reilly, *George Lennon*, p. 162.

13 Liam Deasy, *Towards Ireland free* (Cork, 1973), pp 312, 314.

14 Waterford Brigade correspondence, 22 July 1921 (WCL).

15 Mooney, *Curlew*, p. 322; O'Reilly, *George Lennon*, pp 163–5; Edward Curran (BMH WS 1,359, p. 5); Moses Roche (BMH WS 1,129, pp 15–16).

16 Townsend, *British campaign*, pp 175–6.

17 Barry, *Guerrilla days*, pp 160–1.

18 Reports on Brigades in 1st Southern Division, July 1921 (NLI, O'Donoghue papers, MS 31,217).

19 Memorandum 'Supply of Munitions' from GHQ to all units, July 1921 (UCDAD, Mulcahy papers, P7/A/24).

20 Moses Roche (BMH WS 1,129, p. 16); Patrick Paul (BMH WS 877, p. 57).

21 Henry O'Keefe (BMH WS 1,315, p. 9).

22 IRA Intelligence summary, Nov. 1921 (NLI, O'Donoghue papers, MS 31,210).

23 CI Waterford, Sept. 1921 (TNA, CO 904/116).

24 *Constabulary Gazette*, 1 Oct. 1921.

25 CI Waterford, July 1921 (TNA, CO 904/115).

26 Ibid., Sept. 1921 (TNA, CO 904/116).

27 Ibid., Oct. 1921 (ibid.).   28 Ibid., Sept. 1921 (ibid.).

29 O'Connor, *Waterford*, p. 171.   30 Mac Eoin, *Survivors*, p. 7.

31 Situation report, GOC to C-in-C, 17 Oct. 1921 (TNA, WO 32/9533); Townshend, *British campaign*, p. 199.

32 *WN*, 19 Nov. 1921; *ME*, 19 Nov. 1921.
33 *WS*, 19 Nov. 1921.
34 William Keane (BMH WS 1,122, p. 27); Moses Roche (BMH WS 1,129, p. 16).
35 *WN*, 11 Nov. 1921.   36 *ME*, 28 Oct. 1921.
37 *WS*, 21, 28 Oct. 1921.
38 *WS*, 21 Oct. 1921; *WN*, 28 Oct. 1921; Townshend, *Republic*, pp 322–3.
39 Michael Shalloe (BMH WS 1,241, p. 21).
40 Piaras Béaslaí, *Michael Collins* (2 vols, Dublin, 1926), ii, 271–3.
41 Michael Desmond (BMH WS 1,338, p. 11); *WN*, 26 Aug. 1921.
42 Pax Whelan (UCDAD, Ernie O'Malley notebooks, P17b/95/78).
43 *WN*, 14 Oct. 1921.
44 Waterford Brigade report, 18 Nov. 1921 (UCDAD, Mulcahy papers, P7/B/63).
45 J. Bowyer Bell, 'The Thompson submachine gun in Ireland 1921', *Irish Sword*, 8 (1967), 92–108; Peter Hart, 'The Thompson submachine gun in Ireland revisited', *Irish Sword*, 19 (1995), 161–70; Patrick Jung, 'The Thompson submachine gun during the Anglo-Irish war: the new evidence', *Irish Sword*, 21 (1998), 191–218.
46 Deasy, *Ireland free*, pp 178–81; Barry, *Guerrilla days*, pp 154–9; O'Donoghue, *No other law*, pp 13–15.
47 Greaves, *Mellows*, p. 227; Robert Briscoe, *For the life of me: the adventurous autobiography of the Irish rebel who became the first Jewish Lord Mayor of Dublin* (London, 1959), pp 79–80.
48 Ibid., p. 82.   49 Ibid., pp 90–1.
50 Charles John McGuinness, *Sailor of fortune: adventures of an Irish sailor, soldier, pirate, pearl-fisher, gun-runner, rebel and Antarctic explorer* (Philadelphia, 1935), pp 190–1; Briscoe, *For the life of me*, pp 92–4; Greaves, *Mellows*, p. 232.
51 Briscoe, *For the life of me*, pp 99–102; Andreas Roth, 'Gun-running from Germany to Ireland in the early 1920s', *Irish Sword*, 22:88 (2000), 209–20.
52 Tom Jones, *Whitehall diary* (3 vols, Oxford, 1971), iii, 145; Frank Pakenham, *Peace by ordeal: the negotiation of the Anglo-Irish Treaty, 1921* (London, 1935), p. 138.
53 'Captured British documents' (NLI, O'Donoghue papers, MS 31,212).
54 Briscoe, *For the life of me*, pp 103–5.
55 Greaves, *Mellows*, pp 263–5.
56 McGuinness, *Sailor of fortune*, pp 192–202.
57 'Captured British documents' (NLI, O'Donoghue papers, MS 31,212).
58 McGuinness, *Sailor of fortune*, pp 202–5; Vincent White (BMH WS 1,764, pp 26–7).
59 Michael Mansfield (BMH WS 1,188, p. 29); Mac Eoin, *Survivors*, p. 141.
60 Valiulis, *Mulcahy*, p. 257.

CHAPTER SEVEN *'My constituents suggested … ratification': from Treaty to Civil War*

1 Vincent White, *Dáil Éireann debates*, 6 Jan. 1922, vol. 3, col. 288.
2 J.J. Lee, *Ireland, 1912–1985: politics and society* (Cambridge, 1989), pp 50–1; Laffan, *Resurrection*, pp 346–8.
3 Michael Hopkinson, *Green against green: the Irish Civil War* (Dublin, 1988), pp 89–101.
4 *WS*, 10 Dec. 1921.
5 Patrick Murray, *Oracles of god: the Roman Catholic Church and Irish politics, 1922–37* (Dublin, 2000), pp 34–5.
6 Pax Whelan (UCDAD, O'Malley notebooks, P17b/95/79).
7 *WS*, 10 Dec. 1921.   8 Murray, *Oracles*, p. 458.
9 Minutes, Jan. 1922 (WCA, Waterford Corporation minute book).

10 Minutes, Jan. 1922 (WCoA, Waterford County Council minute book).
11 Hopkinson, *Green against green*, pp 40–4; John M. Regan, *The Irish counter-revolution, 1921–1936* (Dublin, 1999), pp 38–40.
12 *Dáil Éireann debates*, 6 Jan. 1922, vol. 3, cols. 287–8.
13 Ibid., cols. 288–92.   14 Ibid., col. 207.
15 Ibid., cols. 325–31.   16 Ibid., col. 269.
17 *Hansard (Commons)*, 8 Mar. 1922, vol. 151, cols. 1407–15.
18 Joseph M. Curran, *The birth of the Irish Free State, 1921–1923* (Alabama, 1980), p. 138.
19 *WN*, 16 Dec. 1921.
20 *CE*, 17 Dec. 1921; Abbott, *Casualties*, p. 271; Siobhán Lincoln, *Ardmore: memory and story* (Ardmore, 2000), pp 204–5.
21 Anthony Kinsella, 'The British military evacuation', *Irish Sword*, 20 (1997), 275–86.
22 Robinson & Aggett, *Bloody eleventh*, p. 11; *WS*, 8 Feb. 1922.
23 *ME*, 10 Mar. 1922; *WN*, 10 Mar. 1922.
24 Ibid.
25 Patrick Paul (BMH WS 877, pp 57–9); Murphy & Murphy, *Comeraghs*, pp 116–18.
26 Moses Roche (BMH WS 1,129, p. 16).
27 *ME*, 15 Mar. 1922.   28 O'Reilly, *George Lennon*, p. 174.
29 Murphy & Murphy, *Comeraghs*, pp 59–60.
30 Hopkinson, *Green against green*, p. 90.
31 *WS*, 12 May 1922.
32 Murphy & Murphy, *Comeraghs*, p. 29; Mooney, *Curlew*, p. 351; *Last post*, p. 132.
33 O'Reilly, *George Lennon*, p. 174.   34 Mac Eoin, *Survivors*, p. 143.
35 Pax Whelan (UCDAD, O'Malley notebooks, P17b/95/80).
36 Hopkinson, *Green against green*, p. 89.
37 Ibid., p. 70.
38 Gemma Clark, 'Fire, boycott, threat and harm: social and political violence within the local community. A study of three Munster counties during the Irish Civil War, 1922–23' (D. Phil., Oxford, 2010).
39 Compensation claim of Patrick Golden (TNA, CO 762/80/4).
40 Compensation claim of Timothy Gleeson (TNA, CO 762/66/14).
41 Compensation claim of James Coogan (TNA, CO 762/80/3).
42 Michael V. O'Donoghue (BMH WS 1,741, pp 284–5).
43 Compensation claim of Hugh Jones (TNA, CO 762/77/11).
44 Compensation claim of William Roe (TNA, CO 762/108/11).
45 Irish Distress Committee, files and minutes (TNA, CO/762).
46 *WS*, 6 May 1922.   47 *Church of Ireland Gazette*, 25 Aug. 1922.
48 Gemma Clark, *Everyday violence in the Irish Civil War* (Cambridge, 2014), p. 199.
49 Mac Eoin, *Survivors*, pp 141–3, 268–9.
50 McGuinness, *Sailor of fortune*, pp 224–32.
51 *WN*, 24 Mar. 1922; *ME*, 22 Mar. 1922.
52 Ibid.   53 *IT*, 20 Mar. 1922; Curran, *Birth*, pp 174–6.
54 *ME*, 31 Mar. 1922.   55 Ibid.
56 Keohan, *Dungarvan*, pp 56–8.   57 Hopkinson, *Green against green*, pp 56–8.
58 Michael Gallagher, 'The pact general election of 1922', *IHS*, 21:84 (1979), 405.
59 Hopkinson, *Green against green*, p. 110.
60 O'Connor, *Waterford*, p. 202.   61 *ME*, 16 June 1922; *WS*, 16 June 1921.
62 O'Connor, *Waterford*, pp 170–1.   63 *ME*, 23 June 1922.
64 Walker, *Parliamentary election results*, p. 107.
65 *ME*, 28 Jan. 1922.   66 O'Connor, *Waterford*, pp 170–1.

67 *Voice of Labour*, 27 May, 3 June 1922.
68 O'Sullivan & McCarthy, *Cappoquin*, pp 308–12; O'Connor, *Waterford*, pp 167–71.
69 Ussher, 'The true story of a revolution', pp 76–90.
70 Lennon, 'Trauma in time'.   71 Mac Eoin, *Survivors*, p. 4.
72 *Irish Farmer*, 24 June 1922.   73 O'Connor, *Waterford*, p. 171.

CHAPTER EIGHT *'We strove ... to keep a few peaceful things going': Civil War and social strife*

1 Ussher, 'True story of a revolution', p. 60.
2 Hopkinson, *Green against green*, pp 153–5; Eoin Neeson, *The Civil War in Ireland* (Cork, 1966), pp 96–103; Calton Younger, *Ireland's Civil War* (London, 1968), pp 381–6.
3 Pax Whelan (UCDAD, O'Malley notebooks, P17b/95/81).
4 Terence O'Reilly, 'The Battle of Waterford 1922', *Decies*, 26 (1984), 31–7; Dermot Power, 'The Siege of Waterford, 1922', *ME*, 10 Nov. 1955.
5 Nioclás de Fuiteoil, *Waterford remembers* (Waterford, 1946), pp 26–7.
6 Military record of John T. Prout, 8 Dec. 1927 (National Museum of Ireland (NMI), John T. Prout papers).
7 Neeson, *Civil War*, p. 100.
8 Whelan to Lynch, 18 July 1922 (UCDAD, O'Malley papers, P17a/96).
9 *II*, 20 July 1922.
10 De Fuiteoil, *Waterford remembers*, pp 28–9; O'Reilly, *George Lennon*, p. 181.
11 *II*, 22, 24 July 1922.
12 Damage to property (Compensation) Act 1923: register of claims (NAI, OPW/1/18/1–4).
13 Full contemporary accounts of the siege of Waterford are given in *ME* and *WS*, 29 July 1922, and *II* and *IT*, 20, 21 July 1922.
14 Hopkinson, *Green against green*, p. 155; Account by Prout of the Civil War in South Kilkenny-Waterford in July 1922, n. d. (NMI, Prout papers).
15 Hopkinson, *Green against green*, p. 155.
16 Pax Whelan (UCDAD, O'Malley notebooks, P17b/95/81).
17 Hopkinson, *Green against green*, p. 154.
18 *ME*, 29 July 1922.   19 Ibid., 5 Aug. 1922.
20 Hopkinson, *Green against green*, p. 155.
21 Information supplied by Julian Walton.
22 Neeson, *Civil War*, pp 108–11; Hopkinson, *Green against green*, pp 167–8.
23 Murphy & Murphy, *Comeraghs*, p. 143.
24 Ibid., p. 141; O'Reilly, *George Lennon*, p. 195.
25 Patrick Whelan (BMH WS 1,231, p. 9).
26 De Fuiteoil, *Waterford remembers*, pp 30–1; *Last post*, p. 134.
27 Waterford Brigade reports, Aug. 1922 (UCDAD, O'Malley papers, P17a/96).
28 Michael Mansfield (BMH WS 1,188, p. 30), O'Reilly, *George Lennon*, p. 198.
29 O'Reilly, *George Lennon*, p. 200.
30 Waterford Brigade reports, Aug. 1922 (UCDAD, O'Malley papers, P17a/96); Murphy & Murphy, *Comeraghs*, pp 151–2; O'Reilly, *George Lennon*, pp 203–4.
31 *Poblacht na hÉireann War News*, 14 Aug. 1922.
32 'General order no. 9: organisation and activities of Active Service Units', 19 Aug. 1922, in Cormac K.H. O'Malley and Anne Dolan, *'No surrender here!': The civil war papers of Ernie O'Malley, 1922–1924* (Dublin, 2007), pp 526–7.
33 *ME*, 26 Aug. 1922.   34 Ibid., 29 Aug. 1922.
35 *WS*, 26 Aug. 1922.   36 *WN*, 26 Aug. 1922.

37 Mac Eoin, *Survivors*, p. 4; de Fuiteoil, *Waterford remembers*, pp 34–5.
38 *CE*, 25, 26 Sept. 1922.
39 Report from O/C Kilkenny Prison to Prout, 18 Mar. 1923 (IMA, Waterford Command papers, CW/Ops/10).
40 *WN*, 2 Feb. 1923; de Fuiteoil, *Waterford remembers*, pp 38–9.
41 Murphy & Murphy, *Comeraghs*, pp 30–1 quoting Mark Bence-Jones, *Twilight of the ascendancy* (London, 1987), p. 225.
42 *CE*, 4 Sept. 1922; Murphy & Murphy, *Comeraghs*, p. 153.
43 Mick Mansfield (UCDAD, O'Malley notebooks, P17b/117/44).
44 Murphy & Murphy, *Comeraghs*, p. 155.
45 *CE*, 30 Sept. 1922; *ME*, 5 Oct. 1922.
46 *ME*, 22 Sept. 1922.   47 *CE*, 2 Oct. 1922.
48 Ibid., 10 Oct. 1922.   49 *WN*, 8 Sept. 1922; *ME*, 8 Sept. 1922.
50 Waterford Command report, Oct. 1922 (IMA, Waterford Command papers, CW/Ops/10).
51 *WN*, 21 Oct. 1922.
52 Waterford Command, newspaper cuttings, Oct. 1922 (UCDAD, Mulcahy papers, P7/B/64).
53 Waterford Command reports, Oct. 1922 (IMA, Waterford Command papers, CW/Ops/10); *CE*, 29 Oct. 1922.
54 *ME*, 21 Oct. 1922.
55 Waterford Command report, 11 Dec. 1922 (UCDAD, Mulcahy papers, P7/B/64).
56 Ibid.   57 *CE*, 14 Nov. 1922.
58 Ibid., 16 Nov. 1922.   59 *ME*, 17 Nov. 1922; *WS*, 17 Nov. 1922.
60 Waterford Command reports, Nov. 1922 (IMA, Waterford Command papers, CW/Ops/10).
61 *ME*, 5 Dec. 1922.
62 Waterford Command reports, Dec. 1922 (IMA, Waterford Command papers, CW/Ops/10); *WN*, 12 Dec. 1922.
63 Waterford Command reports, Dec. 1922 (IMA, Waterford Command papers, CW/Ops/10).
64 Bernard Share, *In time of civil war: the conflict on the Irish railways, 1922–23* (Cork, 2006), p. 89.
65 Liam Lynch to Éamon de Valera, 11 Jan. 1923 (UCDAD, de Valera papers, P150/1749); Curran, *Birth*, p. 267.
66 *ME*, 6 Jan. 1923.
67 Colm Campbell, *Emergency law in Ireland, 1918–1925* (Oxford, 1994), pp 163–5; Breen Murphy, 'The government's executions policy during the Irish Civil War' (PhD, NUI Maynooth 2010), pp 73–81.
68 Mulcahy to General Murphy (GOC Kerry Command), 13 Dec. 1922 (UCDAD, Mulcahy papers, P7/B/101 & P7/B/26-7); Murphy, 'Executions policy', pp 166–72.
69 *CE*, 6 Dec. 1922.
70 De Fuiteoil, *Waterford remembers*, p. 47; Information on Patrick O'Reilly and Michael Fitzgerald, n.d. (UCDAD, O'Malley papers, P17a/191).
71 Murphy, 'Executions policy', p. 195.
72 Mac Eoin, *Survivors*, pp 144–5.
73 *ME*, 6 Jan. 1923; *WN*, 6 Jan. 1923.
74 Waterford Command, newspaper cutting (UCDAD, Mulcahy papers, P7/B/64).
75 Waterford Command reports, Jan. 1923 (IMA, Waterford Command papers, CW/Ops/10).
76 Martin O'Dwyer, *Seventy-seven of mine said Ireland* (Cork, 2009), pp 224–8.
77 Murphy, 'Executions policy', p. 195.
78 Mac Eoin, *Survivors*, pp 145–7.

79 Hopkinson, *Green against green*, p. 222.
80 Ibid.   81 Ibid., p. 228.
82 Bertie Scully (UCDAD, O'Malley notebooks, P17b/102/130).
83 Letter to P. Murray, 13 Feb. 1923 (UCDAD, Mulcahy papers, P7/B/89).
84 *CE*, 9, 12 Feb. 1923.   85 O'Donoghue, *No other law*, p. 243.
86 W.T. Cosgrave to Mulcahy, 11 Jan. 1923 (UCDAD, Mulcahy papers, P7/B/64).
87 Cork Command reports, Jan., Feb. 1923 (IMA, Cork Command papers, CW/Ops/04).
88 Civil War Intelligence reports, Jan. 1923 (IMA, CW/Operations & Intelligence Collection/01).
89 *ME*, 16 Feb. 1923; *WN*, 16 Feb. 1923; de Fuiteoil, *Waterford remembers*, pp 40–3.
90 *WN*, 9 Feb.1923; Share, *In time of civil war*, pp 107–8.
91 Terence Dooley, *The decline of the big house in Ireland* (Dublin, 2001), pp 187–92.
92 *ME*, 2 Mar. 1923; Cork Command, reports, Mar. 1923 (IMA, Cork Command papers, CW/Ops/04); Damage to Property Act, claims (NAI, OPW/1/18/1); Compensation claim of Sir John Keane (TNA, CO 762/82/11).
93 *ME*, 2 Mar. 1923; Damage to Property Act, claims (NAI, OPW/1/18/1); Compensation claim of C. Fairholme (TNA, CO 762/94/3).
94 Compensation claim of C. Fairholme (TNA, CO 762/94/3).
95 *ME*, 9 Mar. 1923; Damage to Property Act, claim (NAI, OPW/1/18/2).
96 Dooley, *Decline of the big house*, p. 191.
97 Ibid., p. 287.   98 *WN*, 8 Mar. 1923.
99 Murphy & Murphy, *Comeraghs*, pp 160–2.
100 Cork Command report, Mar. 1923 (IMA, Cork Command papers, CW/Ops/04).
101 *WN*, 22 Mar. 1923.
102 Murphy & Murphy, *Comeraghs*, pp 165–6.
103 Hopkinson, *Green against green*, p. 237.
104 Murphy & Murphy, *Comeraghs*, pp 162–3.
105 Mick Mansfield (UCDAD, O'Malley notebooks, P17b/94/80).
106 Cork Command reports, Mar. 1923 (IMA, Cork Command papers, CW/Ops/04); Waterford Command reports, Mar. 1923 (IMA, Waterford Command papers, CW/Ops/10).
107 O'Donoghue, *No other law*, pp 304–7; Murphy & Murphy, *Comeraghs*, pp 165–7.
108 J.A. Gaughan, *Austin Stack: portrait of a separatist* (Dublin, 1973), pp 233–4.
109 Andrews, *Dublin made me*, p. 287.
110 Murphy & Murphy, *Comeraghs*, pp 164–7; Keating, 'The Keatings of Comeragh'.
111 General survey of situation for week ending 19 May 1923 (UCDAD, Mulcahy papers, P7/B/139).
112 Waterford Command reports, May 1923 (IMA, Waterford Command papers, CW/Ops/10).
113 Hopkinson, *Green against green*, p. 257.
114 Cork Command reports, May 1923 (IMA, Cork Command papers, CW/Ops/04); Martin O'Dwyer, *Death before dishonour* (Cashel, 2010), pp 361–2.
115 O'Connor, *Ireland*, pp 115–16.   116 Ibid., p. 113.
117 O'Connor, *Waterford*, p. 177.
118 Ibid., pp 177–9; Dermot Power, 'The Waterford Gas Works Soviet 1923', *Decies*, 68 (2012), 63–94.
119 *ME*, 10 Feb. 1923.   120 O'Connor, 'Agrarian unrest', *Saothar*, 6 (1980), 49.
121 *ME*, 26 May 1923; *WS*, 26 May 1923.
122 *ME*, 2 June 1923.
123 Anthony Kinsella, 'The Special Infantry Corps', *Irish Sword*, 20 (1997), 341.

124 Ibid., 342–3.   125 Ibid., p. 342.
126 *ME*, 1 July 1923.
127 Kinsella, 'Special Infantry Corps', 343.
128 *ME*, 16 June 1923; O'Connor, 'Agrarian unrest', p. 50.
129 *ME*, 30 June 1923.
130 *WS*, 30 June 1923; *FJ*, 10 June 1923; O'Connor, *Labour*, p. 207, note 109; *II*, 20 Sept.
     1923.
131 *ME*, 2 June 1923.   132 O'Connor, 'Agrarian unrest', p. 53.
133 *ME*, 10 Nov. 1923.
134 William O'Brien, *Forth the banners go* (Dublin, 1969), pp 113–14.
135 O'Connor, 'Agrarian unrest', p. 54.
136 Ibid., p. 55; O'Connor, *Waterford*, pp 200–1.
137 General report no. 8, Intelligence Branch, Department of the Chief of Staff, June 1923
     (IMA, CW/Ops/02/11).
138 General weekly summary, 30 June 1923 (IMA, CW/Ops/01/02/12).

CHAPTER NINE *'Ireland shall get her freedom and you still break stone': Waterford in 1923*

1   W.B. Yeats, 'Parnell', *New Poems* (London, 1938).
2   Ciara Meehan, *The Cosgrave party: a history of Cumann na nGaedheal, 1923–33* (Dublin,
    2010), pp 26–9.
3   *ME*, 24 Aug. 1923.   4 Ibid.
5   List of prisoners to be detained Waterford area, Aug. 1923 (IMA, Civil War Prisoners
    Collection).
6   Patrick Lynch (BMH WS 1,237, p. 21); Murphy & Murphy, *Comeraghs*, p. 168.
7   James Mansfield (BMH WS 1,129, p. 24); Michael Mansfield (BMH WS 1,188, pp 33–4).
8   *WN*, 17 Aug. 1923.   9 O'Connor, *Waterford*, p. 194.
10 *ME*, 11 Aug. 1923.   11 *WN*, 17 Aug. 1923.
12 *Times* article was reprinted in the *ME*, 25 Aug. 1923.
13 Ibid.   14 *ME*, *WS*, *WN*, 17 Aug. 1923.
15 *WS*, *ME*, 24 Aug. 1923.   16 *ME*, 2 Sept. 1923.
17 Walker, *Parliamentary election results*, p. 115.
18 Meehan, *Cosgrave party*, pp 13–64.
19 Arthur Mitchell, *Labour in Irish politics, 1890–1930: the Irish labour movement in an age of
    revolution* (Dublin, 1974), p. 190; Ciara Meehan, 'Labour and Dáil Éireann, 1922–37' in
    Daly, O'Brien and Rouse (eds), *Making the difference*, pp 45–6.
20 Alice McDermott, 'Bridget Redmond, the keeper of the Redmondite flame in Waterford',
    Decies, 66 (2010), 87–102.
21 Power, 'Gas Works soviet', 84–5.   22 *ME*, 12 Jan. 1924.
23 O'Connor, *Waterford*, pp 209–12.   24 Ibid., p. 210.
25 *WN*, 29 May 1925; ITGWU, *Annual reports, 1923–1927* (Dublin, 1924–8).
26 O'Connor, *Ireland*, pp 117–28.
27 Niamh Puirséil, *The Irish Labour Party, 1922–73* (Dublin, 2007), p. 17.
28 Andy Bielenberg, 'Exodus: the emigration of Southern Irish Protestants during the Irish
    War of Independence and the Civil War', *Past & Present*, 218 (Feb. 2013), 21.
29 Ibid., 205, table 3.   30 Ibid., 223, table 6.
31 Ibid., 205, table 3.   32 Ibid.
33 C.P. Crane, *Memories of a resident magistrate* (Edinburgh, 1938), p. 223.
34 Ussher, 'True story of a revolution', p. 3.

35 Goff-Davis, *Walled gardens*, p. 38.   36 Ibid., p. 37.
37 *WS*, 10 Dec. 1921.
38 James Healy, 'The civil war hunger-strike October 1923', *Studies*, 71 (1982), 213–26.
39 Copies in author's possession.
40 Healy, 'Hunger-strike', 216; Murphy & Murphy, *Comeraghs*, pp 171–2.
41 Denis Barry, *The unknown commandant: the life and times of Denis Barry, 1883–1923* (Cork, 2010) pp 96–114.
42 Moses Roche (BMH WS 1,129, p. 18).
43 *WN*, 8 Feb. 1924.   44 Ibid., 15 Feb. 1924.
45 Ibid., 19 Apr. 1924.   46 *ME*, 24 Aug. 1924.
47 James Mansfield (BMH WS 1,229, p. 24); Michael Mansfield (BMH WS 1,188, p. 34); Murphy & Murphy *Comeraghs*, p. 168.
48 M. Shalloe (BMH WS 1,241, p. 22).
49 Lee, *Ireland*, p. 112.
50 James Meenan, *The Irish economy since 1922* (Liverpool, 1977), pp 91–2; Johnson, *The interwar economy*, p. 11.
51 P. Breathnach, 'The development of the dairy industry in county Waterford' in Power and Nolan (eds), *Waterford*, p. 708.
52 Cowman, *Perceptions and promotions*, p. 56; J.M. Hearne, 'Industry in Waterford city, 1932–1962' in Power and Nolan (eds), *Waterford*, pp 685–6.
53 Lee, *Ireland*, pp 118–21.
54 Sylvester Ó Muirí, *The state and the sea fisheries of the south and west coasts of Ireland, 1922–1972* (Dublin, 2013), pp 20–4.
55 Dowling, *Housing in Waterford*, pp 26–8.
56 *WN*, 5 Mar. 1923.
57 Minutes, Jan. 1924 (WCA, Waterford Corporation minute book).
58 Vaughan & Fitzpatrick (eds), *Irish historical statistics*, pp 21, 35.
59 Reg Hindley, *The death of the Irish language* (London, 1990), p. 40; Butler, *Gaelic League in Waterford*, p. 57.
60 Butler, *Gaelic League in Waterford*, pp 57–8.
61 Timothy G. McMahon, *Grand opportunity: the Gaelic revival and Irish society, 1893–1910* (Syracuse, 2008), pp 211–15.
62 Census of Ireland 1926, volume 6, tables 4–8.
63 Hindley, *Irish language*, pp 30–36; John Walsh, *Díchoimisiúnú teanga: Coimisiún na Gaeltachta 1926* (Dublin, 2002), pp 12–22, 23–6.
64 Lee, *Ireland*, pp 135–6.
65 The most notable contributions are Fitzpatrick, 'Geography of Irish nationalism', 13–44; Peter Hart, *I.R.A. at war 1916–23* (Oxford, 2003), pp 38–62; Rumpf & Hepburn, *Nationalism and socialism*, pp 38–62.
66 Hart, *I.R.A. at war*, pp 32–3.   67 Regan, *Irish counter-revolution*, pp 94–7.
68 Maume, 'Sir John Keane', *DIB*.   69 Puirséil, *Irish Labour Party*, pp 19–33.
70 *ME*, 8 Mar. 1924.   71 *WN*, 17 Aug. 1923.

Select bibliography

PRIMARY SOURCES

A. MANUSCRIPTS

Dublin

Military Archives

Bureau of Military History witness statements and contemporary documents.
Civil War papers Cork and Waterford Commands.
Civil War Intelligence reports.
Michael Collins papers.
Waterford Brigade reports.
Roll of deceased personnel, National army.
Internment prison books.
Special Infantry Corps reports.

National Archives of Ireland

Chief Secretary's Office Registered papers.
Dáil Éireann loan files.
OPW Files, Register of Claims Property (Compensation) Act 1923.

National Library of Ireland

Piaras Béaslaí papers.
Joseph Brennan papers.
Bulmer Hobson papers.
Rosamond Jacob diaries.
Maurice Moore papers.
Florence O'Donoghue papers.
J.J. O'Connell papers.
Seán O'Mahony papers.
John Redmond papers.
United Irish League, minute book of the National Directory.
Irish National Aid Association and Volunteer Dependants' Fund papers.
Irish Transport and General Workers' Union Lists of Branches 1909–22.

National Museum of Ireland

General Thomas Prout papers.

Trinity College Dublin

Emily Ussher memoir.

University College Dublin Archives Department

Cathal Brugha papers.
Richard Mulcahy papers.
Ernie O'Malley papers & notebooks.

Irish Railway Record Society Archives

Records of the Great Southern & Western Railway Company.

Dungarvan

Waterford County Archives

Waterford County Council minute books.
Waterford County Council Finance Committee minute books.
Dungarvan Urban District Council minute books.
Lismore Town Commissioners minute books.

Waterford

Waterford City Archives

Waterford Corporation minute books 1912–24.
Waterford Corporation Finance Committee minute books.
Waterford National Volunteers papers.

Waterford City Library

Robert Dobbyn diaries.
George Lennon, 'Trauma in time' [unpublished memoir].
Waterford Prison registers, Jan–June 1921.

Waterford Diocesan Archives

Richard Sheehan papers.
Bernard Hackett papers.

London

National Archives

Cabinet papers.
Colonial Office papers.
War Office papers.

National Army Museum

Regimental War Diary, 1st Battalion, The Buffs.

Dorchester

The Keep Military Museum

Regimental records, The Devonshire Regiment.

B. OFFICIAL RECORDS

Census of Ireland, 1901, 1911.
Dáil Éireann debates.
Hansard House of Commons debates.
Local Government Board of Ireland, *Report on the sanitary circumstances of Waterford County Borough, 1910–11*.

C. NEWSPAPERS AND PERIODICALS

Church of Ireland Gazette
Claidheamh Solais
Constabulary Gazette
Cork Examiner
Daily Herald
Dungarvan Observer
Evening Herald
Freeman's Journal
Irish Catholic Directory
Irish Farmer

Irish Independent
Irish Times
Irish Volunteer
Munster Express
Poblacht na hÉireann War News
Royal Irish Constabulary list and directory
Voice of Labour
Waterford News
Waterford Standard

D. PRINTED PRIMARY MATERIAL

Mac Ghiolla Choille, Breandán (ed.), *Intelligence notes, 1913–16* (Dublin, 1966).
Whyte, E. (ed.), *Irish military guide with which the Dublin and the Curragh (official) military directories of Ireland are incorporated, including the navy, the militia and the Royal Irish Constabulary* (Dublin, 1912).

SECONDARY SOURCES

E. PUBLISHED WORKS

1916 Rebellion handbook (Belfast, 1998).
Anonymous, *Fifty years of Liberty Hall* (Dublin, 1959).
aan de Wiel, Jérôme, *The Catholic Church in Ireland, 1914–1918: war and politics* (Dublin, 2003).
Aldridge, A.S., 'Youngest to die', *Decies*, 55 (1999), 185–6.
Andrews, C.S., *Dublin made me* (Dublin, 1979).
Abbott, Richard, *Police casualties in Ireland, 1919–1922* (Cork, 2000).
Augusteijn, Joost, *From public defiance to guerrilla warfare: the experience of ordinary volunteers in the Irish War of Independence, 1916–1921* (Dublin, 1996).
—— 'Why was Tipperary so active in the War of Independence', *Tipperary Historical Journal* (2006), 207–20.

Bance, Michael, *Smokey Joe: the life and times of a provincial newspaper editor* (Dublin, 1994).

Barry, Tom, *Guerilla days in Ireland* (Dublin, 1949).

Béaslaí, Piaras, *Michael Collins* (2 vols, Dublin, 1926).

Bew, Paul, *Ireland: the politics of enmity, 1789–2006* (Oxford, 2007).

—— *John Redmond* (Dundalk, 1996).

Bielenberg, Andy, *Ireland and the industrial revolution: the impact of the industrial revolution on Irish industry, 1801–1922* (London, 2009).

—— 'Exodus: the emigration of southern Irish Protestants during the Irish War of Independence and the Civil War', *Past & Present*, 18 (2013), 199–233.

Bowman, Timothy, *Carson's army: the Ulster Volunteer Force, 1910–22* (Manchester, 2003).

Brennan, Michael, *The war in Clare* (Dublin, 1980).

Breathnach, Proinnsias, 'The development of the dairy industry in County Waterford' in William Nolan & Thomas Power (eds), *Waterford: history and society* (Dublin, 1992), pp 707–32.

Brennan, Niamh, 'A political minefield: southern Loyalists, the Irish Grants Committee and the British government, 1922–31', *IHS*, 30:119 (1997), 406–19.

Brewer, John D., *The Royal Irish Constabulary: an oral history* (Belfast, 1990).

Briscoe, Robert, *For the life of me: the adventurous autobiography of the Irish rebel who became the first Jewish Lord Mayor of Dublin* (London, 1959).

Burnell, Tom, *The Waterford war dead: a history of the casualties of the Great War* (Dublin, 2010).

Butler, Matthew, *The Gaelic League in Waterford* (Waterford, 1944).

Byrne, Brendan, 'Law, order and the RIC in Waterford 1920–21: a chronology', *Decies*, 55 (1999), 117–26.

Callan, Patrick, 'Recruiting for the British army in Ireland during the First World War', *Irish Sword*, 17 (1987–8), 42–56.

Campbell, Colin, *Emergency law in Ireland, 1918–1925* (Oxford, 1994).

Campbell, Fergus, *Land and revolution: nationalist politics in the west of Ireland, 1891–1921* (Oxford, 2005).

Canning, Bernard, *Bishops of Ireland, 1870–1987* (Donegal, 1987).

Clark, Gemma, *Everyday violence in the Irish Civil War* (Cambridge, 2014).

Colum, Padraic & Maurice Joy (eds), *The Irish rebellion of 1916* (New York, 1916).

Conlon, Lil, *Cumann na mBan and the women of Ireland, 1913–25* (Kilkenny, 1969).

Cowman, Des, *Perceptions and promotions: the role of Waterford Chamber of Commerce, 1787–1987* (Waterford, 1988).

Cullinane, David, *Céad Sinn Féin* (Waterford, 2005).

Crane, C.P., *Memories of a resident magistrate* (Edinburgh, 1938).

Curran, Joseph M., *The birth of the Irish Free State* (Alabama, 1980).

Deasy, Liam, *Towards Ireland free* (Cork, 1973).

De Fuiteoil, Nioclás, *Waterford remembers* (Waterford, 1946).

Denman, Terence, *A lonely grave: the life and death of William Redmond* (Dublin, 1995).

Devine, Francis (ed.), *A capital in conflict: Dublin city and the 1913 lockout* (Dublin, 2013).

Dooley, Terence, *The decline of the big house in Ireland: a study of Irish landed families, 1860–1960* (Dublin, 2001).

Dooley, Thomas P., 'Politics, bands and marketing: army recruitment in Waterford city, 1914–15', *Irish Sword*, 18 (1991), 205–19.

—— *Irishmen or English soldiers? The times and world of a southern Catholic Irishman (1876–1916) enlisting in the British army during the First World War* (Liverpool, 1995).

Dowling, Daniel, *Housing in Waterford* (Waterford, 1988).

Fahy, Irene, 'Councillor Mary Strangman and the health of the city', *Decies*, 56 (2000), 189–205.

Fanning, Ronan, *Fatal path: British government and Irish revolution* (London, 2013).

Fewer, T.N., *Waterford people: a biographical dictionary* (Waterford, 1998).

Finan Joseph P., *John Redmond and Irish unity, 1912–1918* (New York, 2004).

Fitzpatrick, David, *Politics and Irish life, 1913–1921: provincial experience of war and revolution* (Dublin, 1977).

—— 'The geography of Irish nationalism 1910–1921', *Past & Present*, 78 (1978), 113–44.

—— *Harry Boland's Irish revolution* (Cork, 2003).

—— 'Emigration, 1871–1921' in W.E. Vaughan (ed.), *A new history of Ireland, vi, Ireland under the Union, II, 1870–1921* (Oxford, 1996), pp 606–52.

Fraser, Murray, *John Bull's other homes: state housing and British policy in Ireland, 1883–1922* (Liverpool, 1996).

French, D., *British economic and strategic planning, 1905–1915* (London, 1982).

Gallagher, Michael, 'The pact general election of 1922', *IHS*, 21:84 (1979), 404–21.

Gaughan, J. A., *Austin Stack: portrait of a separatist* (Dublin, 1973).

Geoghegan, Stannus, *The campaigns and history of the Royal Irish Regiment, Volume II from 1902 to 1922* (London, 1927).

Goff-Davis, Anita, *Walled gardens* (London, 1991).

Greaves, C. Desmond, *Liam Mellows and the Irish revolution* (London, 1971).

Gribbon, Henry D., 'Economic and social history 1850–1921' in W.E. Vaughan (ed.), *A new history of Ireland, vi, Ireland under the Union, II, 1870–1921* (Oxford, 1996), pp 260–356.

Gwynn, Denis, *The life of John Redmond* (London, 1932).

Gwynn, Stephen, *John Redmond's last years* (London, 1919).

Hart, Peter, 'The Thompson submachine gun in Ireland revisited', *Irish Sword*, 19 (1995), 161–70.

—— 'The geography of revolution in Ireland 1917–1923', *Past & Present*, 155 (1997) 142–76.

—— *The I.R.A. at war 1916–1923* (Oxford, 2003).

Hay, Marnie, *Bulmer Hobson and the nationalist movement in twentieth-century Ireland* (Manchester, 2009).

Hayden Talbot, *Michael Collins' own story* (Dublin, 2012).

Hayes, Karl, *A history of the RAF and USNAS in Ireland, 1913–22* (Dublin, 1988).

Hearne, John M., *Waterford Central Technical Institute, 1906–2006: a history* (Waterford, 2006).

Healy, James, 'The Civil War hunger-strike October 1923', *Studies*, 71 (1982), 213–26.

Hepburn, A.C., *Catholic Belfast and nationalist Ireland in the era of Joe Devlin, 1871–1934* (Oxford, 2008).

Herlihy, Jim, *The Dublin Metropolitan Police: a short history and genealogical guide* (Dublin, 2001).

Hindley, Reg, *The death of the Irish language* (London, 1990).

Hobson, Bulmer, *A short history of the Irish Volunteers* (Dublin, 1918).

—— *Ireland yesterday and tomorrow* (Tralee, 1968).

Hopkinson, Michael, *Green against green: the Irish Civil War* (Dublin, 1988).

—— *The Irish War of Independence* (Dublin, 2002).

Jackson, Alvin, *Home rule: an Irish history, 1800–2000* (London, 2004).

Jackson, Daniel M., *Popular opposition to Irish home rule in Edwardian Britain* (Liverpool, 2009).

Johnson, David, *The interwar economy in Ireland* (Dundalk, 1989).

Jourdain, H.F.N., *History of the Connaught Rangers* (3 vols, London, 1926).

Kautt, William, *Ground truths: British army operations in the Irish War of Independence* (Dublin, 2013).

Kelleher, George, *Gunpowder to guided missiles, Ireland's war industries* (Cork, 1993).

Kelly, Matthew, *The Fenian ideal and Irish nationalism, 1882–1996* (Woodbridge, 2006).

Kennedy, Christopher M., *Genesis of the rising: a transformation of nationalist opinion* (New York, 2010).

Keogh, Dermot, 'The Catholic Church, the Holy See and the 1916 Rising' in Gabriel Doherty and Dermot Keogh (eds), *1916: the long revolution* (Cork, 2007), pp 250–309.

Keohan, Edmund, *History of Dungarvan* (Waterford, 1924).

Kinsella, Anthony, 'The British military evacuation', *Irish Sword*, 20 (1997), 275–86.

—— 'The Special Infantry Corps', *Irish Sword*, 20 (1997), 331–46.

Knight, C.R.B., *Historical records of The Buffs* (London, 1951).

Kostick, Conor, *Revolution in Ireland: popular militancy, 1917–1923* (Cork, 2009).

Kotsonouris, Mary, *Retreat from revolution: the Dáil courts, 1920–24* (Dublin, 1994).

Laffan, Michael, 'The unification of Sinn Féin 1917', *IHS*, 17 (1971), 353–79.

—— *The resurrection of Ireland: the Sinn Féin party, 1916–23* (Cambridge, 1999).

—— 'In the shadow of the national question' in Paul Daly, Ronan O'Brien and Paul Rouse (eds), *Making the difference? The Irish Labour Party, 1912–2012* (Cork, 2012), pp 32–42.

Lane, Leeann, 'Rosamond Jacob: nationalism and suffrage' in Louise Ryan & Margaret Ward (eds), *Irish women and the vote* (Dublin, 2007), pp 171–88.

—— *Rosamond Jacob: third person singular* (Dublin, 2010).

Lawlor, Damian, *Na Fianna Éireann and the Irish revolution 1909 to 1923* (Offaly, n.d.).

Lee, J.J., *Ireland, 1912–85: politics and society* (Cambridge, 1989).

Lincoln, Siobhan, *Ardmore: memory and story* (Ardmore, 2000).

Lynch, Diarmuid, *The IRB and the 1916 Rising* (Cork, 1957).

Lyons, F.S.L., *John Dillon: a biography* (London, 1968).

—— 'The watershed, 1903–7' in W.E. Vaughan (ed.), *A new history of Ireland, vi, Ireland under the Union, II, 1870–1921* (Oxford, 1996), pp 111–22.

—— 'The developing crisis 1907–1914' in W.E. Vaughan (ed.), *A new history of Ireland, vi*, pp 123–44.

—— 'The Rising and after' in W.E. Vaughan (ed.), *A new history of Ireland, vi*, pp 207–23.

Mac Eoin, Uinseann, *Survivors* (Dublin, 1980).

Maher, Jim, '1916 in Kilkenny' in John Bradley & Michael O'Dwyer (eds), *Kilkenny through the centuries* (Kilkenny, 2009), pp 465–86.

Mansfield, James, 'The Decies Brigade', *Capuchin Annual* (Dublin, 1970), 377–84.

Marnane, Denis, 'The War of Independence in Tipperary town and district, part 3, the socio-economic background to the Tipperary Town Volunteers', *Tipperary Historical Journal* (2013), 105–13.

Martin, F.X., *The Irish Volunteers, 1913–1915: recollections and documents* (Dublin, 1963).

—— 'Eoin MacNeill on the Easter Rising', *IHS*, 12:47 (1961), 226–71.

Maume, Patrick, *The long gestation: Irish nationalist life, 1891–1918* (Dublin, 1999).

McCabe, Conor, 'The context and course of the Irish railway disputes in 1911', *Saothar*, 30 (2005), 21–32.

McCarthy, Cal, *Cumann na mBan and the Irish revolution* (Dublin, 2007).

McCarthy, Pat, 'The RAF and Ireland, 1919–1922', *Irish Sword*, 17 (1989), 174–88.

—— 'The life and death of Timothy Quinlisk: the Waterford connections to Roger Casement's Irish brigade', *Decies*, 68 (2012), 45–61.

—— 'The Irish rebellion in the 6th Division area', *Irish Sword*, 27 (2007).

McConnel, James, 'Recruiting sergeants for John Bull? Irish nationalist MPs and enlistment during the early months of the Great War', *War in History*, 14:4 (2007), 408–28.

McDermott, Alice, 'Bridget Redmond the keeper of the Redmondite flame in Waterford', *Decies*, 66 (2010), 87–102.

McDowell, R.B., *The Church of Ireland, 1869–1969* (London, 1975).

—— *Crisis and decline: the fate of the southern Unionists* (Dublin, 1997).

McElwee, Richard, *The last voyages of the Waterford steamers* (Waterford, 1992).

McGarry, Fearghal, *The Rising: Ireland: Easter 1916* (Oxford, 2010).

McGee, Owen, *The IRB: the Irish Republican Brotherhood, from the Land League to Sinn Féin* (Dublin, 2005).

McGuinness, Charles John, *Sailor of fortune: adventures of an Irish sailor, soldier, pirate, pearl-fisher, gun-runner, rebel and Antarctic explorer* (Philadelphia, 1935).

McGuire, James & James Quinn (eds), *Dictionary of Irish biography: from the earliest times to the year 2002* (9 vols, Cambridge, 2009).

McMahon, Timothy G., *Grand opportunity: the Gaelic revival and Irish society, 1893–1910* (Syracuse, 2008).

McNally, Brian & Maurice McHugh, *Comhairle Chondae Phortláirge, 1899–1999 comóradh an chéid* (Waterford, 2000).

Meehan, Ciara, *The Cosgrave party: a history of Cumann na nGaedheal, 1923–33* (Dublin, 2010).

Meenan, James, *The Irish economy since 1922* (Liverpool, 1977).

Meleady, Dermot, *Redmond: the Parnellite* (Cork, 2008).

—— *John Redmond: the national leader* (Dublin, 2014).

Mitchell, Arthur, *Revolutionary government in Ireland, Dáil Éireann, 1919–22* (Dublin, 1995).

—— *Labour in Irish politics, 1890–1930: the Irish labour movement in an age of revolution* (Dublin, 1974).

Mooney, Tommy, *Cry of the curlew: a history of the Déise Brigade IRA and the War of Independence* (Dungarvan, 2012).

Muir, Douglas, 'Aerial mail 1919–22', *Irish Sword*, 27:110 (2010), 385–414.

Murphy, Seán & Síle Murphy, *The Comeraghs, gunfire and civil war* (Waterford, 2003).

Murray, Patrick, *Oracles of God: the Roman Catholic Church and the Irish politics, 1922–37* (Dublin, 2000).

National Graves Association, *The last post* (Dublin, 1986).

Neeson, Eoin, *The Civil War in Ireland* (Dublin, 1989).

Nic Dháibhéid, Caoimhe, 'The Irish National Aid Association and the radicalization of public opinion in Ireland, 1916–1918', *Historical Journal*, 55 (2012), 705–29.

Nolan, William & Thomas P. Power (eds), *Waterford: history and society* (Dublin, 1992).

O'Brien, William, *Forth the banners go* (Dublin, 1969).

Ó Broin, León, *Revolutionary underground: the story of the Irish Republican Brotherhood, 1858–1924* (Dublin, 1976).

O'Connor, Emmet, 'Agrarian unrest and the labour movement in County Waterford, 1917–23', *Saothar: Journal of the Irish Labour History Society*, 6 (1980), 40–58.

—— *Syndicalism in Ireland* (Cork, 1988).

—— *A labour history of Waterford* (Waterford, 1989).

—— *A labour history of Ireland, 1824–1960* (Dublin, 1992).

O'Connor, Frank, *An only child* (London, 1961).

O'Donoghue, Florence, *No other law* (Dublin, 1986).

O'Dwyer, Martin, *Seventy-seven of mine said Ireland* (Cork, 2009).

—— *Death before dishonour* (Cashel, 2010).

O'Faoláin, Seán, *Bird alone* (Oxford, 1985).

O'Leary, Cornelius & Patrick Maume, *Controversial issues in Anglo-Irish relations, 1919–1921* (Dublin, 2004).

Ó Gríobhtáin, Nioclás, 'Domhnall Ó Buachalla agus Óglaigh na Rinne', *An Linn Bhuí*, 5 (2001), 185–93.

O'Malley, Cormac K.H. & Anne Dolan, *'No surrender here!': The civil war papers of Ernie O'Malley, 1922–1924* (Dublin, 2007).

Ó Muirí, Sylvester, 'The commercial development of fishing in Waterford' in Criostóir MacCárthaigh & Dónal MacPolin (eds), *Traditional boats of Ireland: history, folklore and construction* (Cork, 2008), 365–7.

—— *The state and sea fisheries of the south and west coasts of Ireland, 1922–1972* (Dublin, 2013).

O'Rahilly, Aodhagán, *Winding the clock: O'Rahilly and the 1916 Rising* (Dublin, 1991).

O'Reilly, Terence, *Rebel heart: George Lennon flying column commander* (Cork, 2009).

O'Sullivan, Daniel, *The Irish constabularies, 1822–1922* (Dingle, 1999).

O'Sullivan, Melanie & Kevin McCarthy, *Cappoquin: a walk through history* (Cappoquin, 1999).

Owens, Rosemary Cullen, *Smashing times: a history of the Irish women's suffrage movement* (Dublin, 1984).

Pakenham, Thomas, *Peace by ordeal: the negotiation of the Anglo-Irish Treaty, 1921* (London, 1935).

Pennell, Catriona, *A kingdom united: popular responses to the outbreak of the First World War in Britain and Ireland* (Oxford, 2012).

—— 'More than a curious footnote: Irish voluntary participation in the First World War and British popular memory' in John Horne & Edward Madigan (eds), *Towards commemoration: Ireland in war and revolution, 1912–1923* (Dublin, 2013), pp 38–45.

Potter, Matthew, *The municipal revolution in Ireland: a handbook of urban government in Ireland since 1800* (Dublin, 2009).

Power, Dermot, 'The Waterford gas works soviet 1923', *Decies*, 68 (2012), 63–94.

Power, Patrick, *A compendious history of the United Dioceses of Waterford and Lismore* (Cork, 1937).

Power, Patrick C., *History of Waterford City and County* (Cork, 1990).

Puirséil, Niamh, *The Irish Labour Party, 1922–73* (Dublin, 2007).

Regan, John M., *The Irish counter-revolution, 1921–1936* (Dublin, 2001).

Reilly, Eileen, 'Women and voluntary war work' in Adrian Gregory & Senia Pašeta (eds), *Ireland and the Great War: 'a war to unite us all'?* (Manchester, 2002), pp 49–72.

Robinson, Roger E. & Walter P. Aggett, *The bloody eleventh: history of the Devonshire Regiment, vol. iii* (Devon, 1998).

Roth, Andreas, 'Gun running from Germany to Ireland in the early 1920s', *Irish Sword*, 22:88 (2000), 209–20.

Rumpf, Erhard & A.C. Hepburn, *Nationalism and socialism in twentieth-century Ireland* (Liverpool, 1977).

Sagarra, Eda, *Kevin O'Sheil: Tyrone nationalist and Irish state-builder* (Dublin, 2013).

Scholes Andrew, *The Church of Ireland and the third home rule bill* (Dublin, 2010).

Share, Bernard, *In time of civil war: the conflict on the Irish railways, 1922–23* (Cork, 2006).

Sheehan, William, *British voices from the Irish War of Independence 1918–1921: the words of British servicemen who were there* (Cork, 2005).

——, *A hard local war: the British army and the guerrilla war in Cork, 1919–1921* (Stroud, 2011).

Smith, John, 'The Oldcastle prisoner of war camp', *Ríocht na Midhe*, 21 (2010), 212–50.

Solar, Peter, 'The agricultural trade of the port of Waterford 1809–1909' in William Nolan & Thomas Power (eds), *Waterford: history and society* (Dublin, 1992), pp 495–518.

Talbot, Hayden, *Michael Collins' own story told to Hayden Talbot* (Dublin, 2012).

Townshend, Charles, *The British campaign in Ireland, 1919–21* (Oxford, 1975).

—— 'The Irish Republican Army and the development of guerrilla warfare, 1916–1921', *English Historical Review*, 94 (1979), 318–45.

—— 'The Irish Railway strike of 1920', *IHS*, 21:83 (1982), 265–82.

—— *Easter 1916: the Irish Rebellion* (London, 2006).

—— *The Republic: the fight for Irish independence, 1918–1923* (London, 2013).

Valiulis, Maryann Gialanella, *Portrait of a revolutionary: General Richard Mulcahy and the founding of the Irish Free State* (Dublin, 1992).

Vaughan, W.E. & A.J. Fitzpatrick (eds), *Irish historical statistics: population, 1821–1971* (Dublin, 1978).
Walker, Brian M., *Parliamentary election results in Ireland, 1801–1922* (Dublin, 1978).
Walsh, John, *Díchoimisiunú teanga: Coimisiún na Gaeltachta 1926* (Dublin, 2002).
Walshe, Eibhear, *Cissie's abattoir* (Cork, 2009).
Ward Alan, 'Lloyd George and the 1918 conscription crisis', *Historical Journal*, 17 (1974), 107–29.
—— *The Irish constitutional tradition: responsible government and modern Ireland* (Dublin, 1992).
Ward, Margaret, *Unmanageable revolutionaries: women and Irish nationalism* (London, 1989).
Wheatley, Michael, *Nationalism and the Irish Party: provincial Ireland, 1910–1916* (Oxford, 2005).
White, Gerry & Brendan O'Shea, *'Baptised in blood': the formation of the Cork Brigade of the Irish Volunteers* (Cork, 2005).
Whittle, Nicholas, *The gentle county, a saga of the Decies people* (Tralee, 1959).
Younger, Calton, *Ireland's Civil War* (London, 1968).

F. THESES AND UNPUBLISHED WORK

Clark, Gemma, 'Fire, boycott, threat and harm: social and political violence within the local community. A study of three Munster counties during the Irish Civil War, 1922–23' (D. Phil., Oxford, 2010).
Dunne, Thomas, 'A history of Waterford labour'.
Evans, Gary, 'The raising of the first internal Dáil loan and the British responses to it, 1919–1921' (MLitt, NUI Maynooth, 2012).
Keating, Lena, 'The Keatings of Comeragh: their part in the War of Independence 1918–1923' (n.d.).
Kenny, Bob, 'The spatial dimension of trade union organisation in Ireland – a case study' (MA, NUI Maynooth, 1985).
Murphy, Breen, 'The government's execution policy during the Irish Civil War' (PhD, NUI Maynooth, 2010).
Ó Faoláin, Domhnall, 'The War of Independence in West Waterford' (copy in author's possession).

G INTERNET RESOURCES

Ulster Covenant online, PRONI: http://www.proni.go.uk/

Index